T0102595

SHOP CLASS
FOR
EVERYONE

SHOP CLASS FOR EVERYONE

EVERYONE

PRACTICAL LIFE SKILLS IN 83 PROJECTS

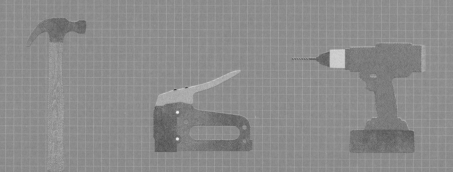

SHARON & DAVID BOWERS

ILLUSTRATIONS BY SOPHIA NICOLAY

WORKMAN PUBLISHING | NEW YORK

FOR HUGH AND PEARSE

Copyright © 2021 by Sharon and David Bowers

All rights reserved. No portion of this book may be reproduced—mechanically, electronically, or by any other means, including photocopying—without written permission of the publisher. Published simultaneously in Canada by Thomas Allen & Son Limited.

Library of Congress Cataloging-in-Publication Data is available.

ISBN 978-1-5235-1238-6

This book has been adapted from *The Useful Book*, © 2016.

Design by Janet Vicario

Workman books are available at special discounts when purchased in bulk for premiums and sales promotions as well as for fund-raising or educational use. Special editions or book excerpts can also be created to specification. For details, contact the special sales director at specialmarkets@workman.com.

Workman Publishing Co., Inc.
225 Varick Street
New York, NY 10014-4381
workman.com

WORKMAN is a registered trademark of Workman Publishing Co., Inc.

Printed in China

First printing March 2021

10 9 8 7 6 5 4 3 2 1

ACKNOWLEDGMENTS

So many people have helped make this book happen and we are so grateful to them all.

Our sincere thanks again to Lynn Cohen, Garth Sundem, Jennifer Griffin, and Angela Miller.

In this latest edition we were thankful to have the watchful eye and steady hand of Sun Robinson-Smith. Thanks also to Megan Nicolay, who has been with this book since it originally stemmed from an idea by Raquel Jaramillo. Sophia Nicolay's lovely and clear illustrations continue to brighten the pages and we are lucky to have her on board.

Warmest thanks to the talented team at Workman, many of whom also worked on the original edition: Samantha Gil, Janet Vicario, Orlando Adiao, Eric Brown, Annie O'Donnell, Barbara Peragine, Kate Karol, Julie Primavera, Claire Gross, Abigail Sokolsky, Claire McKean, Page Edmunds, and Suzie Bolotin.

CONTENTS

DOMESTIC REPAIR 1

Your home tool kit and how to use it

WOODWORKING & METALWORKING 62

The fine art of measuring, cutting, soldering, and making with your hands

PLUMBING

Learn to unplug, seal up, and troubleshoot to make all your "pipe dreams" come true

ELECTRICAL

Untangle and understand those wires, circuits, fixtures, and switches

MECHANICAL

Keep those wheels and gears turning

INTRODUCTION

As technology keeps advancing, it feels like we can do anything if we've got the right device. We can order things online and have them delivered within a couple of hours. We can use our voices to control the lights in our homes. For decades experts have declared that computers were going to make offices "paperless," and the powers that be decided America would henceforth specialize in producing "information workers." Nobody would need to dirty their hands with machinery and grease when technology was the name of the game. Presumably, we'd just leave the repairs to automation while sitting in our cubicles, working diligently at our computers. With an eye on this promised future, many school systems got rid of their Shop and auto repair classes. (While most of us are still waiting on that "paperless" office we were promised.)

Of course, modern life doesn't quite look like a sci-fi movie. And even in space, someone's got to patch a hole or fix a busted rover! Unfortunately, the cancellation of classes that taught essential how-tos and shared practical knowledge has had serious consequences: a whole population of people who never learned to paint, build, do basic plumbing, or complete minor auto repairs. The challenges and global crises of 2020 made it clear that we need more than our screens to stay healthy and keep a household together. We need basic skills that we can build on to adapt to life's unexpected difficulties.

Becoming more self-sufficient is not only easier than many people imagine, it's also extremely satisfying. Work that you do with your own hands is work held to a single standard: Did I fix it? And if the answer is yes, you're finished. It's a feeling of accomplishment that a day spent scrolling through social media, ordering on apps, or poring over spreadsheets can't approach. By the same token, shelves that you've built yourself—made with attention and care and not ordered from a big box store—are well within the reach of anyone who takes a few minutes to learn the basics. Whether you desire the confidence to refinish a floor, fix a leaky pipe, install a dimmer switch, or change a flat tire, those skills are now literally within your grasp. Read on, then get busy.

DOMESTIC REPAIR

One Sunday's to-do list might include anything from fixing a leak, to painting a shelf, to banging down stray deck boards, to putting a new blade on the lawn mower, to hanging a picture. How can you predict what you'll need next Sunday? You can't, which is why your home tool kit needs to be flexible, complete—and organized! A trip to the hardware store for a screw or tool that you know is hiding somewhere in the garage can turn a two-minute fix into a two-hour job. Having the right tool on hand can also be the difference between an easy DIY job and a costly call to the handyman. Spending $200 on tools now can save you many times that amount later.

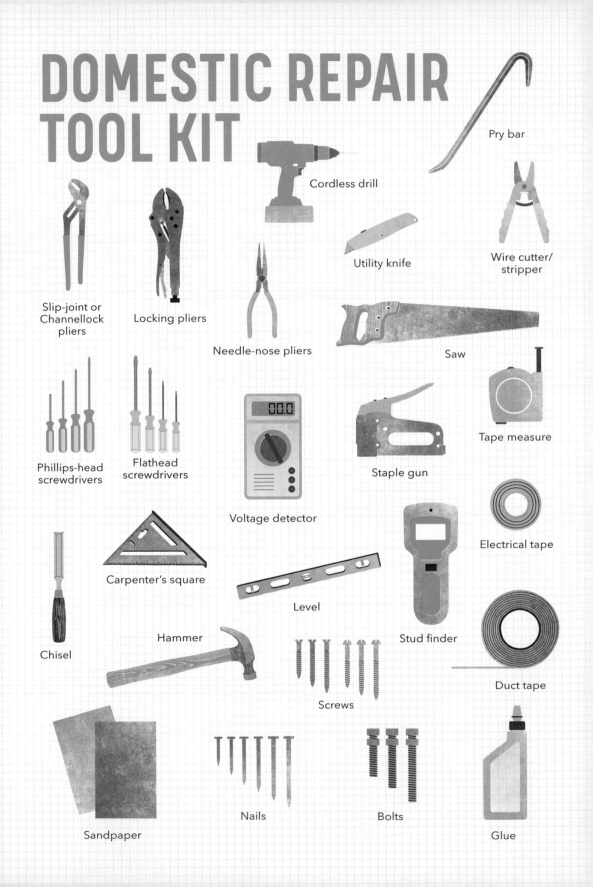

DOMESTIC REPAIR TOOL KIT

Pry bar

Cordless drill

Utility knife

Wire cutter/stripper

Slip-joint or Channellock pliers

Locking pliers

Needle-nose pliers

Saw

Phillips-head screwdrivers

Flathead screwdrivers

Voltage detector

Staple gun

Tape measure

Electrical tape

Carpenter's square

Level

Stud finder

Chisel

Hammer

Screws

Duct tape

Sandpaper

Nails

Bolts

Glue

Hammer. You can't go wrong with a lightweight framing hammer—such as a 20-ounce, smooth-faced model with a straight claw.

Screwdrivers. A medium and a large Phillips (+) and flathead (–) are great places to start.

Tape measure. A 1-inch-wide, 25-foot-long tape measure is indispensable. Make sure it's high enough quality to assure a working lock and well-made retrieval spring.

Pry bar. A short cat's paw pry bar will do just fine to pull nails and lift floorboards.

Locking pliers. Why burn your own grip strength to hold pliers closed? Instead, a pair of versatile, locking Vise-Grips are essential for keeping most things pinched around the house. Consider a pair of Irwin 10-inch curve pliers.

Needle-nose pliers. These are meant for electrical work—to bend and cut wires—but you'll use them for everything from pinching tiny screws to pulling large splinters.

Slip-joint pliers. The most common pliers are two-position, slip-joint pliers that allow you to close tight in one position and grip large objects in the other. Plastic-coated or otherwise, padded handles are a plus.

Wire cutter/stripper. Go with a multi-sized wire cutter/stripper, which you'll use when rewiring lamps and hanging light fixtures.

Voltage detector. You'll need a voltage detector to help locate the source of the trouble in light fixtures, circuit breakers, wires, and cables.

Cordless drill. Look for a variable speed, reversible, twist-lock model with a good set of bits. In addition to a kit of standard bits in a range of sizes, you might want a couple of spade bits, a masonry bit, a hole cutter, and bits used for driving screws (Phillips and flathead).

Chisel. Get a wood chisel, and try to keep it for shaving wood off a loose door jamb instead of opening paint cans.

Saw. A straight handsaw will cut boards quickly and even trim the odd tree branch in a pinch.

Level. You can get a pen-sized laser level for about the same price as a four-foot bubble level, and you will find pros who swear by each. Pick one or the other.

Stud finder. Yes, you can knock on the wall until the hollow sound goes solid, but while you hone your 2 × 4 divination skills, get a stud finder.

Utility knife. A retractable-blade utility knife will do everything from cutting carpet to opening boxes.

Carpenter's square. Carpenters use an L-shaped or triangular steel or aluminum square when building with 2 × 4s. You'll want one around to double-check the angles of the broken picture frame you tacked back together.

Staple gun. A well-made, hand-powered staple gun is essential for hanging holiday lights and tacking upholstered furniture. Make sure the gun you buy accepts staples up to ⅝" and ask a salesperson if you can give the staple gun a few test squeezes before buying. Buy a range of staples—½" and ⅜" are the most useful.

Electrical tape. There are some jobs that require exactly the right gear, and rewiring is one of them. For splicing even the smallest wires, you need vinyl electrical tape, which stretches, adheres to, and insulates wires.

Duct tape. It binds the world together.

Sandpaper. Common aluminum oxide sandpaper runs from the coarse grit of

(continued)

P12 to the fine grit of P220 (and even higher for finish papers). Usually you'll use a coarse paper first and finish with a finer grit, so it's worth buying a set.

Nails, screws, and bolts. Even the most basic home repair tool kit should include a range of nails—ranging from 4d (1½") to 16d (3½")—and screws. Wood and drywall screws have coarse threads, whereas metal screws have finer threads. Get a range of both. It's also worth having a couple of carriage bolts, eye bolts, and screw eyes on hand.

Glue. Super glue, wood glue, Elmer's glue, maybe an epoxy for special projects. Along with duct tape, glue will hold everything together.

#1 How to Hang a Picture

Humans follow a consistent picture-hanging progression. You start putting art on the wall by taping the first concert poster to your childhood bedroom. Then maybe you move on to thumbtacks. In your early twenties you might graduate to a single nail driven into the wall, then you'd hang with wire across the back of the frame. You reach picture-hanging maturity once you deploy the bracket. This section details this method of grown-up picture hanging.

Where to Place a Picture on the Wall

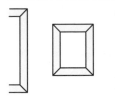
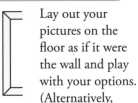

Lay out your pictures on the floor as if it were the wall and play with your options. (Alternatively, make poster board templates the same size as your pictures and then temporarily tack them to the walls with removable adhesive.) Start with the art you imagine as your centerpiece—not necessarily the biggest picture, but the one you most want people to notice—and then add remaining pieces around it. Successfully decorating a wall is about balance. You want neither a tiny piece of art on a vast wall, nor pictures claiming every square inch of wall space. Pictures should be hung so that their center point is at eye level—typically about five feet from the floor—but needn't be hung in frames of matching size. If art is obviously part of the same series, or if displaying a number of photographs, consider using complementary frames—perhaps made of the same material in different colors. The more eclectic your choice of frames, the more your home will look like a gallery; the more standardized your frames, the cleaner it will look.

Keep the following design guidelines in mind: When hanging art above a couch, try to stay 6 to 10 inches from the top of the backrest—any more and the eye goes to the wall, not the art. Unframed, abstract, or "challenging" modern art requires more negative space around it than do portraits, framed pieces, landscapes, and representative art. The darker the room, the more space the art needs (or install accent lights; see page 154). If you have two pictures of the same size, consider breaking up the flow of this art by placing a smaller picture between. Of course, these rules are frequently broken—trust your eye or solicit the opinion of someone whose taste you do trust.

Selecting Hanging Hardware

 Hanging art by a wire stretched across its back is easy—you drive a nail, balance the art on its wire, and then slide it until the art hangs level. However, wire is imprecise and prone to slippage, and is therefore not the first choice of most professional decorators. Instead, consider brackets in which one side mounts to the wall and the other mounts to the picture. They take a little more care going up, but assuming you did your homework before putting holes in the wall, you've got the hang you want for good (or until your taste in art changes). Resist the temptation to hook the back of a picture's frame onto a bare nail head. It's not a secure way of hanging a picture and could cause damage to the wall (and the picture!) if the nail pulls out, as it may. At the very least attach a hoop or tooth-style hanger on the back of the frame, which grabs on to a matched hook on the wall.

TOOLS:

Measuring tape • Pencil • Stud finder • 4-foot level

MATERIALS:

- **Nails**
- **Hooks, brackets, or wire-mounts**

1 Double-check placement. Before you start banging holes in the wall, consider the weight of your art—heavy art should be hung to a stud and not held only by drywall. Art over 50 pounds, such as a large mirror, is best hung on two studs. (See page 7 for how to locate studs.) Does this change your design? Consider the position of your heaviest piece and shift the overall placement of pieces as needed.

2 Measure and mark. Once you're confident in your design, measure up the wall 5 feet and make a light mark with a pencil in a location that will be covered by a picture. We'll call this "eye level." Alternatively, place sticky notes on the wall at the proper height to indicate positions (these are nice because you can also write measurement notes on them). Measure the height of your picture and divide by two—that's the height above your eye-level mark that you want the top of the picture. Measure up from your 5-foot eye-level mark and make a light line with pencil or hang a sticky note.

3 If you're using a hanging wire, measure the distance from the wire to the top of the frame, and subtract this measurement from the above-eye-level height. Mark this spot lightly on the wall, use nails to mount a picture hook over the mark, and hang the picture.

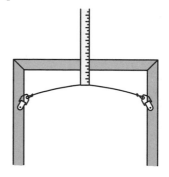

4 To hang with brackets or hooks, you'll need to be a little more precise. Hold the picture up to the wall and lay a 4-foot carpenter's level across the top of the frame. Work to perfectly position the

(continued)

piece and then use a pencil to draw a light line along the top where it should hang.

5 Determine your hardware location. On the back of the frame, measure the distance from the hanging point or points to the top of the frame. Note that if a frame includes two hooks on the back, there is no guarantee these two hooks are equal distance from the top. Measure each separately, as even a ⅛" error in hook height can make a world of difference in how level your art looks. Note also the distance these mounting hooks are from each other (unless there is only one hook).

6 Mount the hardware. Measure down from the top-of-frame line you drew on the wall to precisely mark the locations of the hanging hardware. Mark these locations on the wall and mount the hanging hardware.

7 Hang your art. If you're using a hanging wire, make sure that the wire catches on the hook(s) of the hanging hardware before you remove your hands from the frame.

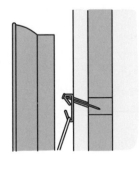

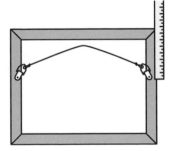

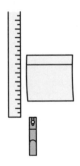

Although a frame may seem to be an arbitrary or replaceable border for a piece of fine art, it's deeply connected to the work itself and intertwined with its history. Changing the frame can de-value a piece of art, so make sure to properly box and store your art *and* its frame to best preserve the original work.

⤬ ⤬

Off the Wall

Hanging art flat on the wall isn't your only presentation option. Instead, consider building or installing a small shelf and setting framed art on it. And plates aren't the only items that can go in a wall-mounted plate display rack. Or turn art into a floor-piece by mounting it on a decorative easel. With a couple of eye screws and some wire, twine, or even yarn, art can be hung from the ceiling, too. ⤬

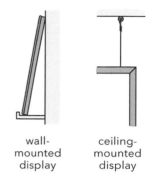

wall-
mounted
display

ceiling-
mounted
display

#2 How to Hang a Shelf

S ome projects—such as advanced joinery—might as well be rocket science. Others, like building a table, are surprisingly simple. Then there's hanging shelves, which seems like it would be easy, but if you want the job done right, turns out to be fairly tricky. How you go about it depends on where you want it hung and what material you'll be drilling into. Here's how to hang shelves that stay put.

What a Stud!

Drywall anchors tend to pull out if they're loaded with more than about 25 pounds, so when you're hanging a shelf in drywall, you'll almost always want to attach the shelf brackets to the wooden studs behind the wall. There are two types of stud finders—magnetic and electronic—and many models can be switched between the two. As the name implies, a magnetic stud finder contains a magnet and the finder beeps when it discovers the steel nails used to hook drywall to the studs. An electronic stud finder measures wall density by electrostatic fields and will sound when the density switches from just drywall to drywall backed by a stud. Because studs are not the only things in your walls that might make a

finder beep, it's worth confirming by checking for studs on either side. The construction norm is to set studs at 16" centers (rarely at 24" centers), meaning that every 16" along your wall you should find the dead center of a stud. Once you discover one stud with your finder, check for additional studs 16" in either direction. Mark the studs lightly with a pencil.

If you don't have a stud finder, look for existing screw or nail holes or for slightly raised nail heads covered in paint. Or look for electrical outlets, which are frequently attached to the studs. Tap with your knuckle as you move across the wall, listening for a solid rather than hollow sound, or push on the wall to check for give. Once you're moderately confident in your clues—from a stud finder or from exploration—probe with a thin drill bit to see if your hunch leads to solid wood. Be ready to close any holes you make with putty and paint.

(continued)

Finding Studs in a Plaster Wall

The walls of most newer homes are made of sheets of drywall mounted with nails to studs, sometimes finished with a thin layer of plaster. Until the late 1950s, however, many builders in the United States and Canada used a technique called lath and plaster, in which narrow wooden strips (laths) were tacked to studs and then covered in thick plaster. A stud finder is completely or almost completely useless in a lath and plaster wall, so instead use the tapping method described above to sleuth your way to stud locations. Once you have educated guesses, drill small exploratory holes, being sure to vary the heights of these holes so as not to weaken large sections of plaster. Older homes with lath and plaster walls may also suffer from imprecise stud spacing, meaning they might vary from 16" centers. In these plaster walls, it's even more important to drill exploratory holes to locate exact stud position before hanging shelves or anything heavy. Mark the edges of studs lightly with a pencil to ensure that you hit the center.

If Your Wall Is Masonry . . .

The good news is there are no studs in a brick or concrete wall. You can hang a shelf or heavy mirror wherever you like. The bad news is, you need specialized tools and a little extra hardware to do it. First, you'll need masonry anchors. Most common are expansion anchors, either nails or screws. If your wall is made of multiple layers of masonry with air between the layers, you can also use masonry toggle bolts, which will push through the first layer and then swivel flat against the layer's back edge (like a drywall butterfly bolt). To hang a shelf, you'll need a bracket at each end and spaced about every 24" in between. Choose anchors that are rated to hold about four times what you expect them to carry—estimate the weight of your loaded shelf, divide it by the number of anchors you plan to use, then multiply this number by four. Because masonry anchors exert force on the wall, they can't be clustered too close to each other for fear of cracking the concrete or brick. The rule of thumb is that masonry anchors should be placed no closer than 10 times the diameter of the anchor—so ¼" masonry anchors should be spaced at least 2½" apart. You'll also need either a hammer drill (rent one from your local home improvement store) or a masonry bit for your electric drill. Make sure the size of your drill bit is appropriate for your anchors. Drill the holes and insert the anchors as specified by the package directions or by hardware store experts.

TOOLS:

Stud finder (optional; see What a Stud!, page 7) • Measuring tape • Pencil • 4-foot level • Power drill • Screwdriver bit

MATERIALS:

- Shelf
- Bracket or mounting hardware
- Wood screws

1 Determine the material of your wall. If your walls are plaster or drywall, locate the studs (see What a Stud!, page 7).

2 Install the brackets on the shelf (the specific procedure will depend on your shelf and brackets— check the instructions that came with your bracket).

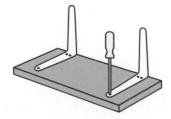

3 Plan the position of your screw holes. The best template for these holes is the shelf itself. With the mounting brackets installed on the shelf, lay a 4-foot level across the shelf and position it against the wall where you want it to hang. For drywall or plaster, make sure your mounting brackets are placed every 16" and aligned with studs. In masonry walls, brackets can be 24" apart. With a pencil, mark the wall through the screw holes in the shelf brackets. Remove the shelf and use a thin drill bit to double-check that each hole hits a stud.

4 Attach the shelves to the wall. Using your drill and screws appropriate to your wall material, attach the bracketed shelf to the wall. Depending on your mounting hardware, you may be able to drive the screws and then hang the shelf directly on them, or you may need to hold the shelf in place while you drive screws through the mounting brackets.

Before they were used to stack books spine-out, shelves held piles of scrolls, and later, books with the spine facing *in*.

#3 How to Install a Closet Rod

T he specifics of hanging a closet rod may vary, but there is one consistent absolute: Hang it strong. Not only are your clothes heavy and the distance the bar spans likely to be wide, but this bar is likely to see abuse as you yank free a shirt or pull pants straight off the hanger. So don't skimp on the mounting hardware, and never try to hang a rod directly from drywall. The instructions here are for hanging the traditional 1¼" wooden dowel closet rod.

Too Clever by Half

There is a fine line dividing genius from gimmick. And that line is practicality. Yes, there are systems that hang from the back of a closet door that allow you to organize 50 pairs of shoes, but if that hanging is going to bang around every time you open the door, making a ruckus and preventing you from closing it, it's not your best option. Likewise, there are hooks that mount to walls, allowing you to hang many items from one attachment, but then you can't see what's in the back. There are battery-powered tie racks and push-button shoe racks—the list goes on. If your stuff is, in fact, overflowing your closet and there is no hope of organizing it neatly in a traditional bar-and-shelf system, you may have to explore other options. First try getting rid of stuff— thrift and consignment stores will gladly accept gently used items. But if your storage needs aren't extreme, bars and shelves are likely your cleanest, easiest options.

(continued)

TOOLS:

Measuring tape • Pencil • Handsaw (optional) • Drill screwdriver bit

MATERIALS:

- 1 × 4 pieces of lumber
- 2½" wood screws (or closet rod manufacturer's hardware)
- Hanging brackets (buy premade or use about 6" chunks of 2 × 4)
- 1¼" wooden dowel

1 Look for studs. Locate the studs in the sidewalls of your closet and mark their location. (See page 7 for instructions on locating studs.) Ideally, you will find them located between 12 inches and 14 inches in from the back wall—enough space to properly hang clothes. If you do find such studs, skip to Step 3.

2 Forget the studs. The chances of finding appropriately placed studs on either side of the closet are about the same as winning the lottery. Instead, it's very likely you'll have to hang the rod from strips of 1 × 4 lumber mounted to the studs. Start by cutting two strips of wood to match the depth of the closet's sidewalls (or have them cut at the lumber store).

3 Mount the brace. Most closet rods are hung at eye level. Either eyeball the height and mark it on the walls, or make a mark on the wall about 5 feet up from the floor. (Be double sure that your measurements match at every point, or you will have a frustratingly slanted closet rod.) Hold a wood strip at this height, level it, and mark the location of the stud(s) on the strip. Screw or nail the wood strip through the side wall into the stud(s). Repeat with the other side. If there is no stud or wood whatsoever behind the closet drywall, use appropriate drywall mounting hardware for the wood strips. Then you'll have to reinforce the rod with supports that

reach out from the wall studs along the back of the closet.

4 Attach the brackets. It's easiest to use commercial rod-hanging brackets, though you can certainly make your own—a chunk of 2 × 4 with a 1¼" hole drilled in the middle makes a fine bracket. One bracket should be closed all the way around and the other should be open at the top. If you're using premade brackets, follow the manufacturer's mounting instructions. If you're using chunks of 2 × 4, use 2½" screws to screw through the 2 × 4 and into the wood strips mounted to the wall.

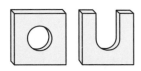

5 Hang the rod. Once you've mounted the brackets to the wood strips, push the dowel into the closed side and set it into the open bracket.

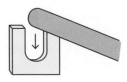

✕ ✕

Closet Overhaul

An organized closet is the first step toward good feng shui and a harmonious life. But don't plunge directly into screwing things to your walls or assembling a one-size-fits-all wire rack system. That's because one size certainly does not fit all when it comes to organizing a closet. Spend ample time planning and figuring out your particular organizational needs before you begin.

Start by evaluating the large items like shirts, pants, and other clothes that need to be hung—this will help define the broad strokes of how your space will be divided. Generally, there are two ways to deal with these clothes: a single horizontal bar or layers of bars. A single bar is easiest—see How to Install a Closet Rod, page 9, for instructions. But if that long expanse is too long for your needs, you're inviting dead space. Imagine other possibilities. Assume you don't want to hang clothes at ceiling height and instead anything above about head level will be home to a shelf of boxes, bins, baskets, or purses.

To "stack" the bars, you'll be dividing the space vertically. Say shirts claim half the available height, and pants and dresses take two thirds. You can either make the shirts double-decker or longer straight across. Decide whether you prefer the usable space to be above or below the pants and dresses—space above can hold shelves for folded clothes and space below can hold bins, drawers, or shelves to hold socks, shoes, and undergarments. If you like, draw a picture of your closet and then fill it in with lines to split this space in various ways. (If you really want to do it right, use graph paper and plot out the precise dimensions.) Then evaluate your construction skills—can you build your vision yourself, do you need to hire a contractor, or can you approximate it with a some-assembly-required closet organization system? ✕

#4 How to Patch a Hole in Drywall

There's a distinctive sound drywall makes when it gets punched with a stray furniture leg or burdened to the breaking point with an improperly secured shelf—a sickening crunch followed by an agonizing cracking noise. If you haven't heard this, you will someday, and when that day comes you'll want to know how to patch a hole in drywall. Depending on the size of your puncture (from nail hole to gaping abyss), there are different techniques to fix it. Pick your poison from the instructions below.

Patch a Tiny Hole

Nail and screw holes, along with other small punctures, can be covered over directly with drywall joint compound, aka putty, patching compound, or mud. (In a move-out pinch, you can use toothpaste on white walls to plug tiny holes. Just don't tell your landlord.)

TOOLS:

Fine sandpaper • Rags • Flexible 4" putty knife

MATERIALS:

- Drywall compound
- Paint

1 Sand around the hole to flatten any rough spots. Wipe away any sanding dust with a wet rag and let the area dry.

(continued)

2 Use a putty knife to apply drywall compound. Place a small amount directly into the small hole and then smooth it flat to the wall with the wide blade of the putty knife. Let it dry for about 2 hours and then apply a second layer if needed.

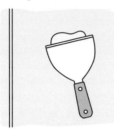

3 Sand the putty smooth, if needed. Dab the patch with paint to match the wall.

Patch Small Holes

If it's bigger than the size of a quarter but smaller than 8" × 8", you'll need to repair the hole with an adhesive wall patch as well as drywall compound.

TOOLS:

Coarse sandpaper • Handheld fine sanding block • Utility knife • 4" putty knife • Rags

MATERIALS:

- **Adhesive wall patch**
- **Drywall compound**
- **Texture spray (optional)**
- **Paint**

1 Remove any loose drywall in or around the hole. Use a utility knife to free any dangling pieces and to trim the edges of the hole until smooth. Finish cleaning the hole with coarse sandpaper.

2 Cover the hole. Fit an adhesive wall patch over the hole, extending around it several inches in each direction. It should look like you've covered the hole with cheesecloth. This is the backing against which you will apply drywall compound. A slightly larger hole, around 8" × 8", would require a galvanized metal patch, also available at your local hardware store.

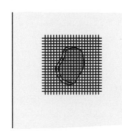

3 Smooth out the patch. Use a putty knife to apply drywall compound over the wall patch. Starting out past the edges and moving toward the center, smooth

the compound to completely cover the patch. You may need to let the edges of the patching compound dry for 15 or 20 minutes so that it can support the putty in the center of the wall patch. Don't worry about making the putty exactly smooth now—you'll sand it in the next step. Let the patching compound dry overnight.

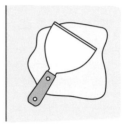

4 Smooth again. Use fine sandpaper stapled to a wood block or a similar sanding tool to smooth the patching compound. Be aware that a somewhat flimsy adhesive patch is the only thing backing your hole, so pushing firmly into it while sanding is likely to crack the compound. Wipe away any sanding dust with a wet rag and let dry.

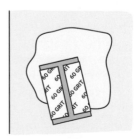

5 Paint the patch. Cover the patching compound with paint that matches the surrounding wall. If the wall is textured, spray it with wall texture spray to match, let dry overnight, and then paint.

Patch Medium Holes

If your hole is greater than 8 inches square, you'll need to repair it with a Sheetrock plug. Common drywall (aka Sheetrock) is gypsum paste poured and hardened between sheets of paper. It can be cut to shape and used to plug large holes for a sturdier fix.

TOOLS:

Utility knife • Measuring tape • Pencil • Handheld fine sanding block • 4" putty knife

MATERIALS:

- **Square piece of drywall**
- **Drywall compound**
- **Texture spray (optional)**
- **Paint**

1 Remove any loose drywall and smooth out the hole as described in Step 1 on page 12.

2 Make the plug. On a square of drywall at least 2 inches wider than the hole on all sides, draw the shape of the cleaned and prepped hole. (Trace it first if it's too irregular to freehand.) Use a utility knife to cut out the shape of the plug through the first layer of paper and also through the gypsum core, but leave the second layer of paper intact. It's better to cut the plug a little too big rather than too small, so cut around the outline to be safe.

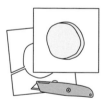

3 Fit the plug. Shave the edges of the Sheetrock plug with a utility knife until it fits snugly in the wall hole.

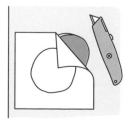

4 Slot the plug into the hole. Position it with the intact layer of Sheetrock paper on the outside. If needed, trim the drywall paper so that it extends about an inch beyond the hole on all sides.

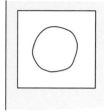

5 Attach the plug. Spread a thin layer of drywall patching compound on the side of the paper that lies flush against the wall and press the paper firmly to stick the plug in place.

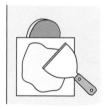

6 Use a putty knife to patch the plug with drywall compound so that it's smooth and flush with the wall. Sand, texture-spray, and paint as described in Step 5, Patch Small Holes.

Patch Large Holes

A hole of more than about a square foot in area requires something more than an adhesive patch or a drywall plug to properly fill it. In this case, you'll need to frame the back of the hole with a 2 × 4, and then attach a larger drywall patch to the frame.

TOOLS:

Utility knife • Measuring tape • Handsaw • 4" putty knife • Fine sanding block

MATERIALS:

- Scrap 14½" 2 × 4
- Framing nails or wood screws
- Drywall
- Drywall screws
- Drywall compound
- Texture spray (optional)
- Paint

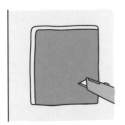

1   Square up your hole. Use a utility knife to cut the hole to a good approximation of a clean rectangle, extending toward the vertical wall studs on either side of the hole.

2   Frame the hole. Cut one or more sections of scrap 2 × 4 to 14¼" lengths. These 2 × 4s will span between framing studs; use enough 2 × 4s to reduce the size of any hole to less than a foot per side. Place these sections in the hole horizontally between the wall studs. Nail or screw the backing wood in place by reaching into the wall and nailing the 2 × 4s diagonally (see Toe-nailing box, below) through the backing wood and into the studs.

3   Plug the hole. Draw the dimensions of the hole onto a piece of drywall and cut out the plug with a utility knife. Use drywall screws to attach the plug to the 2 × 4 backing and to any exposed vertical studs.

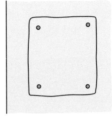

4   Finish the patch. Use a putty knife to patch the plug with drywall compound so that it's smooth and flush with the wall. Sand, texture-spray, and paint as described in Step 5, Patch Small Holes.

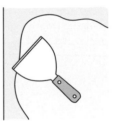

✗ ✗

Toe-nailing: It Has Nothing to Do with Pedicures

Driving a nail into the end of a board at an angle can help you anchor it to another board. This procedure is called toe-nailing. Although it seems straightforward, it can be tricky, so here are a few tips:

- It's best to visualize where the nail will be going—you can do this by holding the nail up next to the boards at an angle.

- Start by tapping the nail in straight on to make the first hole. Then readjust your angle after you've made a small indent.

- If you can drive the nail at an angle through the first board and *then* position it on the other board, that's ideal.

- If you're at a loss for space, try drilling a pilot hole first. ✗

#5 How to Mix Plaster

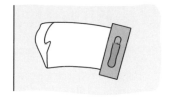

Traditionally, plasterers used putty to create a reservoir on a plastering board. They poured water into this reservoir and then sprinkled it with plaster until it *felt* just right. When the lime in the plaster powder hits water, it creates a chemical reaction that releases heat—so when traditional plasterers felt that the heat was gone, they knew the plaster was ready for use. You can approximate this art in a bucket.

TOOLS:

Bucket • Drill with mixing paddle attachment • Trowel • Spot board

MATERIALS:

• **Patching plaster**

1 Fill a large bucket with water. You'll need enough water for a ratio of one part plaster to one part water. Consider starting with less plaster than you think you'll need and then making another batch once you've been through the process. Traditionally, the first coat of plaster was mixed with a bit of horsehair to help the plaster adhere to itself. Today, lime or gypsum plaster is mixed with sand, fiber, and water. Replacing lime with gypsum removes the need for fiber. Consider mixing three parts silica sand to one part gypsum powder for your first, rough coat of plaster.

2 Add plaster powder until it starts to accumulate on the surface of the water (about half the total plaster you will be using). Use a stirring attachment on your drill to mix until smooth. Add half the remaining plaster powder and again mix until smooth, being sure to scrape the edge of the bucket free of lumps that can be difficult to blend with the smoother plaster. Continue adding plaster and mixing until it reaches a consistency at which it sits on a flat trowel without running off (make it a little thicker if you are plastering ceilings).

3 Pour a workable amount of the mixture onto your plastering spot board. You have about 30 minutes to apply the plaster before it will be too dry to properly mold. See next page for best application practices.

Patching a Hole in Plaster

Use a utility knife to clean the edges of the hole and remove any loose or cracked plaster. Then use a screwdriver to dig out the back of the hole (without further chipping the front!). Trimming behind the hole will allow new plaster to grab the laths behind the hole. Use one rough coat and one finishing coat to first fill and then cover the hole. ✕

#6 How to Plaster a Wall

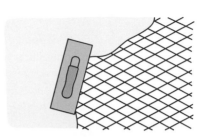

ath and plaster—a technique for building walls that involves nailing narrow strips of wood (lath) across vertical studs to serve as a foundations for spreading plaster—was the dominant method of interior wall finishing in the US and Canada until the 1950s. As was typical of prewar construction, precision in lath-and-plaster work wasn't necessarily of utmost importance. So the laths that span horizontally across a plaster wall are likely to be somewhere around, but not exactly, 2" wide by ¾" thick, leaving about a ⅜" gap between courses. After the laths were laid, builders covered them with a thick layer of plaster, followed by a thinner second coat. The plaster was allowed to push through the gaps in the laths to the back, where it hooked around the boards which, when dry, held the plaster in place.

You may have historic plaster walls in your house, or you might have faux-finish plaster meant to replicate the feel of these walls. Whatever the case, it's useful to know how to repair it. The techniques in this section apply to stucco (usually an exterior finish) as well as to lime plaster (calcium hydroxide mixed with sand and water), though you'll need to add Portland cement to the mix for exterior stucco surfaces (the experts at your local home improvement store should be able to help).

TOOLS:

Bucket • Drill with stirring attachment • Trowel • Spot board • Joint (spackling) knife • Comb or plasterer's rake • Spray bottle of water

MATERIALS:

- **Plaster powder**
- **Sand**

1 Mix the plaster. See How to Mix Plaster, page 15. Apply the rough coat. Use the flat edge of a joint knife to apply the first coat of plaster. Lay it on about ¼" thick (more than that and the plaster will take forever to dry and can be prone to cracking). Force this coat through the laths (or into the bricks) so that when the plaster dries, the hardened pieces that pushed through form "keys" that hold it firmly to the backing. Once you start a layer, work quickly to finish applying plaster to the

Drywall panels are made from a compressed rock known as gypsum. Since gypsum contains water (bound in crystalline form) the material is considered to provide some protection against fire.

wall before it dries, otherwise you're likely to be left with start and stop lines.

2 Rake the plaster. Before the rough coat dries completely, use a sturdy comb or plasterer's rake to score the surface into ridges that will help the next layer bond. Let the layer dry at least 24 hours or, ideally, 36 hours. Use a spray bottle to gently dampen the surface a couple of times to allow the plaster to dry slowly—this will make it stronger.

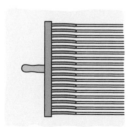

3 Apply the second layer. This next coat is called the brown coat and is mixed exactly like the first, applied ¼" thick, but this time you don't rake the surface.

4 Apply the final layer. For the third layer, leave the sand out of your plaster and, if you like, choose from a range of commercial colors and textures. (Follow manufacturer's instructions to add to the plaster.) Before the brown coat is completely dry, mix the plaster and apply it directly on top. While you apply the finish coat, it's very helpful to keep a spray bottle on hand to lightly mist the area where you're working. That will help this final layer go on smoother rather than having patches dry as you work (although the plaster won't be fully dry for 36 hours or more).

Go Metal

If you're starting a plaster wall from scratch or if your job requires pulling plaster down to the laths, consider replacing wood laths with new metal ones. As wood laths expand and contract with moisture and temperature changes, they can crack the plaster. Metal laths don't have this problem and are also fitted with additional holes and pockets ("keys") that allow the plaster to hold more tightly. If plastering over brick, rather than laths, consider priming with a bonding agent that will help the plaster stick.

#7 How to Repair Cracked Plaster

As the foundation settles, shifting can create hairline or larger cracks in plaster walls. It's easier to repair a wide crack than a hairline, which is too thin to allow plaster to form "keys" and adhere. So your first step in repairing a very thin crack is in fact to widen it.

TOOLS:

Utility knife • Joint (spackling) knife

MATERIALS:

• Patching plaster

1 Use a utility knife or the edge of a trowel to dig into the hairline crack, widening it to about ⅛".

2 Mix up a small amount of plaster (see How to Mix Plaster, page 15). Use a spackling knife to apply a ¼" layer of finish plaster (with color or texture added, as necessary to match), pressing it as deeply as possible into the crack and blending the edges of the new plaster over the existing finish.

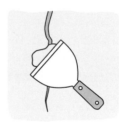

Lime plaster is one of the oldest materials used for building—traditionally it involved mixing horsehair into the water, lime, and sand for reinforcement.

#8 How to Prepare a Surface for Painting

Instead of painting a beautiful color on your walls that's doomed to peel or flake off and will require another coat (or two), always prime first. Any surface you paint should be primed, including walls, wood, concrete, or metal. The only time you may be able to skip priming is when you're painting over an already painted surface—that is, as long as the existing paint is in good condition and the new paint you're applying matches the base (oil or water) of the existing paint. If the existing paint is cracking, peeling, or chipped, or if you're applying oil-based paint over latex or vice versa, you must prime.

The tools you choose will depend on how much existing paint you need to rip off before applying new paint. So tools may range from a paint scraper to a wire brush to just a damp washcloth. Gauge the tools you need, and if at first you don't succeed, try something a little more heavy-duty.

TOOLS:

Paint scraper, wire brush, or damp washcloth (see headnote) • Fine sandpaper

MATERIALS:

• Primer

1 If you are switching from an oil-based to a water-based paint (or vice versa) and the paint is intact on the surface, apply primer evenly and move on.

2 If the existing paint is flaking, it's time to get scraping (or see How to Strip Paint, page 28). Scrape until paint stops coming off.

3 After scraping, you'll want to sand. This helps to get those last few chips of old paint off the surface and will also smooth imperfections.

4 Wipe the surface with a damp washcloth to remove sawdust, dust, spiderwebs, and everything else you prefer not to make a permanent part of the surface.

5 Finally, apply primer. Paint it on as you would a regular coat of paint (see How to Paint a Room, below), and let dry.

Pro tip: Tint the primer with a little bit of the final paint color.

#9 How to Paint a Room

Maybe your attitude doesn't require, as Jimmy Buffett posited, a change in latitude. Maybe it just requires a new color scheme! If those beige walls are dragging you down, change it up. Painting is one of those DIY jobs that looks like a big deal but really isn't. It should only take one day to repaint a room. The techniques here apply to both ceilings and walls. If painting the ceiling, start there (with plenty of drop cloths or newspaper on the floor) since it will drip everywhere. As with many projects, preparation turns out to be at least half the battle.

Picking Your Paint

Paint finishes range in shine from flat to glossy. Flat finish paints are sometimes referred to as wall paint—they're the norm for most interior applications. For trim (baseboards, molding), go shinier—at least satin, if not semi-gloss, or even gloss. The contrast of flat to satin texture adds depth to a room, and glossier paints are formulated to withstand scrubbing—perfect for moldings, kids' rooms, and kitchens. If you do go glossy, be sure to do your prep work—high-gloss finishes highlight imperfections that a flat paint will hide. One gallon of paint covers about 350 square feet of wall space. To estimate how much paint you'll need, multiply the length and height of your walls and add the surfaces together, subtracting 20 square feet for each door and about 10 square feet for the average window.

(continued)

TOOLS:

Drop cloths • Painter's tape • Screwdriver • Rags • 4" putty knife • Paintbrushes (angled, trim) • 50-grit sandpaper • Paint tray and/or small paint bucket • Paint roller

MATERIALS:

- **Putty and/or patching caulk**
- **Soap**
- **Primer (if needed)**
- **Paint**
- **Paint thinner (if using oil-based paint)**

1 Prepare the space. Remove pictures and other hanging art and move furniture to the middle of the room or far enough from the walls to provide easy access. Cover the floor and furniture with drop cloths and tape them down with painter's tape to avoid slipping. Remove all electrical switch plates and then cover the sockets with painter's tape.

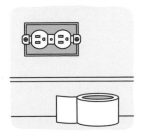

2 Putty or otherwise patch all holes. Caulk or otherwise fill all gaps. Wash your old wall with soap and water to remove all oil, dirt, and accumulated grime. Perhaps more than anything else, this step is the difference between a pristine painted surface and a wall full of imperfections and drips.

3 If necessary, prime the wall. New paint will stick to old paint (as long as you aren't changing from oil-based to water-based, or vice versa—see page 19), but it won't stick so well to bare drywall or plaster. Even if you have existing paint, if you've puttied large holes or otherwise done significant repair, consider priming to put all of your new paint on equal footing. When in doubt, prime. Primer can take anywhere from 30 minutes to 3 hours to dry, depending on the temperature of the room and how thick you apply it. Make sure you allow it to dry fully before moving to the next step.

4 Sand. Whether you are working with a primed wall or an old layer of paint, scuff the surfaces with 50-grit sandpaper to help the new paint adhere. You're not trying to rip away paint with this sanding, so you can do it by stapling your sandpaper to scrap wood and sanding by hand. Wipe down the surfaces with a damp rag to remove accumulated dust.

5 Tape—but don't over-tape! You know that sticking a layer of blue painter's tape to fixtures, baseboards, and crown molding can keep the paint just where you want it. But tape also gives you *permission* to make slips. And inevitably, if you're using tape as your ruler and simply painting over it, paint will sneak underneath and make a mess. If you have hard-to-reach places likely to see significant

painting errors or any surfaces that for whatever reason can't be retouched, tape them. But be stingy with the tape and rely instead on angled brushes and a steady hand.

6 Do your edge work. Pour a small reservoir of paint into a paint tray or small paint bucket (so you don't need to cart around the entire can). Then, starting with an angled brush, carefully paint along all edges, including 3 inches in from junctions with walls, corners, and molding. When you use an angled brush, only wet it with paint about a third of the way up the bristles and then tap it instead of wiping it to clear the extra paint. Run a stroke about an inch away from molding or another unpainted surface and then gently press the longer bristles of the brush close to precisely where the wall meets the base of the molding—hold your breath and draw a very straight line. Either hang a damp rag from your belt or keep one within arm's reach so that you can quickly wipe away mistakes. If you wait until they dry, errors are much more difficult to remove.

Complete the edges of only one wall area and make the switch to rollers. This will help ensure your detail work is still wet when you apply the first rolled coat.

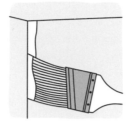

7 Prepare your roller. Fill a paint tray with just enough paint so the top of the puddle reaches the bottom of the ridged grate. Dampen the roller. Use water for latex paint or paint thinner for oils. Smush the roller into the paint and then draw it up the grate to spread it uniformly across the roller. A splotchy roller makes for a splotchy paint job.

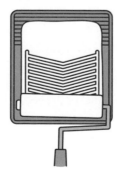

8 Roll out the paint. Slop paint onto the wall in large W shapes. Your goal at this stage isn't to cover the wall, merely to generally distribute the paint.

9 Finish the first coat. Once the paint starts to run thin on your W patterns, go back over the wall with even, vertical strokes. These strokes should spread the initially slopped paint evenly, and should overlap so the strokes bleed into each other. When the roller starts to make a crackling sound, reload it with paint. Remember: The first layer needn't be perfect.

10 Apply a second coat. Let this layer dry thoroughly. Latex paints should dry within an hour; give oil-based paints a full 24 hours. If you need to apply a third coat, clean and sand the second (as in Steps 2 and 4) and then start again with the angled brush and roller (as in Step 8). When you've

(continued)

completed all coats on one wall, move on to the next and start over with Step 5.

11 Paint the trim. If you'd like to paint the molding and other trim, do that after the walls are rolled out. Start with a brush that's slightly narrower than the trim. For wide molding this can be a broad, straight brush but for thinner trim, consider a small angled brush. Once you've painted the front of the molding, finish the sides with a very small angled brush. This can take the steadiness of a surgeon and the patience of Mother Teresa. If in doubt, leave the molding to the pros.

#10 How to Paint a Faux Finish

H ave you ever wanted to sleep in the Sistine Chapel? How about the Taj Mahal? Or the Vatican? Well, you can't—but you can make your walls *look* like a marble sanctuary. Faux painting can do wonders for a room or piece of furniture, whether you are striving to replicate the look of a more expensive finish or simply adding spice to an otherwise monochromatic space. Here are guidelines for a variety of popular faux finishing techniques. Whenever trying a faux painting technique for the first time, experiment first on scrap board instead of going straight to the walls.

Bronze

Recreating the look of bronze requires three slightly adjusted degrees of bronze glaze over a base coat.

TOOLS:

Paint roller and paint tray (optional) • Paintbrushes • 50-grit sandpaper • Rags • 3 buckets • Sea sponge

MATERIALS:

- **Dark yellow latex (eggshell) paint**
- **Acrylic clear glaze**
- **Metallic topcoat glaze**

1 Prep the painting surface. See How to Prepare a Surface for Painting, page 18.

2 Paint the surface. Roll or brush on a latex eggshell base coat in a shade of dark yellow.

3 Prepare the glaze. In three separate buckets, mix the following three solutions: In the first, combine one part yellow base-layer paint with three parts clear glaze; in the second, combine some of the first bucket's mixture with a metallic topcoat glaze to blend. And in the third bucket mix one part of the second bucket's mixture with ½ part water.

1 part base-layer paint & 3 parts clear glaze

some of bucket 1 mix & metallic topcoat glaze

1 part of bucket 2 mix & ½ part water

4 Add the glaze. Use a roller or brush to apply these three mixtures to the wall, over your base coat. If you have three people painting, start at the same time, one with each mixture; otherwise start painting with any mixture and then switch frequently to the others. Patterns should be random and overlapping. Use a sea sponge to push the three mixtures into each other, covering the entire wall with blended glaze.

5 Finish the glaze. Let the wall dry completely and then use a sea sponge to dab on a metallic topcoat glaze.

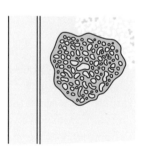

Marble

Marble is a tricky faux finish, so make sure you practice on a (primed) scrap board. There are many colors of marble, ranging from pink to orange to red to green and blue. Replicating the look of marble is more an art than a craft. When choosing your paint, imagine four colors that come together in your ideal marble. Keep a photo of your model marble on hand to review as you paint.

TOOLS:

Paintbrushes • 50-grit sandpaper • 4 paint buckets • Rags • Sea sponge

MATERIALS:

- **Primer**
- **Paint (4 shades, including white: see headnote)**
- **Latex glaze**
- **Varnish**

1 Prep the surface as per Step 1 in Bronze. Prime, and apply a white base coat. Let it dry and then sand it lightly, brushing free any dust with a damp rag.

2 Paint the base coat. In four separate buckets, mix one part paint with one part water and one part clear latex glaze. Start with two somewhat similar colors as your base. Brush wavy patterns of these two colors onto the wall or piece of furniture so they bleed into each other in fairly organic patterns. Use a wet painting sponge to soften and blur the lines between them.

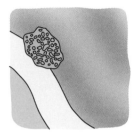

3 Add the marbling. Paint veins with the other two colors. Use a paintbrush or sponge to drip a small ribbon of paint in from the top of the wall and then feather the edges of these veins into the base colors by pulling their edges with a dry brush.

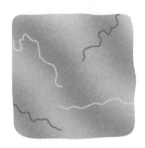

4 Refine the marbling. Review your image of marble—likely there are thinner, crisper veins in addition to the wider, colored swaths you just painted. Use a thin paintbrush to snake appropriately colored veins (likely white) through the multicolored base you laid.

(continued)

5 Add detail. Marble also frequently includes colored mineral intrusions. Using your best artistic sense, add these intrusions by dabbing on your fourth color of paint with a sea sponge and then feather the edges into the background with a dry brush.

6 Finish up—or start over. If your marbling simply didn't work, prime

over it and try again. Once you're comfortable with its appearance, finish the marbling with a layer of protective varnish.

Terra Fresco

For that Italian villa look, cover your walls with a faux finish that replicates this classic Mediterranean plastering technique. Mimicking this surface requires plaster and three off-brown colors of latex paint. Think shades of ochre and café au lait—choose according to your preference and decor. As with other finishes, using an image as a guide can be helpful.

TOOLS:

Rags • 50-grit sandpaper • 3 buckets • Plasterer's blade

MATERIALS:

- **Primer**
- **Drywall compound**
- **3 colors of latex paint in reddish brown, orangish brown, and brick**

1 Prep the surface as per Step 1 in Bronze.

2 Mix the paint with drywall compound. In three separate buckets, add drywall compound to three shades of paint, just until the paint thickens slightly.

3 Apply the base coat. Choose base color—not necessarily the darkest or lightest color, but the color that is closest to the desired finished color—and use a plasterer's blade to apply a fairly thin layer of the plaster mixture to a section of the wall. Cover the wall completely with this base layer. You can make this a slightly thicker consistency than the top layers.

4 Add the layers. While the base plaster is still wet, use the blade to blend smaller amounts of the other two colors into the wall. Use your aesthetics—this step should make the wall look very close to your image of terra fresco. Apply thin coats, being careful not to overload the surface of the wall with plaster.

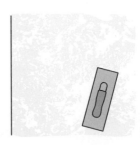

Stone

From fireplace mantels to tabletops, a stone finish adds texture and warmth. As with terra fresco, you combine plaster with paint to get the desired organic look. Faux stone finishes can range from a deep red sandstone to gray slate. Basically, you'll want to pick a base color and two highlight colors—consider looking online at pictures of the rock you plan to mimic and choosing your colors accordingly.

TOOLS:

**50-grit sandpaper •
Plasterer's blade or trowel •
Paintbrush**

MATERIALS:

- **Primer**
- **Drywall compound**
- **3 colors of latex paint**
- **Clear latex glaze**

1 Prep the surface as per Step 1 in Bronze.

2 Plaster the surface. After prepping the wall, spread a thin (¼") layer of drywall compound over it with a plasterer's blade.

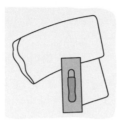

3 Texture the surface. When the compound is tacky but not yet dry, press the blade (or a trowel) flat into the compound and pull it straight out to texture the entire surface. This will take some art—shoot for gentle texture rather than the peaks and valleys of cake frosting. Let the plaster dry fully.

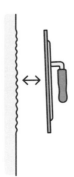

4 Paint the wall. Brush on a base coat that matches your desired color of stone. Allow the layer to dry.

5 Apply accent colors. Use a painter's sponge to dab on each accent color in patterns that match your desired stone look. If necessary, use a dry rag to blend accent colors into the base color.

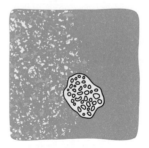

#11 How to Polish Furniture

Wax finishes have been used for a thousand years, but their modern use has waned (pardon the pun). That's because they're not especially protective, as it turns out. Yes, you can coat a console table in wax, but don't expect it to resist water and wear. Instead, a wax finish alone is best reserved for hands-off wood pieces like art. However, paired with a protective finish like lacquer, shellac, or varnish, wax will fill tiny scratches to restore luster, so polishing finished furniture with wax makes it really shine. Wax-based furniture polishes are common—when your finish loses its glow, simply rub on a new layer.

Why Wax?

Stain colors wood. Varnish, lacquer, shellac, and other finishes protect wood. And wax shines wood. Because wax locks in oils and keeps a piece from drying and cracking, it's especially useful for finished furniture that sits in a sunny location. No matter how you use it, wax is rarely worth using alone—it provides no barrier against water, heat, or a wine spill. Instead, combine it with stains and protective finishes to achieve the look you want with the durability you need. Though some woodworkers insist otherwise, protective finishes like lacquer, shellac, and varnish shouldn't be applied on top of wax—they simply won't grip. Instead think of wax as the finishing touch.

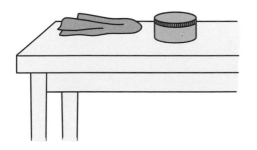

Which Wax?

Like oil finishes and varnishes, many wax furniture finishes are derived from natural sources. Chief among these are carnauba wax, derived from the leaves of the carnauba palm, and beeswax, which is derived from, well, bees.

Most waxes are sold in a tin similar to the kind you would expect to hold shoe polish. That's no accident—wax finishes, in fact, work very much like shoe polish, and are applied in the same way. And like shoe polish, you should match the color of the wax to the color of the piece. Wax in a complementary color can make a finish shine; contradictory wax color will cloud it. You can find paint-on wax finishes, but they're traditionally (and still most commonly) sold as pastes.

Be sure that whatever wax you get, it's compatible with the existing finish. Some waxes include a solvent that makes the wax easier to work with and can help create a more uniform finish, but solvent-based wax will eat into a water-based finish. Likewise, make extra sure that your protective finish has dried completely before applying a solvent-based wax, otherwise you risk harming the finish.

TOOLS:

Lint-free rags

MATERIALS:

- Oil soap, like Murphy brand
- Furniture wax

1 Apply the wax. Before application, thoroughly wipe the piece clean with a rag dampened with soap and water. Wipe the piece dry with a lint-free cloth to be sure no dust, dirt, or other impurities remain. Start with a small dollop of paste wax on a clean cloth covering your first two fingers. A little wax goes a surprisingly long way and it's easier to apply wax a little at a time than to end up with gobs of wax that must be scrubbed away. Like polishing a shoe, rub the wax onto the wood piece with circular motions. If applying wax directly to bare wood or to stained (but not protected) wood, focus on pushing the wax down into the wood grain. The most forceful stroke should go with the wood grain, but continue to work the polish in a circular pattern. If applying wax over a protective finish like a lacquer, varnish, or shellac, the wood's grain will already be hidden and you can wax the piece just as you would wax a car or shoe. Apply wax until you see it start to build up on the surface of the piece.

2 Buff the furniture. After applying wax, wait for the wood to turn hazy—this indicates dried wax remaining on the surface, instead of sinking into the pores, which must be wiped from the piece. However, if you wait too long, wax will dry into a fairly impervious shell that can be difficult to remove. Buff when wax is cloudy but not yet firm. Use a clean piece of lint-free, cotton cloth to rub the waxed furniture until it shines. Don't be shy: You should expect to remove the bulk of the wax you just applied. If you accidentally wait too long, consider applying another layer of wax, which can help to significantly loosen the dried first layer.

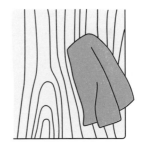

Beeswax was so highly coveted in the ancient world that it was considered a valuable form of currency. When the Romans conquered the island of Corsica in 181 BCE, the defeated Corsicans were taxed 100,000 pounds of beeswax.

#12 How to Strip Paint

You know for a fact that there's a gorgeous oak chair underneath that hideous hot-pink paint, and you need to set it free. Or perhaps you'd like to expose the wood trim in your old farmhouse. There are so many reasons to want to remove paint, and the results are almost always worth the hassle.

Chemical Warfare

For years, the standby chemical for stripping paint has been methylene chloride; however, it's exceedingly toxic and can even be fatal. Opt instead for benzyl alcohol or soy-based strippers, which are safer for you and the environment. (If you do use a methylene chloride–based paint stripper, you must wear a respirator, chemical-resistant gloves, and protective clothes, and catch all excess chemicals with a drop cloth and rags.)

Some paint strippers are spray-on liquids while others are paint-on gels. Liquids are good for removing one or two coats of paint and for hard-to-reach or irregular surfaces. Gels generally sit on the paint longer and fight gravity better—they can be painted on walls and even overhangs. Because gels sit longer, they work better for tough projects, like removing 15 layers of paint from century-old clapboard.

The Sanding Option

You can also sand away old paint. But for a large job like the side of a house, sanding is a fairly inefficient method. Likewise, it may not be the right method for a delicate job like fine furniture, because it removes a layer of the underlying wood along with the paint. For those Goldilocks jobs that are neither too big nor too fine, scouring the paint away with coarse-grain sandpaper helps you avoid the use of chemicals.

Get the Lead Out

In 1978, lead was outlawed as a paint additive. Before that, however, it was used widely. So if you're stripping layers of old paint, be aware that it might contain lead. In that case, stay away from sanding, which can create inhalable lead-tinged dust. While stripping, make sure you catch lead paint flakes on a drop cloth, and bag and dispose of them properly at a hazardous waste collection center.

✂ ✂

Some Like It Hot

If you want to avoid chemicals, you can also strip paint with a heat gun. Hold the heat gun in one hand and a paint scraper in the other as you heat and then scrape away the paint, one small section at a time. Be sure to keep the heat gun moving constantly so it doesn't scorch the surface or create dangerous embers. On small jobs, you can even substitute a hair dryer for the heat gun; just hold it very close to the paint and don't expect it to peel off in sheets. ✂

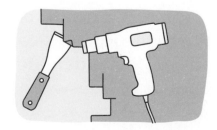

TOOLS:

TOOLS:

Safety goggles • Chemical-resistant gloves •
Drop cloth • Disposable paintbrush • Rags •
Paint scraper • Wire brush

MATERIALS:

• Paint stripper (see Chemical Warfare, opposite)

1 Safety first. Before using any corrosive chemicals like paint stripper, put on safety goggles and chemical-resistant gloves (thin latex won't do it) and make sure the work area is well-ventilated. Open windows and doors, or move the item to be stripped outside (onto a drop cloth).

2 Coat the surface with paint stripper. Spray or brush the paint stripper onto the surface to be stripped until thoroughly covered with an even layer. Let sit, as per the manufacturer's instructions.

3 Remove the paint. With a rag, wipe away the paint stripper, gently scraping any stubborn spots. The paint should come off in sheets or globs.

#13 How to Prepare a Wood Surface for Painting

That old deck chair or thrift-store bookshelf may be weather-worn, but with a coat of paint it could be good as new. Before you go to town on it, though, you need to determine: Is the wood bare or is it coated with a non-paint finish? This is an important question, because latex paint won't stick to an oil-based varnish. If upon closer inspection the wood does in fact have a finish, consider a varnish remover or prime it with a primer matched to oil-based varnishes (see Which Primer is Prime?, below). But here's what to do if the wood really is bare.

TOOLS:

Rag • 50-grit sandpaper

MATERIALS:

• Oil soap, like Murphy brand
• Bleach (if needed)
• Primer

1 Prepare the surface. Wash the wood with oil soap, and water and wipe away any grime with a rag. If the wood has been outside or in a damp area, look for mildew spots. These are more than mere discolorations—they're alive! Rather than sanding or scraping or simply painting over the spots, you need to kill the spores or the mildew is likely to regrow. Scrub the affected area with a solution of one part household bleach and three parts water and let dry. Likewise, remove any rust, splinters, and obvious imperfections that may affect the paint job.

2 Sand the surface with 50-grit sandpaper. You want to rough up the surface

(continued)

and thoroughly degloss it so that the primer and paint have more to grip on to. When you're finished sanding, wipe the surface again with a damp rag to remove any sawdust. Let the surface dry.

3 Apply primer evenly over the surface to be painted.

⨯ ⨯

Which Primer Is Prime?

When painting over an oil-based stain, a bonding primer will keep your paint from rolling off like water from a duck's back. Use an oil primer for unfinished or weathered wood, distressed paint, varnish, or woods like redwood that bleed tannins and so require an oil-based primer to lock the juices inside. Use a latex-based primer on non-wood surfaces like drywall, masonry, or metal, and also on softwoods like pine. Remember, before you prime, always thoroughly degloss the surface with sandpaper. ⨯

#14 How to Refinish Furniture
(or, Giving New Life to Old Wood)

S ay you just inherited the desk that was in your room as a middle schooler—complete with scars, pencil tracks, and chipped varnish. Before you can allow the desk to leave the garage, you simply have to refinish the surface. The process of refinishing wooden furniture involves removing the old finish, sanding the wood to a near-pristine state, and then protecting it with a new finish—in this case, that would be varnish, though you can see a complete list of wood finish options on page 71.

Choosing a Varnish

Like paint, varnish comes in a variety of styles, including gloss, semi-gloss, matte, satin, and flat. It's up to you how shiny you want the finished piece, but the degree of gloss doesn't only affect shine—it also determines how smooth and how saturated with color your piece appears. A high-gloss finish accentuates a piece's lines, but also highlights its imperfections. If your piece is slightly chipped or otherwise more "rustic" than you would like, consider a flat varnish to smooth out the appearance of those rough edges.

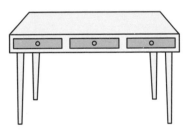

You can also choose between natural-resin and synthetic, and oil- and water-based varnishes. It used to be that water-based varnishes were shorter-lived, but newer water-based varnishes have greatly improved on their predecessors and are now a viable, less toxic alternative to oil-based varnish. Water-based varnish doesn't yellow over time like an oil-based varnish, but it can be prone to clouding when applied in more than three layers. Also consider polyurethane varnish—a variety of synthetic. Other synthetic varnishes, like phenolics, are specifically for marine use.

Buy only as much varnish as you need for the project you have planned—once you've closed a can of varnish and let it sit in the garage for a year, dried flakes from the edges are likely to fall into the product next time you open it. A can of varnish should describe how much surface area the can will cover; if you have any leftover, properly dispose of the remainder (at a household hazardous waste collection center). Rags soaked in varnish should be hung to dry (never balled up—they can catch fire) and disposed of with other hazardous waste.

Safety First

Varnish works by combining resin with a solvent that keeps the resin in liquid form until painted onto your wood surface. Once applied, the solvent evaporates, leaving behind the hard, translucent finish. Working with varnish necessarily releases fumes into the air—that's the solvent evaporating—so most varnish solvents are harmful to breathe. Always work outdoors or in a well-ventilated area. For a longer job, or if you plan to work with varnish frequently, consider using a respirator to protect your lungs.

TOOLS:

Rags • Random orbital sander (or paint stripper) • Medium to fine (80- to 100-grit) sandpaper • Putty knife • Steel wool • Disposable brush • Chemical-resistant rubber gloves • Respirator (optional) • Drop cloth (or newspapers) • Stir stick • Paint tray

MATERIALS:

- **Paint stripper (or random orbital sander)**
- **Grain filler (optional)**
- **Wood stain (optional)**
- **Varnish**

1 Remove the old finish. Wipe down the piece with a damp rag to remove any accumulated dust and dirt. Follow the instructions in How to Strip Paint on page 28, and opt for a gel and not a liquid stripper (it is prone to drain off furniture before it can work properly). Use a putty knife and steel wool to remove as much paint or varnish as possible. If you don't want to use a chemical stripper, reach for the random orbital sander (or spend hours building muscle and character sanding by hand).

2 Sand the wood. Even if you use a chemical stripper, you'll still need to sand to get a smooth finished surface. See How to Sand Wood on page 70—and remember, always sand with the grain! If your wood has a particularly high grain, consider applying grain filler before moving on to varnish. If you do, pick a filler color that either contrasts with the desired finish (to highlight the grain pattern) or matches it (to hide the grain).

3 Stain the wood. If you would like to add color to your piece, now's the time to stain it. It's stain that provides the color you want and varnish that protects it. Consider testing stain on scrap wood first, both to see the dried color and also to see how many coats of stain it will take to get the color you want. When applying stain, brush with the direction of the wood grain. Let the stain

(continued)

dry for 3 to 6 hours, then wipe with a slightly damp rag before continuing.

4 Apply the varnish. Once dried, varnish is extremely difficult to remove, so lay down a drop cloth or newspapers to guard the floor. Likewise, protect your hands with thick rubber gloves. The mixture of resin and solvent in a varnish means it can separate—make sure

to mix the can thoroughly before applying varnish and periodically while working, Pour the varnish into a paint tray and apply it as you would a coat of paint, using light strokes to avoid streaking the finish.

5 Apply multiple coats, waiting 6 hours between each coat. Sand very lightly between coats with fine-grit sandpaper—you don't want

to rub off all the varnish you just applied, but slightly roughening the finish will allow the second coat to stick better. Between coats, check the surface to ensure that there are no flies in the ointment, or accumulated dust, which can severely mar the finish. If the surface is going to see heavy, everyday use, consider applying a fourth coat of varnish.

#15 How to Caulk a Bathtub

C aulk has two major predators: mechanical damage like gouges and peeling, and mildew. You know the look of the first and hopefully your bathroom is ventilated enough so that you don't know the look of the second. Mildew is a generic name for any mold that grows in damp places. There are a couple of kinds of mildew, and once any one of them gets a toehold in your bathroom caulking, it can be almost impossible to kill. If your caulking is speckled black, consider replacing it.

In your bathroom, the most common mildew is *Cladosporium*, a speckled black or dark green mold that sometimes appears around the tub. It's different from the highly toxic "black mold" that haunts every homeowner's nightmares, but you'll still want to remove it.

TOOLS:

Caulk removal tool or putty knife and screwdriver • Razor blade • Vacuum cleaner • Rags • Caulking gun • Utility knife or sharp scissors

MATERIALS:

- **Caulk softener**
- **Mineral spirits or rubbing alcohol**
- **Caulk (silicone-based)**
- **Caulking tape**

1 Remove existing caulk. First wipe down the existing caulk and then spray, wipe, or squirt on a commercial caulk softener, letting it sit as per the manufacturer's instructions. A caulk removal tool should cost less than $10 and is a useful, but not necessary, addition to this project. Using the tool or a putty knife and screwdriver, gouge away the old caulk. If using a metal tool, be careful not to scratch the surface around the caulk, both for cosmetic reasons and because any imperfections in the finish provide footing for future mildew. Make another pass with the caulk removal tool to scrape free as much residue as possible. If needed, finish with a razor blade—you want no caulk remaining. Use a strong vacuum cleaner to suck free as many caulk pieces and other gunk as possible. Then aggressively wipe the seam with mineral spirits or rubbing alcohol.

2 Prepare the tub. Fill the tub with water to expand the space around it to its maximum size. (Empty it after the caulk has dried.) Use caulking tape along the surfaces directly above and below the seam. In addition to protecting neighboring surfaces, tape should also help you visualize, define and plan the size of the caulk bead you will draw.

3 Apply the new caulk. Ideally, use a caulking gun, which allows you the best control for drawing a consistent, even bead. Most manufacturers also offer caulk in squeezable tubes, which are good for small jobs, and some caulks also come in aerosol form. Load the caulk into the caulking gun and cut off the tip of the tube at a 45-degree angle. Puncture the seal with a nail and test the bead. If the bead is too small, cut off another short section of the tip. Squeeze the trigger of the caulk gun and run a slow, consistent bead from one end of the seam to the other. If caulking a vertical seam, start at the bottom. This can take practice—if you break the bead or are unhappy with its evenness, you'll have to start over. In that case, wipe away your first attempt with a rag before it dries. Once you're happy with the bead, wet your finger and run it down the seam, pressing the caulk into the seam.

4 Gently peel away the tape and let the caulk dry thoroughly (following the instructions on the tube) before allowing it to get wet.

⚹⚹

Types of Caulk

There's a caulk for every job. Here are some of the most common.

Silicone: This is the best caulk for bathrooms and other damp areas. It doesn't stick to wood or other porous surfaces but is ideal for ceramic and tile. Silicone caulk can't be painted, so choose a color that matches your decor.

Latex: Easier to apply but not as long-lasting as silicone caulk. It can be painted, however, and can also be used on porous surfaces. It's also better for gaps that don't flex–i.e., not for the space around your tub that expands slightly with the added weight of water.

Polyurethane: Best for window and door use, as it bonds to wood. Unlike silicone, polyurethane caulk dries hard.

Acrylic and vinyl: Good options for filling the gaps around windows that remain closed. These caulks adhere to wood and porous surfaces and can be painted. They also come in a variety of colors to match existing paint.

Painter's caulk: An inexpensive latex caulk used to fill small holes in Sheetrock or plaster walls prior to painting.

Mortar caulk: A special formula for filling holes or cracks in brick or concrete. ⚹

#16 How to Replace a Cracked Tile

How broken is a broken ceramic tile on the floor or bathroom wall? If the answer is "Not so broken," you might be able to avoid replacing it (see "A Simple Fix," opposite). But if the ceramic tile now carries a star-shaped pattern of cracks as if struck with a hammer or if sections of tile have been crushed or lost, you'll have to replace it. If you live in an older home, it may be a major challenge to find just the right replacement tile. If you don't have any leftover tiles, bring broken pieces with you to a tile store, where you should be able to find a reasonable replacement.

TOOLS:

Rag • Hammer • Chisel • Putty knife • Grout removal tool • Craft stick or old toothbrush

MATERIALS:

- **Replacement tile**
- **Tile adhesive**
- **Tube of grout to match existing grout**
- **Grout sealer**

1 Remove the broken tile. Cover the tile with a rag and smash it to bits with a hammer. (Be careful not to smash the nearby tiles.) Chisel out the bits of tile and clean out the old glue, ideally with a putty knife or chisel.

2 Evaluate the grout. If it's chipped or decaying, use a grout remover to scrape it free. Wipe the edges of the hole with a rag to clear away any additional debris. Dry thoroughly.

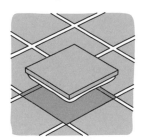

3 Affix the replacement tile. Spread tile adhesive onto the back of a new tile and push it into place.

4 Replace or refresh the grout. If you removed grout, now is the time to add new. If you didn't remove grout, now is the time to augment the existing grout so that it holds the edges of the new tile. Select a squeeze tube of grout in a color that matches the existing grout. Pack the grout around the replacement tile with a craft stick or the handle end of an old toothbrush. Once the grout is mostly dry, wipe off the tile with a damp rag.

5 Seal the grout. Apply grout sealer to protect the fresh grout and its tile. Let dry completely before getting the tile wet, as per the sealer manufacturer's instructions.

If you can't find the right tile in the tile store (and if you don't have any extras around the house), you could look into made-to-order tiles, or consider replacing multiple tiles in an "accent" pattern.

✕ ✕

A Simple Fix

A crack may not necessitate replacement. If the crack hasn't deformed the shape of the tile or if there aren't chunks missing, try painting over it. Mix paint that exactly matches your tile color with tile filler, then dab it onto the crack with a cotton swab. If the crack is more than a hairline, try to push the filler into its depths. Don't worry about filler spilling over the edges. Once the mixture is tacky but not dry, wipe the area with a damp cloth. Ideally, you'll be able to pull the filler and paint down to the level of the crack, leaving a smooth repair. ✕

#17 How to Patch Linoleum

Repairing a damaged section of linoleum is a lot like fixing damaged tile—though perhaps even easier because there's no finicky ceramic or grout to deal with. It's a manageable fix with modest DIY skills, so there's no need to put up with ugly cracked linoleum.

TOOLS:

Measuring tape • Utility knife • Putty knife or flathead screwdriver • Rags

MATERIALS:

- Scrap linoleum
- Soap
- Linoleum adhesive
- Acrylic seam sealer

1 Cut the patch. Do you have matching scrap linoleum in the garage? If so, you're in luck. If not, consider cutting a patch from an unseen area (such as under the refrigerator or stove) or seek out matching material from a flooring specialist. Use a utility knife to cut a square patch of linoleum about an inch larger on all sides than the damaged area.

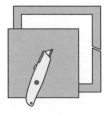

2 Match the patch to the damage. Set the linoleum patch on top of the damaged area and use the utility knife to cut out the damaged linoleum in exactly the same dimensions as the patch.

3 Remove the damaged linoleum. Use a putty knife or flathead screwdriver to pry free the damaged area. If the damaged linoleum refuses to budge, take a tip from your ceramic tile skill set and chop the damaged area into smaller, more manageable sections, which you can then pry out. You can also try heating the damaged area with a heat gun or hair dryer to loosen it. With the damaged section removed,

scrub the area aggressively with soap and water and rinse with clean water. Dry the area thoroughly.

4 Dry fit the patch. Place the patch into the hole you cut to ensure proper sizing. If needed, trim the patch or the hole so it fits without buckling.

5 Affix the patch. Apply linoleum adhesive to the back of the patch and press it into place firmly to squeeze out any air bubbles trapped underneath.

6 Seal it up. Coat the seams with seam sealer (in a finish that matches your floor, be it high-gloss or matte), and let the area dry for at least a couple of hours before walking on it.

#18 How to Replace a Damaged Section of Carpet

There are so many ways to ruin a piece of carpet—a dropped candle, a glass of red wine, a pet with unfortunate habits. Of course, replacing wall-to-wall carpeting is an exceedingly high price to pay for one little area of damage. Fortunately, it's simple to replace just a piece of it, and no one will be the wiser—especially if the carpet is on the shaggy side, the repair is nearly invisible.

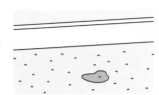

TOOLS:

Measuring tape • Utility knife

MATERIALS:

- **Carpet scrap**
- **Double-sided carpet tape or adhesive**

1 Cut a patch. Locate or purchase a piece of carpet scrap that is identical or very similar to the damaged section. (If the patch is very visible, you'll need to be especially careful about matching.) Cut a rectangle from the carpet scrap that is about an inch larger on all sides than the damaged area. In order for the patch to blend with the surrounding carpet, make sure you cut the patch so the direction of the pile (the upper layer, also called the nap) matches that of the carpet.

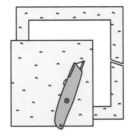

2 Match the patch to the damage. Set the patch on top of the damaged area and use it as a guide as you cut out the damaged area with a utility knife. If possible, try not to cut into the carpet pad underneath.

3 Dry fit the patch. Place the patch into the hole and trim, if needed, so that it fits snugly, with no gaps.

4 Stick the patch in place. With either double-sided carpet tape or an adhesive, press it into the hole. Allow ample time for drying before walking on it.

#19 How to Refinish a Wood Floor

Drop a bead of water on your hardwood floor. What happens to the droplet? If it beads against the wood and then slowly soaks in, try a thorough cleaning and polishing before reaching for the drum sander. If the water fails to bead and instead soaks directly into the wood, it's time to refinish.

TOOLS:

Drum sander (plan to rent)
• Extra-coarse (24-grit) sandpaper • Medium (60-grit) sandpaper • Fine (100-grit) sandpaper • Random orbital sander • Wet/dry vacuum
• Finish applicator, such as lambswool

MATERIALS:

• Plastic trash bags
• Masking tape
• Floor finish of your choice (consult your local home improvement store)

1 Remove everything from the room. Put plastic trash bags over any light fixtures (work during the day so you don't need to turn them on) and secure with masking tape.

Tape over all electrical sockets and any other wall openings.

2 Procure and prepare the sander. Rent a drum sander from a hardware store, and load it with extra-coarse sandpaper. If you haven't used a drum sander before, begin in an area that will be covered by a rug or furniture. Tip the drum sander back before you start it; once the sanding pad reaches speed, gently lower it onto the floor. Keep the sander moving, never letting it rest in a single spot while the sanding pad is moving.

3 After a thorough pass with extra-coarse sandpaper, switch to medium. Sand until the floor is level and smooth.

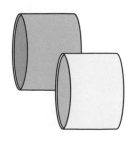

4 Sand the edges and corners of the room. Switch to a random orbital sander with medium sandpaper for the areas that the drum sander won't reach. Use any available means to clean the sawdust, including a wet/dry vacuum.

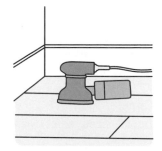

5 Just as there are many ways to finish a deck (see How to Refinish a Deck, opposite), there are many ways to finish hardwood floors. Popular options include wax, water-based polyurethane, and oil-based polyurethane. Or, you can even hire a pro to acid-finish your floors (also called "Swedish finish"). Follow all directions listed on your chosen finish. The process is similar to refinishing furniture (page 30), but you may need to allow up to 24 hours for drying.

#20 How to Refinish a Deck

So you finally got around to power washing your deck to expunge the layer of mildew and bird poop. But now the wood grain is standing high and you can't walk across your deck barefoot without risking the puncture wounds of a thousand splinters. It's time to sand and refinish the deck. Not only will it smooth down those splinters, but it will extend the life of the deck and keep your home looking spiffy. Use any power sander—a 5" random orbital sander with medium sandpaper works well.

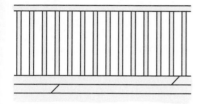

TOOLS:

Orbital floor sander (plan to rent) • Coarse to medium (20- to 50-grit) sandpaper • Medium to fine (80- to 100-grit) sandpaper

MATERIALS:

• Deck finish of your choice (consult your local home improvement store)

1 Clean the deck. Remove all furniture, including the grill, and thoroughly sweep the deck clean of all leaves and debris. Start sanding the deck. Plan the course of your sanding so that you can cover all areas evenly (start

in a corner and work your way around). Run the power sander with the grain of the wood and apply light, even pressure as you let the sander do its work. If the wood of your deck is especially weathered or warped, start with a 20-grit sandpaper. If not, start with 50-grit and then make another pass with 80-grit.

2 Sand the railing and balusters by hand. Use 80-grit to 100-grit sandpaper for handrails and other surfaces that people will touch with their hands. Using a sandpaper finer than 100-grit

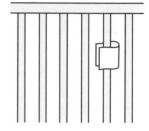

can close the wood's pores, making staining and finishing less successful.

3 Stain or paint your deck. There are many, many options for finishing your deck. Consider taking a picture of your deck and talking with your local home improvement store about finishing options. Your store can also offer application tips.

#21 How to Catch Mice
(or, Pests Be Gone!)

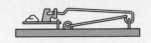

M ice are like teenagers: They go where there's food. So the first step toward keeping mice out of your house is to remove the incentive for their invasion. Find another place to store that birdseed in the garage, and never leave a kitchen messy overnight. Keep food in sealed glass or metal containers and clean up that food waste, and your mice *might* magically disappear. Also keep in check the clutter that hides mice—clean out the garage and be especially sure to keep a woodpile a couple of inches off the ground and away from the house.

Keep Out!

For all their flaws, mice are rational little creatures— make it too hard for them and they'll go elsewhere. That said, mice have soft cartilage that allows them to slip easily though openings that you swear wouldn't fit an ant. It's worth doing your best to plug any and all gaps and cracks in walls, ceilings, floors, foundations, and the backs of cabinets and pantries. There are a number of ways to plug these holes, including the somewhat rustic but effective strategy of cramming the hole full of steel wool and then duct taping over it. You can also try filling smaller or hard-to-reach gaps with expanding foam, though mice may chew through it. If you want to do it right, cover holes with metal sheeting or grating or plug them with cement. If you fail to secure their food sources, however, the little buggers may still find another way in. So remove the temptation.

There Is No Better Mousetrap

There are seemingly dozens of so-called "mouse repellants" on the market, in spray, liquid, and even electronic form. But do any of these repellants work? Overwhelmingly, they don't. In fact, there's almost no evidence that they do any good at all. Stick with removing food sources, clearing out potential nesting spots, closing off access points, and trapping the few mice that remain. Poison can quickly wipe out a large-scale infestation but should be used as a method of last resort. That's because in addition to the danger of ingestion by children and pets, poisons allow mice to wander off and expire in places you would rather they didn't, namely in walls and other hard-to-reach places.

Trap Types

There are two types of people in this world: Those who kill mice and those who relocate them (or make their spouse do it for them). Actually, there's a third type, too: cat people. Which are you? If you'd rather not kill the little buggers, use one of the many commercially available humane traps and then steel yourself for the job of release. If you're the killing type, there are a number of tools to choose from. Most exterminators recommend staying away from glue traps, which are less likely to catch mice than the common snap trap and less humane once they do. Snap traps can be messy but they are inexpensive and generally effective. If none of the preceding options sound spectacular, consider an electronic trap, which seems the most effective and humane way to deal with a small number of mice.

MATERIALS:

- Talcum powder
- Bait
- Traps

1 Become a mouse sleuth. Look for the telltale signs of droppings and evidence of chewing. If you know mice are present but can't immediately discover their path, sprinkle a thin layer of talcum powder or flour over suspect areas—then watch for mouseprints. Mice like to follow natural contours like the edges of walls or pipes.

2 Bait the traps. Use more traps with less bait rather than fewer traps with more bait, and position them with the catching mechanism pointing along one of these pathways. Use bait that doesn't pull free easily, like peanut butter (rather than cheese). If you have a larger infestation, try previewing the traps as feeding stations by placing food in the traps without setting them at first. Then, once the mice are

habituated, bait and set the lot of them all at once.

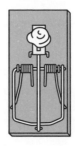

3 Check the traps. Once baited, check the traps daily. If you fail again and again, ask yourself how well you know your rodents. A mousetrap won't catch a rat and a rat trap may not be sensitive enough to catch a mouse. Consider setting a range of sizes and seeing what works.

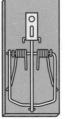

4 Dispose of the mouse. If you're using a cheap snap-trap, you can pick whether you want to open the jaws and release the dead mouse into the trash or just ditch the whole trap, mouse and all. If you used a live trap, follow the trap instructions to release the mouse in a field or other uninhabited area (not in the driveway outside your neighbor's garage).

Note that this is not a job for the squeamish. If you're overmatched or under-brave, call in the professionals.

✕ ✕ ✕ ✕ ✕ ✕ ✕ ✕ ✕ ✕ ✕ ✕
The Rest of the Pests

Mice are far from the only pests that like your house more than the outside world (especially in fall and winter). Additional visitors may also include cockroaches, ants, fleas, or other insects exotic and familiar (if you have termites, DIY time is over—call an exterminator). The first rule remains the same for them all: Make whatever it is they want inaccessible. Discover their food source and remove it. Beyond that there are species-specific traps. And beyond that, fumigation. But start with an aggressive campaign of prevention. ✕

Peppermint oil offers a more pleasant prevention tactic to safeguard against mice. A cotton ball soaked with a generous amount, placed near potential entry points, may deter a curious creature.

#22 How to Repair or Replace a Screen

Some things seem to happen in slow motion—the first time you rode a bike without training wheels, the kiss at your wedding . . . all the way to watching a toddler smash through your screen door. Even if you don't have a blundering kid, pet, or spouse, your screen door is likely to accumulate nicks and punctures. You can patch tiny holes, and if you do so when you first see them, you might be able to stop them from getting bigger. But a screen is easy to replace, so as soon as bugs start to find passage through the holes or you're sick of unsightly rips, pull the old and install the new. Here's how to repair or replace a wire screen.

TOOLS:

Measuring tape • Scissors • Screwdriver or awl • Spline installation tool • Utility knife

MATERIALS:

* Replacement screen
* Replacement spline (optional)

Fix Holes in Wire Screen

1 Make the patch. Use scissors to cut a piece of screen a couple of inches wider on all sides than the hole from a roll of extra screen or use a patch from a repair kit.

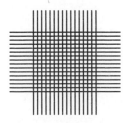

2 Bend the wires. Screen is made of wire woven horizontally and vertically. Pull out the horizontal wires for ½" around the edges of the patch, leaving the vertical wires poking free. Bend these free wires directly backward at a 90-degree angle.

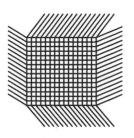

3 Attach the patch. Push the patch onto the screen so that the bent wires go through to the other side of the screen (most people choose to patch from the outside, with the

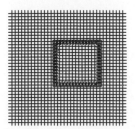

bent wires pushed inside, but the choice is yours). Bend these wires down on the other side of the screen to hold the patch in place—use your fingers or needle-nose pliers. Push the wires down completely so they won't snag.

Replace a Screen

1 Remove the screen from the window or door. Remove any hardware that intrudes on the face of the screen—most will come free easily with a screwdriver. Evaluate screen hardware for dings and discoloration and replace if damaged. If you're working on a sliding screen, check the frame's rollers while you're at it. If they are worn or tend to stick, consider replacing them. Most rollers are held in place with clips that you can pop free with a flathead screwdriver. If there is a latch, check its attachment point and replace if needed. If you are repairing a sliding door, take this opportunity to

thoroughly clean the track on which it runs.

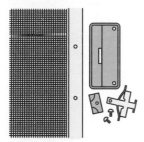

2 Remove the spline. The screen's edges are almost certainly held in place by a thin line of rubber called the spline. This piece presses on top of the screen into a tight groove, and the friction of the spline in the groove holds the screen taught. To remove the screen, you'll have to remove the spline first. Use a thin screwdriver or awl to pick at the spline near one of the screen corners, trying to lift it free without breaking it. If possible, pull the spline free

in one long strip. Repeat this procedure to remove all four sides of the spline, checking to see if there might be splinc on either side of the screen.

3 Lay the new screen across the frame. Start with a piece of replacement screen at least 2" larger than the opening—later you'll trim it to size. For now, align one edge of the new screen along the corresponding edge of the frame to make sure you don't start installing the screen cockeyed.

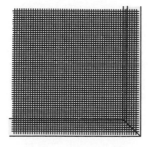

4 Install the screen. A spline installation tool should have small, pizza-cutter-like circles on each end. One circle has a convex edge (it bulges outward), and the other circle has a concave edge (it is grooved inward). Run the convex edge of the

spline installation tool on top of the screen to push it into the groove that runs along the frame edge. Press the screen firmly into the groove without ripping it.

5 Reinstall the spline. Use the concave side of the spline installation tool to push old or new spline into the groove on top of the screen. Pushing too firmly can make the tool's wheel run against the screen and potentially damage it. Slightly angle the tool away from the inside of the screen so that any rips

(continued)

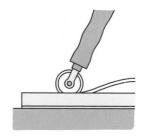

By the 1950s, screen doors and windows were common in the United States and were so useful in keeping bugs out of the house that parasitic diseases were almost eradicated.

---

occur on the overhang rather than inside the spline. As you push the spline into the groove with the roller, use your other hand to pull the screen taut beyond the edge of the side you're rolling. However, be careful not to pull so hard that you tilt the screen in the frame.

6 Use a utility knife to trim the excess screen. To avoid scratching the frame, you can cut directly into the outside gap created by the spline.

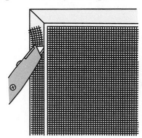

7 Replace any needed hardware, including rollers or the handle of the door. Most rollers clip in place and most handles attach with screws. Reinstall the screen with the hardware you removed in Step 1.

✕ ✕

If Your Screen Is Vinyl . . .

Vinyl doesn't bend like wire, so you'll need to glue or sew vinyl patches. Cut a patch from material that matches the screen—unlike wire, it need only be ½" wider on all sides than the hole. Once you cut the vinyl, paint the edges with clear nail polish to keep them from fraying. Use rubber cement to hold the patch in place. For a more aesthetically appealing patch, sew the patch in place with thread that matches the color of the vinyl. ✕

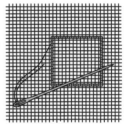

#23 How to Weather-Strip Windows and Doors

The thermostat is set to 70 degrees, so where's the chill coming from? Think of windows and doors as holes punched in your house—improperly sealed, they are going to let cold air in. In order to keep drafts out and your heat in (and your heating bill *down*), weatherstrip them. The technique for weather-stripping casement windows (which are hung on hinges) varies slightly from double-hung (which slide); doors have their own technique.

On the Strip

By far the most common forms of weather stripping are adhesive foam or tubular vinyl. Foam alone is rarely appropriate for exterior weather stripping and is better used as a barrier against drafts inside the home. Tubular vinyl

weather stripping resists weathering and is better for outside use. For both, the adhesive backing may or may not need to be reinforced with tack nails in order to remain in place. Other types of weather stripping include felt, which is usually nailed in place, and a variety of metal strips that can be spring-loaded or interlocking. Foam and vinyl strips are appropriate for installations where they will be compressed but nothing will slide sideways across them (the lower sill of a leaky window that opens and closes vertically, but not the lower edge of a door that swings closed). Spring-metal interlocking strips can be used in situations where they are rubbed, for example on the sides of sliding windows. Another option is V-channel strips—usually plastic, these strips can be used to insulate the sash channels on double-hung windows.

Like a Candle in the Wind

Cracks in the seal around a door or window can be nearly invisible, so you may need to do some sleuthing to find them. It's best to explore for leaks on a windy day. Carefully run a lighted candle around the edges of doors and windows, watching for the flame to flicker. If Mother

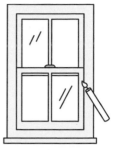

Nature refuses to provide wind, make your own. Recruit a helper to blow from the outside with a handheld hair dryer while you check the integrity of the seals with a candle on the inside. Be careful with the flame, and keep a damp rag on hand to wipe away any carbon smudges (or spot fires).

TYPES OF WEATHER STRIPPING

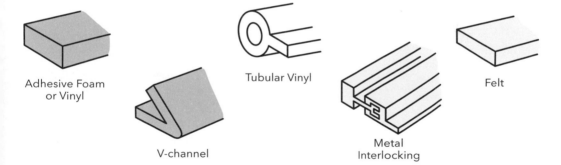

Adhesive Foam or Vinyl

V-channel

Tubular Vinyl

Metal Interlocking

Felt

TOOLS:

Measuring tape • Tin snips (for double-hung windows) • Utility knife • Screwdriver • Drill

MATERIALS:

- Soap
- Adhesive-backed weather stripping
- Spring metal weather stripping (for doors and double-hung windows)
- Finishing nails

For Double-Hung Windows

These are the most common windows in modern homes—they slide rather than swing into place. Adhesive-backed weather stripping like foam is perfect for the bottom of these windows, where the base of the window may leave a leaky gap against the sash. Use weather stripping that is narrow enough to sit against the desired edge and thick enough to close the gap.

1 Clean the surface. Remove any old stripping and wash the desired edge with soap and water. Dry thoroughly.

(continued)

2 Seal the lower edge. Peel off the adhesive back and affix a strip cut to match the length of the lower edge. If you've prepared the surface correctly, you shouldn't need to nail or otherwise reinforce the adhesive.

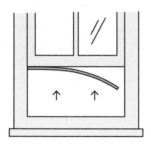

3 Seal the tracks. The sides of these windows slide on a track, which shouldn't but sometimes does leak air. Protect against these leaks with plastic V-channel weather stripping. Make sure you buy the correct width of weather stripping for your windows and then cut the V-channel into strips about an inch longer than your sash height. Slide the weather stripping down the tracks on the sides of your windows, between the window frame and the sash (you will have to stuff it in). Use finish nails to attach the V-channel to the

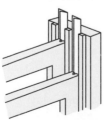

jamb (make sure the window doesn't get caught on the nails).

For Casement Windows

Because casement windows swing instead of slide shut, they are much easier to insulate.

1 Clean the surface. Remove any old weather stripping or sealant, thoroughly wash the surface that forms the window's seal with soap and water, and let it dry.

2 Measure the faces of the window sash that come into contact with the window. Cut pieces of adhesive-backed foam insulation to these sizes with a utility knife. Remove a small bit from the backing and stick the end in place. Pull off the backing as you

press on the strip, using additional strips as needed.

3 If needed, trim the strips to fit. If you struggle to keep adhesive strips stuck to your window sashes, add finishing nails.

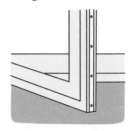

For Doors

Unlike some kinds of windows, all four edges of a door can be fitted with weather stripping.

1 Ensure that the door is hung properly. Look from the outside to see if the door hangs square in the frame. If it sags, try tightening the hinge screws. After enough openings and closings, a door's hinges can pull so much against the mounting screws that they may enlarge their holes. In that case, consider replacing them with larger screws that fit the new hole size (as long as these larger screws also fit through the hinges!). You can also try filling the screw holes with toothpicks dipped liberally in wood glue and then cutting the toothpicks flush. Now evaluate the squared door. If

gaps remain around the edges, it's time for weather stripping.

2 Seal the sides. Because the door must swing freely across the sides of the door frame, consider using "spring bronze" weather stripping instead of foam or vinyl adhesive strips here, which would quickly pull free or degrade as the door is swung across them (okay, if it's a rarely opened garage door, you might start with adhesive stripping and see how long it lasts). Measure the doorjamb and cut lengths of spring bronze to fit. Press the spring bronze in place, tight against the doorjamb. Use finishing nails about every 8 to 10 inches to hold it in place.

3 Prepare the top and the threshold. Adhesive-backed foam or vinyl weather stripping will work along the top and bottom—surfaces where the door applies direct instead of crosswise pressure. Remove any old weather stripping or sealant and thoroughly clean the surfaces with soap and water. Let dry completely.

4 Seal the top and threshold. Use a utility knife to cut a length of foam weather stripping just longer than the doorstop that runs along the top of the doorframe. Peel only a bit of the backing from the weather stripping, then press the adhesive to firmly attach it to the top of the doorframe, removing the backing as you go. Do the same along the bottom.

5 Install the door sweep. The door sweep hangs down from the bottom edge on the outside of the door, covering the gap at the bottom when the door is closed. Measure your door and buy the proper sweep at your home improvement store. Hold the sweep up to the bottom edge of the door so that it hangs at the desired height (it should deter drafts but not stop the door from opening). Mark through the holes on the sweep onto the door. Now use your drill and the mounting screws that came with the sweep to attach it.

#24 How to Caulk a Window

Caulking drafty windows will not only make your home more comfortable, but will cut down on heating and cooling bills and can keep out pesky insects that wiggle their way in through loose seams. If the seam isn't going to move, caulk it. If the window opens and closes onto the seam, you'll need to use weather stripping (see page 44).

TOOLS:

Putty knife or 5-in-1 painting tool • Caulking gun

MATERIALS:

- **Candle**
- **Polyurethane caulk**
- **Craft stick (optional)**

1 Test for drafts. Following the instructions on page 45, carefully run a lit candle along window seams, watching for the flame to

flicker and reveal any drafts. An interior draft may in fact be due to imperfections in the exterior window caulk. Check outside first, as repairing a cracked or damaged outside seal should allow you to open and close the window, without inviting in a draft.

2 Remove the old caulk. Once you locate the failed seal, use a putty knife or the long, sharp edge of a 5-in-1 painting tool to remove it. Once you start removing window caulk, it's best to remove it completely and re-caulk the entire seam. Once you've removed the old caulk, wipe the surface clean with a damp rag and let dry.

3 Apply new caulk. Load the caulk into the caulking gun and cut off the tip of the tube at a 45-degree angle. Puncture the seal with a nail and test the bead. If the bead is too small, cut off another short section of the tip. You needn't be as precise with polyurethane caulk as you are with silicone caulk in the bathroom. Especially with exterior use, you may need to vary the size of the bead to fill an uneven gap. In any case, squirt caulk in the gaps to fill them. Finish by running a wet finger or craft stick along the bead to smooth the seam.

#25 How to Replace a Windowpane

Be it from bird or baseball, your windows are in constant danger from flying objects. Fixing a broken pane is either fairly simple or completely impossible, depending on your windows. With older, wood-frame windows, pulling the old pane and inserting a new one requires only a bit of skill with putty and glaze. With a vinyl window, you'll most likely have to replace the entire sash.

First evaluate your broken window—is it fixable, DIY or otherwise? Is the pane attached with putty or clips, or is it an integral part of the window assembly? If it looks like the pane will pop free, keep reading. If you have a new vinyl, double-paned window, get ready to shell out to replace the entire assembly.

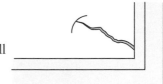

Temporary Fixes

You may be able to temporarily repair small cracks and holes in a windowpane until you are able to replace it. To stop a crack from spreading, try using a glass cutter to draw a shallow arc in the path of the crack. Again, this is a temporary fix, but "capping" the crack can keep it contained. Likewise, tiny holes like those from pesky pellet guns or a slingshot pebble may be patchable with clear nail polish. None of these fixes will restore a window to its previous luster, but they can keep a problem from getting worse until you find the moxie, time, and money for a real fix.

TOOLS:

Glass-handling gloves • Safety goggles • Measuring tape • Screwdriver • Pliers • Heat gun or hair dryer • 2" putty knife

MATERIALS:

- **Glass pane**
- **Window putty**
- **Paint**

1 Buy a new pane of glass, cut to size. Both lumber and hardware stores should be able to provide sized glass.

If in doubt about the size you need, read on to learn how to pop the sash free of the house and bring it with you when buying a new pane. If it's possible to measure the pane while it's still in the frame, measure it precisely and ensure you replace it with exact dimensions. With glass, even $\frac{1}{16}$" matters.

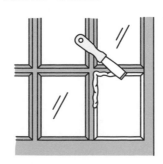

2 Gear up. When working with broken glass, wear not only protective glass-handling gloves but eye goggles as well. Especially when removing a broken pane, it is possible to fling glass shards. Unlike sawdust, a glass shard in the eye can do immediate, permanent damage.

(continued)

3 Remove the broken pane and its sash (if possible). With an older window, this might be as easy as unscrewing the hinges that connect the sash to the casing. On newer windows, it may be easier to remove the pane from the frame than to remove the frame itself. Modern double-paned windows will need to be replaced completely, sash and all.

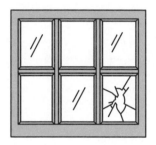

4 Loosen the pane. Make sure you're wearing gloves and then use pliers to remove broken glass that may have fallen. Evaluate how the pane is attached to the frame. With older windows, it might be held fast with glazing compound. In this case, use a heat gun or hair dryer to loosen it. Work a putty knife

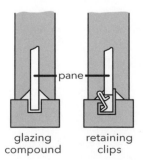

glazing   retaining
compound   clips

into the loosened compound and gently pry the glass free. Scrape excess compound from the frame. With newer windows, the glass pane is likely attached to the frame with retaining clips. Use a screwdriver to press the clips and pop the pane free.

5 Clean the frame. In an older, wooden window, scrape out the rabbet groove that forms the seat for the windowpane. If the wood is degraded, consider replacing the frame or chiseling away a layer to make a new, level rabbet (in that case you would need a slightly larger pane).

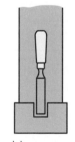

rabbet groove

6 Attach the new pane. Run a bead of window putty along the rabbet. Set the new pane in place and gently press it down into the putty. Note

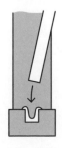

that at this stage, it's very easy to crack the glass. Press with care, waiting for a complete seal to form between the glass and the sash.

7 Adjust the pane. Move the pane in the putty until it is centered, with a $\frac{1}{16}$" (putty-filled) gap on all sides between the glass and the sash.

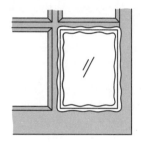

8 Lock in the pane. Like most picture frames, wood-frame windows generally use small metal tabs to hold the glass in place. These tabs push into the wood, flush to the glass, about every six inches. Put a tab in place by hand, and use a flathead screwdriver to shove it into the wood. Avoid angling it into the glass, which can easily chip the pane.

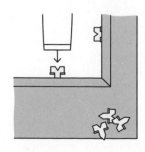

9 Seal the pane. Roll a ½" rope of putty and press it into the back of the glass, over the tabs, to seal the edge of the pane. Free the pane of any excess putty with a putty knife or razor blade. Let dry for at least three days.

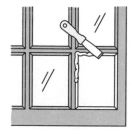

paint to the very edge of the glass to hide the repair.

10 Repaint the frame with paint that matches the rest of the frames. Run the

#26 How to Unblock a Gutter

For reasons that should be obvious, it is never a good idea to climb onto the roof and lean out over the edge in order to clear leaves from your gutters. It is equally dangerous to imagine that a blocked gutter will somehow unclog itself—this mind-set can lead to corrosion or, in extreme cases, the gutters ripping free from the house. Instead, follow the steps here to clean the gutters safely.

Proper Drainage

The purpose of a gutter is to drain water away from the foundation of the house. If your downspout is releasing water into an impromptu pond that drains back toward the house, it's not doing a very good job. If needed, add another horizontal section of downspout to eject water farther away. And make sure the ground around the foundation slopes away from instead of toward it. If it doesn't, you may need to take out a shovel and do some digging so the water has a place to go. (Some homeowners make channels and line them with gravel, bricks, or stones.)

Before a Blockage Occurs . . .

Does a tree overhang your gutters? If so, you'll need to be diligent about cleaning the gutters at least once every fall and then checking them again in the spring to see if the winter wind

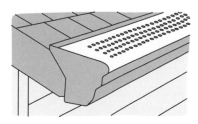

whipped any unexpected leaves or branches into the system. If the gutters seem to clog often, be proactive: Consider installing gutter guards, which are strips of steel or plastic with holes or pores for filtering water. They attach under the last course of shingles and protect the open tops of the gutters, while allowing rain from the roof to pass through. Plastic gutter guards are inexpensive and easy to install—find them at your local home improvement store.

(continued)

TOOLS:

Rubber gloves • Bucket or heavy-duty trash bag • Freestanding ladder • Hand trowel (optional) • Garden hose with sprayer

1 Get a helper. You'll need someone to stabilize the base of the ladder while you work. It is best to use a freestanding ladder to avoid leaning it against the gutters, which aren't meant to support significant weight.

2 Detach the downspouts. Before you go shoving muck around, consider detaching the downspouts so the debris doesn't make its way in and cause an even larger problem. Most downspouts will detach from the roof with a screwdriver, and then sections should come apart with a tug. That said, if the downspouts are generally clear of debris and the problem sits in the gutters, just detach the downspouts enough that muck will fall instead of washing into them.

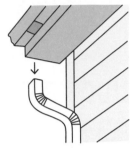

3 Scoop out the debris. Put on your rubber gloves and hold a sturdy trash bag or bucket in one hand. Starting at the downspout locations and working toward the middle of the gutters, scoop out all the leaves and muck. If it's been a while or if you live in a climate where significant dust washes from the roof, you may also need a hand trowel to dig into the mud that accumulates in the gutters. If muck-grabbing isn't your thing, you can blast out the gutters with a pressure washer—this is a messy job but easier than scooping them out by hand.

4 Reattach the downspouts and rinse the gutters. Once you've cleaned out the major debris (sticks, leaves, Frisbees) by hand, use a garden hose with a sprayer attachment to rinse the remaining dirt into the downspouts. (Watch to ensure that the water flows smoothly out with no obstructions.)

✕✕✕

Troubleshooting a Blocked Downspout

There are as many folk remedies for unblocking a downspout as there are for curing hiccups. Start by trying to blast away a clog by aiming your hose's sprayer attachment up the blocked pipe. If the water breaks the clog into pieces, clear these bits and then keep squirting until you've mined through the entire clog. If that doesn't work, haul the garden hose up a ladder (have a helper hold the base!) to the top of the clogged spout and try to blast it out from there. If the pipe is still clogged, remove the hose's sprayer attachment and feed the length of the hose down the pipe. Turn on the water and wiggle as needed until leaves, twigs, the odd squirrel and

other goodies come geysering out the bottom of the pipe. If that *still* doesn't work, you have a serious clog. At this point, weigh the difficulty of taking apart your downspout against the difficulty of feeding a plumber's snake up the spout to auger the clog. Some downspouts will disassemble easily with the removal of a couple of screws. Others are composed of a single length of pipe, which would require cutting and sweating to fix. ✕

#27 How to Repair a Cracked Gutter

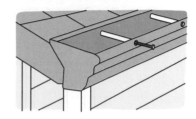

Eventually, even despite careful maintenance, gutters will corrode, crack, or take a hit from a falling branch and require repair. It's easy to repair a small hole, though more significant damage may require replacing the gutter. Another common problem is gutter sag, often a result of detached hardware. When a support pulls free, it allows the outer lip of the gutter to fall outward and can affect the slope of the gutter. There are long screws just for fixing this problem—ask for gutter screws at the hardware store and use them to pinch the gutter back into position.

TOOLS:

Freestanding ladder • Tin snips • Wire brush • Rags

MATERIALS:

- **Metal patch or scrap**
- **Roofing cement**

1 Get a helper. You'll need someone to stabilize the base of the ladder while you

work. Use a freestanding ladder to avoid putting extra weight on the gutters.

2 Prepare the crack for repair. Use tin snips to cut free any rust clinging to the edges of the crack or hole. Thoroughly clean the affected area by scrubbing it with a wire brush and then wiping it with a damp rag.

3 Apply the patch. For this repair, you need a metal patch a couple of

inches larger than the crack or hole. You can buy flexible metal patching material at the hardware store or you can make your own patch by using tin snips to cut a piece from scrap metal flashing. Make sure the metal of the patch matches the metal of the gutter. Cover one side of the patch with roofing cement and stick the patch in place, centered so it completely covers the damaged area.

#28 How to Prevent Ice Dams

Keeping your home toasty as the temperature outside plummets is only one good reason to properly insulate your attic. Yes, you will save on heating costs if you aren't paying to keep your attic warm, but warm air rising through the attic to the roof can have an even more costly repercussion: a potentially catastrophic ice dam. There's a good chance your roof is peaked or otherwise slanted. Combine that with imperfect insulation and you're likely to have a hot spot at your roof's apex. In the winter, this warmer area can melt the snow, which then runs down the roof . . . until it meets a colder section of roof below and freezes solid. This is an ice dam, and it can cause serious damage (see How to Remove an Ice Dam from the Roof, opposite). The key to preventing an ice dam isn't keeping your roof warm, but rather keeping it cold enough to avoid melting the snow and creating a dam in the first place. This means not only insulating your house from the cold roof, but insulating the attic and roof from your warm house. Home improvement centers carry Styrofoam baffles specifically for this purpose. When installed, they create air channels between the attic insulation under your roof and the roof itself. Insulate the attic right, and keep ice dams at bay.

TOOLS:

Caulking gun • Roof rake

MATERIALS:

- Styrofoam attic baffles
- Fiberglass batt insulation
- Safety mask and gloves
- Window caulk

1 Install the baffles. Wear your mask and gloves and remove the fiberglass batt insulation by pulling it up in strips. Press the Styrofoam ventilation baffles up into the

space that was insulated and reapply the insulation—while you're at it, add an extra layer.

2 Insulate the floor. Also focus your insulation on the floor of the attic and not just the underside of the roof. If needed, pull up old insulation and replace with new. Consider laying a second layer of insulation, rolling it down in strips perpendicular to the first layer.

3 Ensure that your roof is properly ventilated—cold air should sneak into the Styrofoam air channels from the eaves, pass through, and

exit at the ridge to keep the roof properly chilled. Look for soffit vents under the eaves. If you don't have vents, consider an evaluation by a roofing expert.

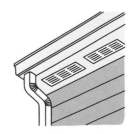

4 Insulate ducts, pipes, and cables. Wrap fiberglass batt or foam pipe insulation around any ventilation or other pipes, including dryer vents or ducts connected to

the kitchen or bathroom. Caulk around any cables that penetrate the attic.

5 Keep the roof and gutters clear and free of debris (see How to Unblock a Gutter, page 51), which can form an anchor for a dam. If snow looks to be accumulating, use a roof rake to scrape it from the edges of the roof and around gutters.

#29 How to Remove an Ice Dam from the Roof

Even with proper insulation, when melting snow flows from the roof into the gutters, it's likely to refreeze and can eventually build up into a wall. Left alone, the weight of the dam will increase until it finally rips free, creating a major safety hazard and probably taking your gutters with it as it cascades onto your parked car below. Before it does that, an ice dam can trap water behind it, pooling it on your roof where it will degrade your roofing material and might create leaks. Do what you can to prevent ice dams, but don't let them linger once they form. Here's how to clear an ice dam if you, unfortunately, find one attached to your roof.

Danger Ahead!

Stop! *Never* walk on a snowy or icy roof. Working from below isn't safe either—as soon as you start hacking at an ice dam, you increase the likelihood of the entire thing releasing, at which point it can slide down the roof onto you and your ladder. (Not to mention the danger inherent in wielding an ax from atop a ladder resting on snowy ground.) So resist the temptation to just whale away on the dam with an ax. Likewise resist the urge to torch the dam with a propane flame in an attempt to melt it. It doesn't work. By far the safest method of dealing with an ice dam is preventing it from forming in the first place (see How to Prevent an Ice Dam, opposite). If you're past that point, here's what to do. And remember that a partially melted ice dam can break free and slide.

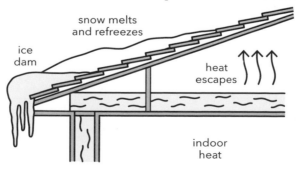

snow melts and refreezes

ice dam

heat escapes ↑↑↑

indoor heat

(continued)

TOOLS:

Freestanding ladder • Heat cables

MATERIALS:

- **Calcium chloride pellets**
- **Pantyhose**
- **De-icing salt**

1 Try ice-melting pellets. These may or may not work, but they're relatively inexpensive, completely safe, and so easy they're worth a try. Don't use salt pellets, as they can corrode metal gutters and flashings. Instead, look for calcium chloride pellets. Hurl them onto your roof, preferably directly onto the dam itself, and then hope for the best. The pellets are likely to melt into the dam until reaching the roof, but the melt won't necessarily branch out from the holes the pellets create. However, if you have a pool of water trapped behind the dam, it may only take one small hole melted through with a calcium chloride pellet

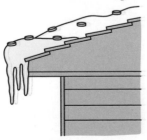

to allow the trapped water to burst forth, likely melting out the remaining dam.

2 Next, try heat cables. If the pellets don't work, carefully climb a freestanding ladder (have a helper hold the base) to reach the roof, where you can lay heat cables on the ice dam. Lay cables on the dam, plug in below, and then stay far away as the heat cables melt the ice. Again, if you have any question about the integrity of the dam and fear there's any chance it may break free, don't risk working below it. Call an expert. Alternatively, some homeowners with foresight choose to leave zigzags of heat tape in place just above the gutters throughout the winter, turning them on when ice dams start to form.

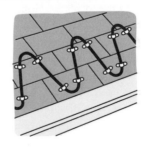

3 Finally, try pantyhose. Heat cables or tape should solve the problem, but sometimes they are too thin to completely melt an ice dam, in which case it's time to go with pantyhose.

Fill pantyhose with de-icing salt to form long, unattractive sausages. Lay these sausages on the ice dam. (And then come up with a good story to tell the neighbors.) Stay far away as the ice starts to melt the dam. Note that this isn't the best long-term strategy, as over time salt can erode gutters and other metal parts of the roof. But in a pinch, it's worth a shot.

⌘ ⌘ ⌘ ⌘ ⌘ ⌘ ⌘ ⌘ ⌘ ⌘ ⌘ ⌘

Keeping Steps and Pathways Ice-Free

Roofs are certainly not the only spot where ice likes to form in the winter—steps and walkways are prime territory for ice sheets. As with roofs, the best way to keep your walkways free of ice is to keep it from forming in the first place. As soon as it snows, shovel. This keeps the bottom layer of snow from compacting, melting against the warmer ground, and then refreezing into perilous ice patches. If you already have ice or if ice forms despite your efforts with a shovel, consider throwing down sand, gravel, or even kitty litter onto the ice to increase your grip. For tougher cases, try rock salt. Sprinkle just enough to loosen the ice and then scrape it free with a snow shovel. ⌘

Is It Time for a New Roof?

When in doubt about your roof, it's tempting to call in the pros for a consultation—but the pros are more than a little biased toward replacement. Unless you know a roofer and know that said roofer already has enough work to stay busy for the next fifteen years, it's hard to trust the opinion of someone with a vested interest in the disrepair of your roof. Instead, check it out yourself before calling in a professional. It's imperative, of course, to keep your roof in tip-top shape—not only does a good roof keep the outside out, but it's a must for maintaining your home's value.

Light (or Rain) in the Attic

The first job of a roof is to keep precipitation out. If water is coming in, blame it on the roof. Head up to the attic to look for spots where the structure of the roof deck sags inward and, on a rainy day, look for leaks. On a sunny day, check for places where light shines through. Beyond these obvious failures, look from the attic at the underside of the roof deck for dark spots and black streaks that can indicate the locations of slower leaks. Mildew can also be a sign that moisture is making its way past the roof.

Shingled Out

From outside at ground-level, look up at the roof from below and see if you can spot any of the following problems:

• **Missing shingles.** These will have to be replaced. When you notice a bare spot, check from the attic to make sure it hasn't already led to rot in the wood decking of the roof itself.

• **Loose shingles.** If you notice shingle tabs flapping in the breeze, cement them down before they rip free entirely. Use roofing cement, also called

flashing cement, to apply two quarter-sized dollops to the underside of each tab. Press the tabs down against the course below. Don't use too much cement or it will squeeze out when pressed.

• **Damaged flashing.** Flashing is the (metal) sheeting that closes the gap between your roof and things that poke out of it, like a chimney. Damaged or punctured flashing can allow water to sneak in. In most cases, you simply replace the damaged flashing and then the surrounding shingles.

• **Curling shingles.** The most common cause of curling shingles is improper fastening. Unfortunately, once the undersides have been exposed, there's a good chance the backing will crack and you'll have to replace them. Another common cause is an improperly ventilated roof (see How to Prevent Ice Dams, page 54, for instructions on ventilation).

(continued)

Asphalt shingles are expert at keeping water off the roof, but they're not nearly as waterproof from below. If water is condensing from a warm house underneath the roof, it can make shingles curl upward.

• **Algae.** Especially in humid climates, algae can grow on the roof (so your roof should already include algae-resistant shingles). Most often, though, an algae infestation is an eyesore and nothing more—it won't affect the integrity of the roof. Kill algae with a bleach solution in a spray bottle. Scrub vigorously, but don't pressure wash the roof, as it can shorten the life of asphalt shingles.

• **Blistering.** Are there small bubbles and knobs on the shingles? They're likely the result of a defect in the shingles themselves. Sometimes moisture becomes trapped inside shingles during manufacture, which later bubbles and then bursts free. These shingles will need to be replaced. You should be able to get your money back from the manufacturer.

The Verdict

As with an old car, it eventually stops being cost-effective to patch over the problem, and the root of the issue must be addressed. At some point, you'll need a new roof. Before making that determination, consider the problem: Is it the boards of the roof decking or the shingles that are to blame? If it's the shingles, you might get away with laying a new layer of shingles directly over the existing layer. Most often, it's the decking that will dictate when you need a new roof. Look for rot, water spots, sagging, and cracks in the wood. Then find out how long it has been since the roof was replaced—a properly installed roof should last 20 years. If you're finding problems at 10 years, turn a very careful eye on your shingles, flashing, and other roof coverings. At 15 years, start getting suspicious of your decking. With harsh winters or high humidity you might be pushing into replacement territory. At 20 years, count your blessings if you can get away with spot repairs, but be ready to replace the whole thing if these repairs start to become frequent. The cardinal rule of roof replacement is to get it done before a leaky roof causes damage to the rest of the house. A typical roof replacement with asphalt shingles will cost about $100 for every 100 square feet, though this varies widely in different areas of the country. Make sure you get at least three quotes from roofers before deciding—both to explore for lower prices and for the information that an inspection can provide.

#30 How to Repair a Crack in a Concrete Driveway

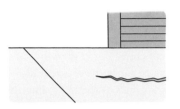

Concrete is not especially malleable, so when something pushes on it, instead of bending, it cracks. Typically, cracks in a driveway are due to tree roots burrowing underneath like attackers digging under the walls of a medieval castle. Cracks can also come from imperfect compression of the soil when the driveway was laid, resulting in uneven settling. Needless to say, when the ground falls out from beneath a driveway, it cracks. Cracks can also come from water that seeps under the driveway and expands during a winter freeze. In rare cases, you'll have to break up the slab with a jackhammer and pour a new driveway. But before you go to that extreme, try repairing the crack with concrete resurfacer.

TOOLS:

Pressure washer (plan to rent) • Masonry chisel • Air compressor or wet/dry vacuum (optional) • Bucket • Drill with mixing paddle • Flat-edge trowel • Concrete float • Rubber floor squeegee • Push broom (optional)

MATERIALS:

• Masonry cleaning solution
• Concrete resurfacing powder

1 Clean the concrete. Add masonry cleaning solution to a pressure washer and scour the driveway, focusing on removing any dirt, debris, and mildew from in and around the crack. If loose material inside the crack proves difficult to blast loose, you'll need to chisel it free using a masonry chisel. If possible, after pressure washing and chiseling, let the crack dry and then hit it with an air compressor or vacuum out any dust with a wet/dry vacuum.

2 Mix concrete resurfacing powder in a bucket, according to the package directions. Use a mixing paddle on a drill to stir the mixture until no lumps remain. The consistency of the concrete mixture should be that of a thick paste.

3 Coat the crack. Pick up the bucket and pour the mixture roughly and liberally onto the crack. Use a flat-edge trowel to aggressively pack the mixture down deep into the crack.

(continued)

4 Smooth the concrete. Use a concrete float, which is like a large metal paddle, to flatten the resurfacing material to the surrounding concrete. If you plan to stop after filling the crack, feather the edges of the patch into the driveway with the concrete float and stop here. If you're up for a bit more resurfacing, you can leave the edges slightly rough and proceed to Step 5.

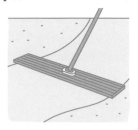

5 Prepare to resurface. Let the patched crack dry overnight. Now you can resurface the rest of the driveway up to the level of the crack patch. Mix another batch of concrete resurfacer, this time much thinner than the first batch, to about the consistency of runny pancake batter. Because you'll be applying this second batch in a thin layer, wet down the driveway to keep it from drying too quickly.

6 Cover the entire driveway. Pour the thinned resurfacer onto the driveway and spread it around with a rubber squeegee. If the driveway is especially wide, be strategic about how you pour resurfacer and then squeegee before moving on to the next section—avoid "painting yourself into a corner." The edges of the squeegee can be tricky and it takes practice to avoid leaving edge marks in the resurfacer.

7 Scuff the surface. If you like, once the resurfacer is set but not dry, use a push broom to scuff the surface so that the driveway has more traction when wet. Let the resurfaced driveway set for at least 24 hours before using.

Sealing out the Seasons

Though it is optional, sealing a driveway can help reduce cracking and will improve the overall appearance of your driveway. These instructions for sealing concrete and asphalt assume that you've already pressure washed the entire driveway surface and repaired all cracks. If that's not the case, do it now. This also assumes it's a beautiful summer weekend with no rain in the forecast for the next few days— apply sealant only if you expect at least 36 dry hours with a temperature over 60 degrees. Also be sure you completely rope off the driveway from friends and family who might unknowingly drive into the middle of your wet project with catastrophic consequences for both the project and any tires that might touch it. With the preparation handled, applying sealer is fairly straightforward: Pour what looks like a workable amount of sealant onto the driveway (about two gallons at a time works well) and spread it around with a rubber squeegee. Let it dry overnight. And cross your fingers against an unexpected summer thunderstorm. ✕

#31 How to Patch Cracked Asphalt

Patching asphalt starts out exactly the same as patching concrete. Before you begin, pressure wash the driveway (see Step 1 of How to Repair a Crack in a Concrete Driveway, page 59), being sure to blast free any dirt and debris in the crack. If the crack is thinner than ½", patch it according to the instructions for concrete, but with asphalt patching material. If the crack is more than ½" wide, you'll need to follow a slightly different set of steps, detailed below.

TOOLS:

Bucket • Steel tamping rod (optional)

MATERIALS:

- Crushed, angular gravel
- 4 × 4 post
- Asphalt repair compound
- Asphalt sealant

1 Fill the base of the crack with gravel. The best gravel to fill a large asphalt driveway crack is crushed, angular gravel. (Round gravel shifts too easily.) Fill the crack until it is only 2" deep. Use a 4 × 4 post to tamp down the gravel to a firm underlayer, adding more

gravel as necessary to reach the 2" mark.

2 Mix the asphalt repair compound in a bucket, according to the manufacturer's instructions.

3 Pour the compound on top of the gravel underlayer. Compact the compound firmly into the crack with the 4 × 4 post (or with a steel tamping rod designed for the purpose).

Add more compound as needed to bring the surface of the repair up to the level of the surrounding driveway. Tamp the compound aggressively for a durable repair.

4 Let the blacktop asphalt dry. While it will feel dry after 24 hours and you can expect it to hold weight, there's a good chance the bottom of the patch will still be slightly pliable. Wait a couple of weeks before applying asphalt sealant (see Sealing Out the Seasons, page 60), which prevents air from penetrating beneath the surface.

WOODWORKING & METALWORKING

I still have a wooden stool I made in shop class as a teenager, with turned legs and a woven seat. It's a nice piece, and what it taught me at a tender age is that the things we make with our hands are valuable to us. It also taught me how much fun tools can be! Some items, such as hammers, planes, and saws, are great basics to have on hand for minor repair jobs, but with the addition of some (carefully used) power tools, a whole world of wood- and metalworking opens up.

A Visit to the Lumberyard

If you need real wood, you can't beat the selection, quality, price, and expertise of a lumberyard. After you've found your closest lumberyards, call ahead to ask how things are done. Do they offer delivery, or might you have to rent or borrow a truck? Is there someone to show you around and help you? Can you place an order and have it show up at your house, or should you expect to go through the piles and load the wood yourself? What does the yard offer in terms of ripping boards to size? Is there a different procedure for home owners than for contractors? With a little know-how, going to a lumberyard can be like visiting with friends.

HARD VS. SOFT

Hardwoods come from deciduous trees and include maple, mahogany, cherry, oak, and teak. Softwoods come from cone-bearing trees and include types like pine, cedar, and fir. Softwoods grow faster and make up about 80 percent of the world's timber, and so tend to be significantly cheaper. Most general construction work is done with softwoods, including home construction and inexpensive furniture.

Softwoods are graded according to the American Softwood Lumber Standard. First, softwoods are divided into "select" and "common" categories. Select starts with grades A and B, which are appropriate for natural finishes and are completely or almost completely free of blemishes. Select softwood grades C and D may have significant blemishes but are still aesthetically pleasing when painted. Common lumber is rated 1 through 5. For general projects, stick with grades 1 and 2—tight-grained lumber with good structural integrity, usable in most types of building. Grade 3 common lumber is used for crates, sheathing, and subflooring. Grades 4 and 5 barely hold together—you'll have a tough time finding them in most lumberyards.

Hardwoods are graded according to the National Hardwood Lumber Association guidelines, which specify the percent of surface area that must be free of blemishes to earn each grade. The grade FAS stands for firsts and seconds, and requires a board at least 6 inches wide and 8 feet long with more than $83\frac{1}{3}$ percent of both faces free of blemishes. Most common uses for FAS hardwoods are furniture and moldings. FAS One Face (F1F) boards must meet FAS requirements on one face. Selects is the same as FAS, but boards can be sold in smaller sizes. Number 1 Common hardwood boards must be at least $66\frac{2}{3}$ percent free of blemishes. This is the most common grade used for cabinetry and furniture. Number 2 Common (aka Economy Grade) must be at least 50 percent blemish-free and is primarily used for smaller furniture parts, which allow you to cut around the blemishes.

BE CHOOSY (OR, HOW TO PICK A PIECE OF LUMBER)

When checking a 2 × 4, look down its length and spin it to check for curves and twists. Check for cupping, in which the board starts to take on a U shape. Check that the edges are square and that the board isn't cracked or split. With boards you plan to use in cosmetic projects, look for blemishes. Otherwise, structural integrity is the only thing that matters.

BRING ON THE PRESERVATIVES

As a rule, untreated wood shouldn't see moisture—it can't touch the ground or be the outside layer of construction. Preservatives protect against fungal, microorganism, and insect decay and can be applied with or without pressure. Pressure-treated lumber lasts significantly longer (20 years or more) than wood treated with a brush-on preservative. For decking applications, you might want to consider plastic composite lumber, which lasts even longer and won't ever give you splinters.

(continued)

WOODWORKING TOOL KIT

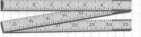

Rulers

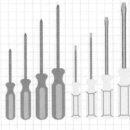

Carpenter's square

HAND TOOLS

Crosscut saw

Rip saw

Level

Screwdrivers

Files and rasps

Nails

Screws

Clamps

Plane

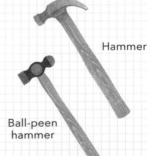

Hammer

Ball-peen
hammer

Measuring tape

Chisels

Workbench

Sharpening stone

POWER TOOLS

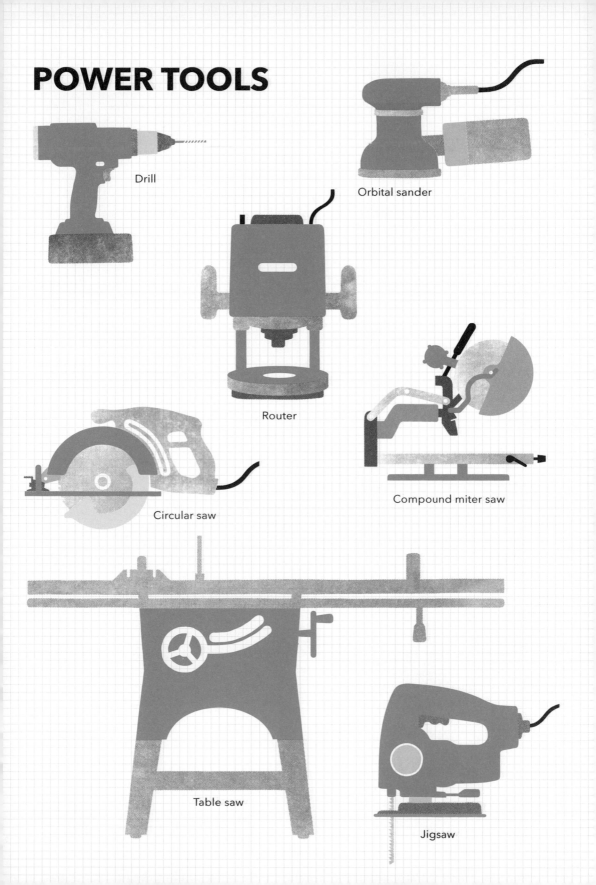

Drill

Orbital sander

Router

Circular saw

Compound miter saw

Table saw

Jigsaw

Hand Tools

Watch a National Geographic film on primates and you'll see hand tools in action—chimps using thick sticks to break open nuts or long twigs to fish for ants and termites. We humans take it a few steps further. In fact, if you don't mind adding a little extra elbow grease to a project, hand tools can do anything their electric cousins can do. (Some woodworkers swear that hand tools do an even better job.) Here are the essential hand tools (see page 64 for visual reference) in any woodworking tool kit, including the trusty measuring tape, the main measuring tool you need for woodworking, along with a ruler (or two) and a carpenter's square.

Hammer and nails. Put a glob of metal at the end of a stick and you've got a hammer. But beyond that basic design, there is a dizzying array of hammer varieties. Eventually, you can populate your tool kit with a whole quiver of them, but to start, decide if your first hammer is going to do double duty for household fix-its or if you can justify a hammer specifically for woodworking. If you're getting just one for all uses, go with a medium-sized framing hammer with a mallet face on one side and a claw on

✕ ✕ ✕ ✕ ✕ ✕ ✕ ✕ ✕ ✕ ✕ ✕ ✕ ✕ ✕ ✕ ✕ ✕ ✕

Shopping for Tools

You don't have to complete your woodworking tool kit all at once. Although you can easily spend $1,000 or more on tools, a few hundred dollars is enough to get you started with a handful of essentials. Build from there as your budget, needs, and interests evolve.

Most tool manufacturers offer three or more quality levels, and even as an amateur or hobbyist, you don't want the lowest level. (You'll likely spend more money replacing cheap tools than you will investing in quality ones.) Consider buying a few good tools, rather than a bunch of cheap tools you'll end up replacing after your first project. ✕

the other. If you're buying one specifically for woodworking, you'll need your hammer for more than driving and pulling nails—you'll use it to drive chisels, tap joints into place, and sink nails slightly below the surface of wood—so you'll want something with a little more finesse. Everyone has his or her favorite hammer, but consider a mid-weight mallet with a flat face opposite a ball-peen. You'll have your go-to hammer in hand more often than any other tool, so whatever you get, make sure it *feels* right. Add a set of nails in a range of sizes, and you'll be well on your way.

Screwdrivers and screws. You'll want to use wood screws for projects specific to woodworking—they're thicker than drywall screws and less likely to snap in half. While you may be drilling screws most often, a screwdriver is also handy.

Chisels and a sharpening stone. A sharp chisel lets you change the shape of wood. You'll need the four basic sizes: ¼-, ½-, ¾-, and 1-inch. With these, you can make joints, gouge, carve, bevel, and even pry in a pinch. Whatever chisels you choose, make sure they're *sharp* (get a good sharpening stone). Even a new chisel is likely to need sharpening. Putting a fine edge on your chisel will keep slippage to a minimum and keep your thinner chisels from breaking.

Level. Keeping your projects aligned during construction can make the difference between a wobbly step-stool and one you can actually use. As in your domestic repair tool kit (see page 2), choose between a bubble and a laser level.

Plane. Basically, a plane is a sharper, heavier version of a deli cheese slicer. It makes a rough piece of wood into something nice to touch, reducing its thickness or smoothing it out before sanding and finishing. Hand planes are a quicker and less dusty way to do some of the work you might do with an electric sander. Your first plane should be a low-angle block plane, which cuts at an angle of about 37 degrees (as opposed to the standard 45 degrees). A shallower cutting angle allows you to plane all three grains of wood (face, edge, and end grain), making the shallow plane a more versatile tool.

Files and rasps. Rasps have sharp teeth used to aggressively shape wood. Files have parallel, diagonal rows of teeth of various sizes and are generally used as an intermediate between a rasp and sandpaper. Start with a few flat and half-round rasps and files ranging from "bastard cut" (the coarsest) to "smooth cut" (the smoothest)—you can go a long way with an 8-inch, medium cut flat file.

Saw. There are two basic kinds of saw: a rip saw and a crosscut saw. The rip saw has larger, more aggressive teeth for cutting quickly *with* the grain. A crosscut saw has finer teeth for cutting *across* the grain. You can also find a saw with teeth halfway between rip saw and crosscut, and still others have rip saw teeth on one side and crosscut teeth on the other. Buying a combination saw as your first saw may mean you have to do a little more sanding to get the smoothness you want from crosscutting, but it'll give you the versatility to cut things other than wood, like PVC pipe.

Clamps and a workbench. Even the mightiest woodworker can't hold a piece of wood and work it at the same time. Start with two 24-inch bar clamps, and then buy more as needed. Not only will clamps—and a good workbench!—keep wood from shimmying while you're hammering, chiseling, planing, and sawing, but you'll need clamps to hold pieces together while glue dries. Bar clamps are for clamping longer pieces; spring clamps (smaller, and shaped more like a clothespin) are for clamping shorter spans; and C-clamps (like bar clamps, but heavier and less adjustable) clamp within the fixed width of the "C" shape.

Power Tools

Power tools can be intimidating, but as long as you learn to use them safely, there's nothing like the convenience of ripping an inch off the long edge of a stock board without breaking a sweat. There's no need to spend thousands of dollars on specialized woodworking power tools—basic power tools will do 95 percent of those jobs just as well.

Drill. If your drill will be doing double duty around the house, go cordless. But if you can justify a drill specifically for woodworking, it's worth giving up mobility for the power of a plug-in drill. You'll want a reversible drill with a variable speed trigger and adjustable clutch. The bigger the chuck—the piece that holds the rotating bit—the more torque the drill offers—a ⅜-inch chuck is enough. If you'll be drilling metal or concrete, you'll need a ½-inch chuck, while the ¼-inch chuck is only for fine projects. Keyed or keyless chuck shouldn't affect your choice, unless you're prone to losing things—in that case, go keyless.

Circular saw. Carpentry isn't the same as woodworking (building infrastructure as opposed to building items to populate that infrastructure), and the circular saw probably fits better in the first category. That's because a circular saw is generally used for rougher cuts. There are two basic kinds: the sidewinder, in which the motor sits next to the blade and turns it directly, and the worm-drive, in which the motor sits behind the blade and is geared for higher torque. For most woodworking projects, a high-quality sidewinder is as good

(continued)

as a worm-drive, but beware the underpowered sidewinder (15 amps is standard)—when a blade slows, it heats up and will dull more quickly. A slow blade can also catch on a cut and jump, meaning it won't deliver a clean line.

Jigsaw. You'll need a jigsaw to cut curves. As with a drill, the choice between corded or cordless comes down to the trade-off between convenience and power. If you imagine working with hardwoods (or anything besides wood), a corded jigsaw is best. If you're only working with softwoods (see page 69), a cordless jigsaw with one speed option (high) is fine. All jigsaws are *reciprocal,* meaning the blade goes up and down. Better jigsaws are *orbital* as well, meaning that the blade also goes slightly forward and backward, pulling the cutting edge away from the wood on the downstroke and putting it back against the wood on the upstroke (the cutting stroke). You'll want a range of blades to go with it— invest in a set that includes taper, wavy, and side-set teeth (for fine to rough cuts).

Orbital sander. The genius of a random orbital sander is a sanding belt that moves so that any single grain on the belt never travels the same path twice. The result is a much smoother finish than a belt or disc sander, but it also means you can't remove as much material as quickly. A palm sander will handle most basic needs, and whatever model you choose, make sure it has dust control—either self-contained or with a hose connection to your wet/dry vac.

Table saw. A table saw lets you push wood under a spinning blade. It's best for technical cuts, and it's a tool you'll likely use every day you set foot in your workshop. So if you're going to splurge on anything, splurge on a table saw. (Spend time learning about the proper use of it, too. Nothing sends hobbyists to the emergency room as often as a misused table saw.) Make sure your table saw has a blade guard (almost all do), and then look for a good rip fence and miter gauge. The rip fence is the metal bar against which you'll slide wood when cutting. A secure rip fence with quality tuning controls can help ensure a safe, straight cut. The miter gauge allows you to cut wood at an angle, though it's an accessory you can also buy separately. The table saw is a surprisingly versatile tool that you can use for many kinds of cuts, including with the grain (ripping), across the grain (crosscutting), and at an angle (for cuts like miters and bevels).

Router. With a single round blade sticking out below a flat baseplate, a router is used to hollow out sections in a face of wood, to round corners, and more. Make sure you buy at least a 2-horsepower router, with variable speed control and a soft start, which will keep it from bucking if you try to start it while the tooth is stuck. Most routers now come with the ability to accept ¼- or ½-inch shank router bits (smaller bits are less expensive, but the extra mass of a ½-inch bit makes for a smoother cut). You'll see both stationary routers and plunge routers—the difference is all in the base. With a stationary router, you set the base to allow a cut of defined depth, and that's where it stays. A plunge router allows the shank to dive into the wood and back out again.

Compound miter saw. When joining wood to wood, a couple of degrees can make a big difference. A good compound miter saw can help you ensure your angles are spot-on. With that in mind, make sure your saw has a high-quality miter gauge—the scale that shows the angle of your cut. The gauge should have accurate hard-stops at the common cutting angles of 0, 15, 22.5, 30, and 45 degrees. A 10-inch blade is enough for most projects, but, if you can afford it, a 12-inch blade will let you use your miter for slightly longer cuts.

#32 How to Measure Hardwood Boards
(or, *Determining Board Feet*)

Hardwoods are measured and sold by the board foot, which is 1 foot long, 1 foot wide, and 1 inch thick. For your project, you may need a board of 1 × 10 of a certain length—in that case, skip to the next section and just go buy it. You can say, "I'd like an eight-foot, one-by-ten pine board." More complex projects, especially those that require widths other than the standard 1-inch thickness, may require ordering in board feet. Here's how to figure it out.

1 Board feet is calculated by multiplying a board's width in inches by its length in feet by its thickness in inches and then dividing by 12. This means that a *thicker* board contains more board feet than a thinner one of equal surface area—board feet is a measure of volume, not area. So, a 16-inch-wide, 8-foot-long, 2-inch-thick board would be 16 × 8 × 2 ÷ 12 = 21.3 board feet.

2 First, list the rough-cut sizes of the boards you need. Start by determining how thick you want the finished board, then add ⅛ or even ¼ inch to account for surface planing.

3 Do the same thing with width, again adding ¼ inch.

4 Add an inch to the length of each finished board to determine the rough-cut length—you'll make the end cuts last, and the plane or router (see pages 66–68) has a nasty habit of chipping board ends before you get to them.

5 If you aren't sure, you can always order your hardwood from the lumberyard S4S—"surfaced both sides"—in which case you don't need to add a cushion—just ask for what you need.

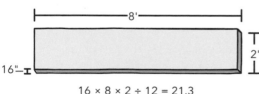

16 × 8 × 2 ÷ 12 = 21.3

✕ ✕

Buying Softwood Boards

Softwoods are sold in standardized board sizes, not by surface area and board feet. You don't get much more standard than a "2 × 4," but a 2 × 4 actually measures 1½ × 3½ inches, the size of the board after being planed down from the rough stock. The same is true of all standard softwood boards, including the 1-by series (1 × 2, 1 × 3, 1 × 4, 1 × 6, 1 × 8, 1 × 10, and 1 × 12), the 2-by series (2 × 2, 2 × 4, 2 × 6, 2 × 8, 2 × 10, 2 × 12), and bigger wood, including 4 × 4, 4 × 6, 6 × 6, and 8 × 8. All the 1-inch dimensions are actually ¾ inch; all the dimensions from 2 to 6 inches lose exactly half an inch (e.g., a 2 × 6 is in fact 1½ × 5½). Dimensions over 6 inches lose ¾ inch. These widths and depths all come in the standard lengths of 6, 8, 10, 12, 14, 16, 18, 20, 22, and 24 feet. ✕

#33 How to Sand Wood

(or, How to Make a Sanding Block)

anding wood is an ancient art, and it is one that is crucial to all forms of woodworking. From finishing a board to flattening a deck (see page 39) to smoothing a sculpture, sanding makes your projects shine. Ancient as it is, there is a right and a wrong way of doing it. When sanding a flat surface, start with rough-grit sandpaper and continue stepping down the grit until you reach the desired smoothness. Sandpapers run from extra-coarse grits of 12-grit, 24-grit, 30-grit, and 36-grit (sometimes marked as P12 to P36), coarse grits of 40-grit to 50-grit (P40 to P50), medium from 60-grit to 80-grit (P60 to P80), fine from 100-grit to 120-grit (P100 to P120), and very fine from 150-grit to 180-grit and 220-grit (P150 to P220). It's rarely worth sanding with anything finer than about P180, as finishes penetrate slightly rougher woods better and the finish becomes the smooth surface of your piece anyway. Here are the Zen-like basics of sanding wood properly.

TOOLS:

Range of sandpaper (coarse, medium, and fine) • **Staple gun**

MATERIALS:

- **Wood glue**
- **Felt or lightweight cardboard**
- **Scrap 2 × 4 board**

1 Make a sanding block. Commercial sanding blocks are flat on the bottom with a nice grip and padding to spread the force of your downward pressure. Glue a layer of felt or thin cardboard to a small piece of scrap 2 × 4—anywhere from 3 to 4 inches. To get a better grip on the block, cut a second, smaller piece of 2 × 4 and glue it to the top for a handle.

2 Prepare the sanding block. Cut a piece of sandpaper of the desired grit slightly larger than your block. Lay it on the flat part of the block (grit side out), then fold the ends over and staple them to the top of the block.

3 Start sanding a test piece of wood. Sand in the direction of the wood grain, applying light, even pressure. When the sandpaper gets clogged with particles or loses its grit, staple a new sheet over the old one. As you step down the coarseness of your sandpaper in stages, wipe away any accumulated sawdust from the board. Before the final sanding, wet the wood and then let it dry to raise the edges of the grain pattern. Use a fine sandpaper and light pressure to finish sanding the piece.

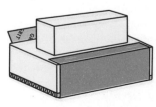

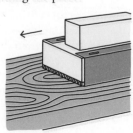

Wood Finishes

Some modern furniture is designed to be assembled, used, and discarded. That's not the case, however, for the table with the hardwood joinery that you just spent a month slaving over, or for that heirloom antique—so you need to protect it. Finish your tabletops or other special wood surfaces with a protectant to ensure that they bring as much joy to the robot overlords of 2147 as they bring to you today.

Finishes are distinguished mostly by the solvent used as the base. You apply the finish as a liquid, but then the liquid solvent goes away, leaving the color and texture of the finish behind. Finishes lose their solvents by evaporation or reaction. In the former, the water or other emulsion liquid vaporizes, leaving just the finish itself behind. The material left after evaporation will dissolve in the original solvent, meaning that if you spill water on a water-based evaporative finish, you will lose the finish. A reactive finish, such as tung oil or varnish, changes at the chemical level while it cures. Once the finish is dry, you don't have to worry about accidental water spills. Choose based on the preferred finished look, and on your willingness to work with harsher chemicals.

Wax. Some consider wax a finish, while others consider it merely a polish to be used over a true finish, like lacquer or shellac. Paste waxes like carnauba and beeswax aren't necessarily waterproof and also don't create a hard shell to resist dents and dings, but they do make a piece *shine*. (Antique furniture may have remnants of an original wax finish, and it can be hard to replicate the color without applying more wax.) To apply paste wax finish, wrap a piece of cotton-based cloth around your fingers and rub on the wax as you might when polishing a pair of shoes. Rub the wax into the grain, and don't be shy about applying multiple coats.

Oil. Like wax, some woodworkers choose to use an oil finish as a topcoat after first applying a more durable, protective finish, like a varnish or lacquer. Also like wax, oil finishes are best applied with a cloth wrapped around your hand. Due to the long drying time of oil finishes—especially linseed oil, which can take three days—don't apply too much at once. Work the oil into the grain, and when you see the grain refuse to accept more finish, stop and let the coat dry.

Varnish. The durable, shiny surface of a varnish is made of resin, which is combined with drying oil and a thinner or solvent. The solvent keeps the resin in liquid form, and then evaporates to leave the hard finish. A common mistake when applying varnish is brushing it on over dust or other specks, which become permanent additions to the wood finish (until they rip free, chipping the varnish). Thoroughly clean the surface before applying varnish.

Shellac. Shellac is a versatile finish with a long history. It's nontoxic and can be used to seal wood before staining, or it can itself be mixed with colors. Basically, shellac is bug poop. The female lac bug of India and Thailand secretes a resin that dries on trees and can be scraped free in flakes. The flakes are dissolved in ethyl alcohol to make a liquid. After the liquid is applied to the wood, the alcohol evaporates, leaving your project covered in a thin, protective layer of lac bug secretion. Cool, huh? Shellac can be brushed or padded onto wood. Brushing is straightforward, but consider using a disposable brush, because it can be especially difficult to clean shellac from the bristles. To pad shellac, wrap cotton muslin around an old sock and then pour shellac into the sock. Gently squeeze the sock to force

(continued)

shellac into the muslin and then apply it to the wood with long, smooth strokes.

Lacquer. Lacquers come in brush-on and spray-on forms, and both dry very quickly. Lacquer is very similar to shellac, only while shellac is made from bug excrement found on lac trees, lacquer comes straight from the lac tree itself. A chemical additive cements multiple coats together, even after the first coat dries. Use a natural-bristle brush and apply a quick, thin layer first and follow with additional, thicker layers. Lacquer and polyurethane (see below) are used in much the same way, but should not be used on the same piece.

Polyurethane. This forgiving finish is available in water-based or oil-based formulas. Oil-based polyurethane requires fewer coats than

water-based polyurethane but takes longer to dry and can hold the patterns of brush marks. Water-based finish requires at least three (and up to five) coats, and even then remains susceptible to water marks. That said, water-based stain won't smell up the room with toxic fumes. Water-based finish also self-levels, so it tends not to hold brush marks. When mixing polyurethane finish in preparation for application, go with the reverse James Bond—stir, don't shake, which would introduce thousands of tiny bubbles. Work with the grain and gently brush away any lingering bubbles. Inevitably, you will leave a few, but don't worry—the marks will disappear in a month.

#34 How to Build a Birdhouse
(or, an Introduction to Measuring, Cutting, and Nailing)

A bird could probably live in just about any box that keeps it warm and dry, but if you decide to put one in your yard, why not give it a bit of charm? Here it is: the classic birdhouse. The perfect project on which to cut your woodworking teeth. Your woodworking skills will build on each other, like stacking stones for a tower. At the base of this tower are measuring, cutting, and nailing, so as you work on this project, focus on getting these essential skills just right. The first rule of woodworking is "measure twice; cut once." Take your time in preparation and assembly will be easy.

TOOLS:

Pencil • Tape measure • Ruler or carpenter's square • 2 bar clamps • Jigsaw or handsaw • Drill • Spade bit • ½" bit (for optional perch) • Hammer • Paintbrush • Safety goggles

MATERIALS:

- One 6-foot 1 × 8 cedar or pine board
- Fifty 1¼" finishing nails
- One 4" × ½" dowel (optional)
- Wood glue
- Paint, polyurethane, or varnish finish
- Galvanized wire

1. Start by drawing the shapes of your largest pieces, the front and back, onto the board. Lay the 1 × 8 board on a flat surface and

hook the metal end of your tape measure on a long edge of the board, near one end. The front and back of your birdhouse will be 7¼" wide, so measure exactly 7¼" on the short (8") edge and make a small tick mark with your pencil. Each piece will be 9½" tall, so use the tape measure to measure and mark 19" along the long edge of the board. At the 19" mark, line up the carpenter's square along the bottom of the board so one side of the L points exactly perpendicularly across it. Draw a line all the way across the board. Measure along this line, and make a mark at exactly 7¼". Use the long edge of the carpenter's square to draw a line connecting your two marks at 7¼". You will have a 7¼" × 19" box.

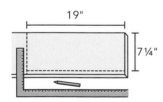

2 Use the tape measure to make a mark in the middle of the long box, at 9½". Use the L of the carpenter's square to draw a line across the board at this point, splitting the box into two halves. To draw the triangular peaks of your birdhouse, measure and mark 5⅞" along each of the 9½" edges. Make another mark in

the exact center of the 7¼" width, at 3⅝". Now draw diagonal lines connecting the edge mark at 5⅞", with the center mark at 3⅝". You should have now drawn the front and back of the birdhouse.

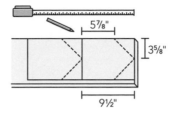

3 Measure and draw two pieces for the roof. One roof face will be 7" × 6½". Measure 7" from the farthest line you drew in the previous step. Then measure 6½" across the width of the board. Use the carpenter's square to draw the sides of the 7" × 6½" rectangle. The other roof face will be shorter—6½" × 6¼". As before, measure 6½" up from the farthest pencil line. Then measure 6¼" down the board and use the carpenter's square to draw the sides of your rectangle.

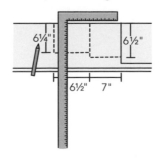

4 The two sides and the bottom of the birdhouse will all be 5¾" × 4" rectangles. Measure 5¾" from the last line you drew, 4" across the width of the board, and use the carpenter's square as before to draw the sides. Repeat for all three pieces.

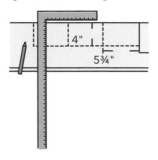

5 Now it's time to cut. Clamp your board to a fixed surface like a workbench, making sure that your first cutting line doesn't overlap the bench. Keep in mind that you will start by cutting the end you marked in Step 1. Put on your safety goggles and line up your jigsaw or handsaw at the end of your board, at the 7¼" line. If you like, lay the carpenter's square or a metal ruler parallel to the line to guide the saw. Keeping the face of the saw tight against the board, cut straight to the 19" line and then stop.

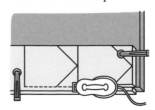

(continued)

6 Unclamp, adjust, and reclamp the board to free up the lines at 9½" and 19", and then cut the front and back of your birdhouse. Clamp these cut pieces to your workbench to make the diagonal cuts, as marked.

7 Continue adjusting and clamping the board and making one straight cut at a time, eventually freeing all your birdhouse pieces from the board.

8 Use a drill fitted with a spade bit to cut an entrance circle in one of the identical faces. (To add a perch, drill a smaller hole right below it and add a piece of ½" dowel.)

9 Assemble the four walls of your birdhouse. Run a thin line of wood glue along the 5¾" edges of your two side pieces and attach them to the front and back pieces. Let the glue dry until it's tacky and then use three finishing nails along each edge.

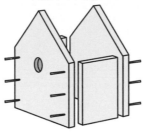

10 Attach the floor. Place the floor piece about ½" up from the base of the house walls. Glue it to hold it temporarily in place. After the glue has dried, nail it into place with three evenly spaced nails on each side. Make sure the nails from the wall hit the edge of the floor.

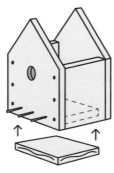

11 Add the roof faces. Glue along the top of the walls and place the 6½" × 6¼" piece in place

against the glue so that it ends flush with the top of the roof angle. Use three nails to fix the roof panel permanently in place. Then use three nails to add the 7" × 6½" piece so that it overlaps and ends flush with the shorter piece.

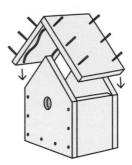

12 Finish and hang. Use an outdoor (oil-based) paint or clear finish to protect it from the elements. Drill two holes in the back of each of the two side walls, just below the edge of the roof and above the base. Thread a piece of wire horizontally through the two higher holes and another through the two lower ones, then tie the birdhouse securely around a tree or fencepost, preferably facing east.

Drill Bits and How to Use Them

As with any choice you make in woodworking, material matters. You may need a different type of drill bit depending on what you're boring holes in. Steel bits work well in softwood but don't hold up as well against hardwood. Their cousin, high-speed steel bits, are so named because they can withstand higher temperatures than other types of steel—and thus will cut through materials like wood, fiberglass, PVC, and soft metals faster. Even tougher than high-speed steel is titanium-coated HSS, and moving up the spectrum, the hardest drill bits—carbide-tipped—are primarily used for tile and masonry. They stay sharp a long time! When you insert a bit into the drill chuck, make sure the shaft is straight and then tighten the chuck around it well.

Twist bits. The most common type of bit, twist bits are the kind you probably got in a starter set of bits. Twist bits are an all-purpose bit that can be used in just about any material. The spiral groove—or flute—helps to remove sawdust from the hole as you go.

Spade bits. These bits (they're not the kind for horses) have a pointy tip in the center of a flat edge, and they're made for ripping quick holes through soft wood. They can leave ragged edges but get the job done quickly.

Auger bits. Auger bits look a little like thinner twist bits but have a tip that starts the drill hole for you. Augers are often used with hand-powered drills because they require less torque and are easy to turn. They are typically used for drilling deep holes in wood (the large flute gets chaff out of the hole easily).

Countersink bits. Sometimes called screw pilot bits, these are specialty bits that look like a regular bit with a sheath around the base. This type of bit is a multitasker—it drills a pilot hole, so you don't split the wood when you put in a screw—at the same time as it drills a countersink hole, a conical hole that allows you to conceal the head of the screw with sawdust or a wooden plug, lending the whole project a more refined look.

#35 How to Build a Picture Frame

(or, an Introduction to Mitering and Using Moldings)

Decorative moldings give your home character—baseboards where walls meet the floor, crown molding where walls meet the ceiling—you get the idea. But before you jump into installing yards of intricate molding, it's worth practicing on simpler projects. Like a picture frame—or ten. Pay special attention to the tips that will enable you to miter cut molding—that is, beveling it so it fits snugly together at an angle—without chipping it. Being able to put a perfect end angle on a piece of molding is a skill that'll serve you well down the line.

(continued)

TOOLS:

Measuring tape • Calculator • Miter box and handsaw, or miter saw • 2 bar clamps • 4 corner clamps • Hammer • Utility knife • Safety goggles

MATERIALS:

- **Picture frame molding**
- **Wood glue**
- **Backing board**
- **½" to ¾" brad nails**
- **Sandpaper and stain or paint to finish (optional)**
- **Hanging or standing hardware**

1 Measure the mat or picture to determine the interior dimensions of your frame.

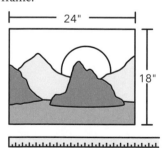

2 Call ahead to frame shops to find out if they sell picture molding in lengths. Bring along to the store your measurements, a calculator, and an idea of the style you want.

In the Frame Shop

1 First, order a piece of glass and a backing board sized to the art you want to frame.

2 Choose the style of picture frame molding that best complements your art. Keep in mind that the more intricately a piece of molding is patterned, the more prone it is to chipping and cracking. The width of the molding should be listed on the sample. If not, the store should assist you in getting an accurate measurement.

3 To determine how much molding to get, add twice the molding width to each length of the interior dimensions. For example, if your interior dimensions are 18" × 24" and you plan to use 2" molding, get two 22" and two 28" lengths of molding. The shop can cut the molding to length or you can add these lengths together, plus a couple of inches for scrap, and carefully transport the long length back to your shop. That said, there's a good chance a shop will have molding samples on hand, but not the actual molding. If you're in a hurry, ask to see only what's in stock. If you're not, plan on waiting to have the molding of your choice shipped to you or to

the shop for pickup. The shop very well may offer to miter the molding for you. Don't let them. For the purposes of this project, that's cheating. But you can get the molding rabbeted. This will precut the inside groove that will hold your picture in place.

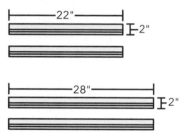

Back in Your Wood Shop

1 Cut the molding to length, if necessary (see Step 3, In the Frame Shop).

2 Lay out your four lengths of molding and double-check that each is twice the molding width longer than the interior dimensions of your frame. Miter the corners to 45-degree angles before joining them to make your frame. First, make sure that your saw blade is sharp. Use clamps (not just the pressure of your hand) to hold the molding securely to the saw. Finally, position your molding piece in the miter box or on the saw molded-side-up, so that the visible edge is pressed against the top of the box or saw table. Now line up your cuts. Put on your safety

goggles, turn the blade to 45 degrees, lock it in place, load your wood, press it tight against the saw's back fence, and make the exact same cuts on one end of all four pieces of molding.

3 Reverse the 45-degree angle of your miter box or saw and repeat, cutting the opposite ends of your molding. Be careful with the direction of your cuts—it's worth laying out the wood as it will eventually be assembled and drawing rough pencil lines showing the direction you want your angles. Mitering the mirror image of the angle you planned is a quick way to turn your usable molding into scrap.

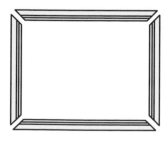

4 Once you've mitered the corners, dry fit your picture frame, using the corner clamps to hold the molding in place. Remember, the picture and the glass should sit against the small ledge called the rabbet, running around the inside of the molding. If your frame pieces are slightly too big, unclamp the frame and miter again to shave the extra, being sure to cut exactly equal amounts from opposite sides of the frame. If your frame is slightly too small, cry, swear, and then start over from the beginning (or trim your art . . .). If needed, continue shaving your frame until your art fits into the rabbeted frame.

5 Glue the frame pieces together at the joints and hold them in place with your corner clamps. While the joints are drying, cut your backing board to the size of your art with a utility knife.

6 Once the joints are dry, reinforce them by carefully tacking them together with brad nails. This isn't the time to swing away and risk cracking your delicate project. Light taps with thin nails should do the trick.

7 If you like, sand and stain or paint your finished frame and, once it's dry, install the hanging or standing hardware on the back.

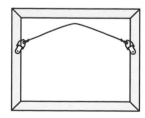

A Few Relevant Woodworking Terms

If you're going to be making your own bookshelves, stools, and wood frames from scratch, it's also worth learning to talk the talk. Here are a few basic vocabulary terms that will help when you're shopping for materials, making the project, or asking for help along the way.

CROSS CUTS

These cuts run perpendicular to the grain of the wood.

RIP CUTS

These cuts run parallel to the grain of the wood.

FENCE

A guide at the back of a tool (like a saw) that stops whatever you're cutting, keeping it a set distance from the blade.

MITER BOX VS. MITER SAW

A miter box is a simple tool that has slats that helps you hold the saw at an angle and clamps the wood in place. Using a miter box, you can make angled cuts on a piece of wood with a handsaw.

If you want to upgrade to a power tool, consider a power miter saw if you have the need for a crosscut chopsaw that makes it easy to shave off bits of wood with precision. Some models tilt for bevel and miter cuts. Compound miter saws can make angled cuts to the edge and face of the board (you'd want that for crown molding).

BEVEL ANGLE VS. MITER ANGLE

Although it may sound like these terms can be used interchangeably, they do have different meanings. The bevel angle is the tilt of the saw blade from vertical on the table saw, while the miter angle is the horizontal angle. Typically the maximum bevel on a miter saw is 45 degrees.

RABBETING

Cutting a deep groove or a notch into a wood so that you can fit and attach another piece to it. Rabbeting describes both the act of cutting the groove, and also fitting in the joining piece. A rabbet is also the name of the joint made thus. Rabbeting usually also includes gluing or fastening the grooved pieces.

#36 How to Build a Doghouse
(or, an Introduction to Framing and Roofing)

Building a sturdy and comfortable doghouse splits the difference between wanting what's best for your best friend and not necessarily wanting your best friend hogging your bed. Build the house a little bigger and you've got a storage shed or small barn. A little bigger than that and you've got a garage. That's to say, the techniques you learn here are the same ones you'd use to build any framed wooden box with a top that points at the sky. Note that standard shingle size is 12" by 36", but the package size depends on the weight of the shingle, so you may want to ask for help at your home supply store.

TOOLS:

Measuring tape • Pencil • Carpenter's frame • Circular saw or handsaw • Jigsaw • Drill and bit larger than your jigsaw blade • Sandpaper or orbital sander • Staple gun and ⅝" staples • Utility knife • Safety goggles • Paint brush

MATERIALS:

- **One 8-foot pressure-treated 2 × 4 board**
- **One 8-foot 2 × 2 board**
- **One 4' × 8' sheet exterior-grade plywood**
- **3" galvanized deck screws**
- **1¼" galvanized deck screws**
- **Four 15-inch 1 × 1 framing strips**
- **Four 13-inch 2 × 2 framing strips**
- **15-pound tar paper**
- **½" galvanized roofing nails**
- **Asphalt shingles (to cover roof)**
- **Exterior-grade paint**

1 Measure, mark, and cut an 8-foot, pressure-treated 2 × 4 into four pieces to make the rectangular base. You'll need to cut two lengths of 22½" and two lengths of 23". Measure, mark, and cut an 8-foot 2 × 2 into four lengths of 13" and four lengths of 15", to make the frame of the walls and roof.

2 Use a tape measure, carpenter's frame, and pencil to draw the following template onto the 4' × 8' sheet of exterior-grade plywood. Adjust the size of the opening to fit your dog—it should be about ¾ of your dog's height. (Keep in mind that the smaller the opening, the less quickly the house will lose heat.) Either freehand the arch at the top of the entryway or use something round to stencil it—a Frisbee works well for this shape.

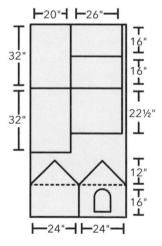

3 Cut out the pieces from your plywood template. Clamp the plywood securely to sawhorses (best) or to your workbench and use a circular

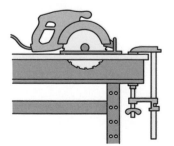

saw or a handsaw (more arduous) to make all of the straight cuts.

4 To cut out the entryway, first drill a hole big enough to fit the blade of your jigsaw in the piece to be removed (the hole can go anywhere). Start your jigsaw cut in this drilled hole and follow the lines of your entryway to cut it out. Support the flap you're cutting out so that it doesn't tear free and splinter once the weight of the detached piece is too heavy.

5 Decide whether you want the roof of your doghouse to end at a mitered 45-degree angle or whether you'll overlap one roof face on top of the other. If mitering, set the blade of your circular saw to tilt 45 degrees before cutting the line that will be your roof apex on both faces. Because the roof faces are exactly the same size, you can cut both faces at the same 45-degree angle and then just

(continued)

flip one to join the cut sides. Sand the edges of these pieces to remove any splinters.

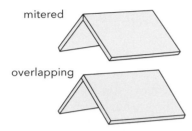

mitered

overlapping

6 Assemble the base framing. The pressure-treated lumber will sit against the ground, with the floor of the house sitting on top of it. Not only does this keep untreated wood from molding and rotting, and keep the treated wood away from Fido's teeth, but it also traps air underneath the house to act as insulation. The 22½" pieces are the front and back, and the 23" pieces are the sides. Laying the lumber on its edge, fit the 23" pieces inside the front and back pieces, and predrill two screw holes per joint so that you're drilling through the face of the 22½" pieces and into the ends of the 23" pieces (remember, the finished floor dimensions should be 22½" × 26"). Use 3" galvanized deck screws to hold the frame of the base together.

7 Screw on the floor. Lay the piece of plywood that is the floor of the doghouse on top of your frame. Use 1¼" galvanized deck screws spaced about every 8" to 12" to hold the plywood floor to the frame.

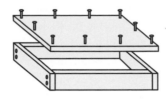

8 Attach the framing strips to the side walls, top, and back. Lay a 15" framing strip along the 26" length of one of the side pieces. Leave 1" of plywood extending past the strip at the bottom. Use 1¼" deck screws spaced about every 8" to fix the framing strip to the side wall. Repeat for the other side wall. Lay a 15" framing strip across the bottom edge of what will be the back of the doghouse, again leaving 1" of plywood past the strip. Lay the final 15" framing strip along the bottom edge of the doghouse front, again leaving 1" extending past the strip.

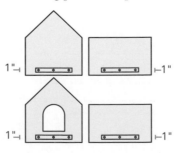

9 Attach the side walls to the base. Place a side wall against the base so that the framing strip sits on the top of the base and the 1" overhang of plywood along the lower edge of the side wall extends down to the pressure-treated lumber. Use 1¼" deck screws spaced about every 5", screwed down through the framing strip and into the base to hold the pieces together. Repeat for the other side wall. Then, use 1¼" deck screws to screw through the overhanging 1" of plywood along the lower edge of each wall, into the pressure-treated lumber, spaced about every 8".

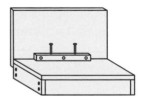

10 Attach framing strips along the insides of the roof angles of the front and back plywood pieces. Center one of the 13" 2 × 2 framing strips along the inside of a sloped roof edge so that the top of the strip is flush with the top of the plywood. Use three 1¼" wood screws,

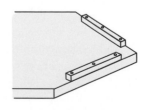

driven through the plywood into the framing strip, to hold the strip in place. Repeat for the remaining three 13" framing strips.

11 Attach the back. Tip the house on what will be its front and lay the back piece against the rear edges of the side walls. Seat the framing piece attached to the back down against the base. Screw it in place as you did with the side walls. Repeat to attach the front.

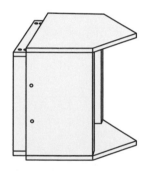

12 Attach the roof panels. Lay a panel flush against the framing strips you attached to the wall pieces in Step 10, making sure that if you chose to cut a 45-degree bevel to miter the top of the roof in Step 5, to place the

angle appropriately at the apex. Also make sure the roof panel sits square to the walls and that the eaves hang over an equal amount on both sides. Use 1¼" wood screws spaced about every 8" to screw the roof panel to the framing pieces. Repeat with the other roof panel.

13 Now shingle the roof. Run 15-pound tar paper up one side of the roof and down the other, staple it in place, and use a utility knife to trim it flush with the roof panels. To install the asphalt shingles, start with an upside-down row of shingles (tab up) along both lower edges of the roof panels, using roofing nails to hold them in place. The shingles should overhang the plywood edge of the

roof panel by about ¾". Then nail another layer of shingles, right-side up, directly over this first row. Install another row slightly higher, making sure it overlaps the first. Continue installing rows until you've completely covered both roof panels. Cap the roof ridge by cutting smaller rectangles of shingles, bending them over the roof peak and nailing them in place so they overlap each other slightly, covering the nails in the previous tab.

14 To finish, paint the walls of your doghouse with an exterior-grade paint. Let dry.

#37 How to Build a Shaker Stool
(or, How to Use a Template)

There are things that are unlikely, like winning the lottery, and there are things that are impossible, like cutting two identical, irregularly shaped pieces of wood without a template. A template and the skills to use it ensure that you can mass-produce complicated cuts —in this case, two identical legs for a Shaker-style step stool.

There are a couple of ways to use woodworking templates, but here we'll draw directly on a piece of ¼" plywood, trace it against our wood, and rough-cut it to shape with a jigsaw. Finally we will use what's called a "flush trim bit" mounted in a router to smooth the wood to the template. One reason cutting to a template is such a useful skill is the ubiquity and convenience of online templates. For nearly any project you can imagine, a template is but a quick search away, so you can produce professional-looking designs in your own shop. This Shaker stool is a great place to start—and the wood should set you back only about $15.

TOOLS:

Tape measure • Pencil • Table saw or handsaw • Jigsaw • Router • Clamps • Flush trim bit with bearing • Drill • Countersink drill bit • 4-foot level • Safety goggles

MATERIALS:

- One 4-foot 1 × 12 pine board
- One 1-foot 1 × 4 pine board
- Scrap ¼" plywood, at least 10" × 11"
- Double-sided tape (optional)
- Fifty 1" wood screws
- Wood glue (optional)
- Paint or finish (optional)

1 Measure and mark 14" from the end of a 4-foot 1 × 12 board. Cut it off with a table saw and rip the piece down to exactly 11" wide. This will be the top of your stool. Measure, mark, and cut a 1-foot 1 × 4 into a piece 11" long and 3" wide. This will be your brace.

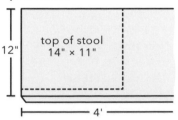

2 Cut a 20"-long section from the 1 × 12 and rip it to exactly 10¼" wide. Cut

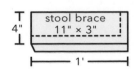

this piece in half, making two 10" × 10¼" rectangles. Once shaped, these will be the legs of your stool.

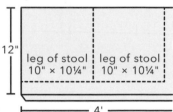

3 Make a template for the legs. Measure, mark, and cut a section of ¼" plywood into a 10" × 10¼" rectangle. Draw a shape for your stool legs onto this plywood rectangle. One common cut is to taper the legs slightly toward the top, marking ¾" in from the top sides and drawing a straight line to the bottom corners. You'll also need to cut some sort of decorative arc from the

bottom center of your legs. Some ideas are shown here, but feel free to experiment with the shape of this arc. If you make an irretrievable mistake, it only costs another 10" × 10¼" scrap of plywood to start again. Use a frisbee or another rounded household object if you need something to trace.

4 Measure about 3" from the top edge to find the exact center of your template. Draw a 3" × ¾" rectangle that, when cut out from each leg, will secure the brace.

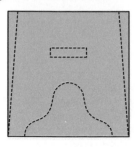

5 Cut out the plywood shape that you'll use as a template to sculpt your stool's legs. Consider using your table saw for long, straight cuts and the jigsaw for more ornate, curved cuts (and drill a hole to cut out the rectangle

for the brace, as you did in Step 4 of How to Build a Doghouse). Sand or use your router to finish the template to the exact shape you want the legs.

6 When the plywood template is ready, lay it on top of one of the 10" × 10¼" pieces of pine that will be your stool's legs. Trace around the template with a pencil, put on your safety goggles, and then use the jigsaw to rough-cut the stool leg to shape.

7 Place the plywood template beneath the rough-cut stool leg and clamp them together to your workbench. To prevent slippage, use double-sided tape to stick the template to the wood before clamping.

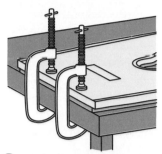

8 Make sure the router is unplugged and insert the flush trim bit. Set the router on top of the clamped piece and template and look at how the bit and bearing hit the side of the stacked pieces. Adjust the bit so that when the router is flat against the piece, the bearing hits the template and the bit hits the rough-cut board.

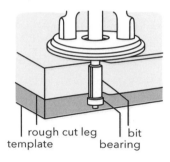

rough cut leg   bit
template   bearing

9 Prepare to drive the router along the rough-cut board, using the template below it as a guide. Place the router flat against the board, with the bit safely away from the edge of the wood. Plug in and turn on the router, and once the bit is up to speed, bring it into the board, stopping when you feel the bearing contact the template.

(continued)

Using the feel of the bearing against the template, run the router around the edge of the board, making an exact copy of the template, including the space between the legs and the brace support holes. Repeat Steps 7 to 9 with the other leg.

and wiggle slightly until all four feet sit flush against the ground. Lay the top of the stool across the legs and use a level to check that it lies flat. If all four feet aren't snug to the ground or if the top of your stool isn't level, use your table saw to shave your cuts accordingly. If your brace seems unsturdy, use wood glue to secure it in the hole.

evenly spaced pilot holes and use 1" wood screws to attach the top to the legs. Again, if you like, use wood glue and sawdust to camouflage the holes.

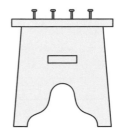

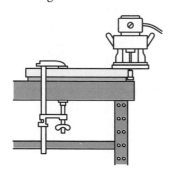

10 Assemble the stool. Insert the brace into the rectangular holes, connecting the two legs. Place the legs on the ground

11 Attach the top. Lay it atop your legs and make sure it's exactly centered and level. Countersink four

12 If you like, paint or finish your Shaker stool. Traditionally, this kind of furniture would be finished with oil and wax (talk to your local home improvement or woodworking store, or see Oil Finishes for Wood, page 92).

✕ ✕

Sanding Furniture

Sanding furniture or shaped pieces follows the same essential strategy as sanding a flat board—always go with the grain of the wood and progress from coarser to finer paper.

For flat surfaces, use a padded sanding block. For curved surfaces, use a thick sponge covered with sandpaper, which will help you exert even pressure while conforming to the shape. To sand rounded pieces like spindles or thin chair legs, cut a long strip of medium- or fine-grit sandpaper and wrap the paper around the piece so that you can hold the two ends together. Pull the sandpaper wrap back and

forth, as if using a bow and stick to start a fire.

For rounded edges, use a piece of fine-grit paper folded onto itself. For detail sanding, wrap fine-grit sandpaper around the tip of a sharpened pencil. For even finer work, use a toothpick. When sanding delicate pieces, brace both the hand doing the sanding and the hand doing the holding so that your sanding materials don't slip. Sanding can lead to chips and dings as well as scratches, especially when working with fine edges. When you're finished, blow the sawdust from the crevices or use a clean toothbrush to free it. ✕

#38 How to Build a Chessboard
(or, Learning to Veneer)

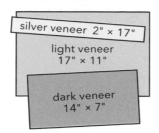

The interior decorators of King Tut's tomb used ebony and ivory veneer. So did the builders in the French Renaissance court of King Louis XIV, who used exotics and burl wood to make intricate veneer patterns called marquetry. Today Ikea continues this great tradition, as veneer is widely used in commercial furniture to stretch the use of valuable hardwoods. Done right, veneer—a thin slice of wood applied to another piece of wood as decoration—can greatly enhance a project. Here you'll apply the technique to create a chessboard.

TOOLS:

Pencil • Craft or utility knife • Table saw, circular saw, or jigsaw (optional) • Carpenter's square • Metal straightedge • Miter box and handsaw, or miter saw • Clamps • Safety goggles

MATERIALS:

- At least 14" × 7" sheet of dark veneer (extra preferred)
- At least 17" × 11" sheet of light veneer (extra preferred)
- At least 2" × 17" sheet of silver (or contrasting) veneer (extra preferred)
- Painter's tape
- Clear tape
- 17" × 17" sanded plywood
- Wood glue
- Scrap wood

1 There are many ways to cut veneer, and each cut tends to give a different, distinctive pattern to the grain. So when you go to the home improvement store or lumberyard, explore not only the colors of veneers but also their grains. Pick 1-ply light and dark hardwood veneers that are exactly the same thickness. Then choose a third piece of contrasting 1-ply veneer—silver works well—for the trim that will go around the outside edges of your board. You may be able to use veneer scraps. Veneer comes with or without paper backing. For this project, raw (unbacked) veneer is preferable, but paper-backed will work as well.

silver veneer 2" × 17"

light veneer 17" × 11"

dark veneer 14" × 7"

2 Cut the veneer into strips. Depending on your tools, use a saw or a craft or utility knife to cut your veneer to size. If you use a table saw, be sure you know how to use it safely, because you'll be making narrow cuts. Like molding, veneer tends to chip and crack when cut. Whatever saw you use, pick the blade with the smallest, most closely spaced teeth, and make sure it's sharp. To guard against splintering, put scotch tape over the lines you will cut, and then slice through the tape. Remove it carefully once you've made your cuts. Measure, mark, and cut four strips each of light and dark veneer. The standard dimension of chessboard squares is 1¾" on a side, so, for now, make eight strips that are 1¾" × 14". Measure, mark, and cut four ¼" × 17" strips of silver veneer, and another four strips of 1" × 17" light veneer for your border.

(continued)

3 On a flat surface, lay the 1¾" × 14" light and dark veneer strips exactly side by side with the face side down, starting with a light strip. Push the strips against a carpenter's square to ensure that they are exactly square on all sides. If squaring the strips is impossible, shave strips as necessary or replace badly cut strips with new ones. The precision of this step will determine the success of your project. Using the carpenter's square to keep them flush, use a liberal amount of clear tape on the backs of the strips to hold them all together in a square.

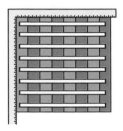

4 Cut your strips into squares. First, make marks every 1¾" along your first light strip and then make corresponding marks at every 1¾" along the final dark strip. Lay the metal straightedge between the corresponding marks and run your craft knife along the straightedge, being sure to hold the knife exactly vertically. It's fine if your cuts require multiple strokes with the knife. As long as you run true against the straightedge, it's better to make multiple light cuts

than risk cracking the veneer. Because you backed your strips with clear tape and then cut through the tape, the cuts in this step will again make strips (held together with the tape), only this time your strips are made of alternating light and dark squares.

5 Pick up these strips and, as before, lay the strips side by side, but this time alternate the pattern so that it looks like the standard chessboard. Square these strips against the carpenter's square and again join them together with tape into a perfect square.

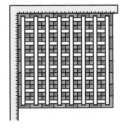

6 Lay the ¼" strips of silver veneer alongside your squared, chessboard-patterned strips to form a border. Use the craft knife to miter the corners at 45-degree angles (see How to Build a Picture Frame, page 75). Do the

same with the 1" × 17" strips of light veneer, to complete the border.

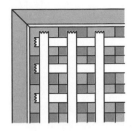

7 Mount your veneer chessboard surface on your 17" × 17" sanded plywood board. To do this, pick off the tape from one piece of veneer at a time, apply a dot of wood glue to the back of each piece and place it on the board. Once all pieces are in place, clamp them in place to dry. Place scrap wood against the clamp pads to spread the force of the clamp across a wider area—this will help you avoid scratching, denting, or cracking your veneer.

If you are feeling ambitious, flip to page 93 (How to Build a Storage Chest) and use the techniques there to build what is effectively a small chest to hold your chess pieces and on top of which you can mount your veneer.

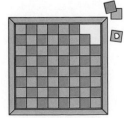

#39 How to Make a Butcher Block
(or, Laminating 101)

A butcher block is a serious hunk of wood, used as the solid base for heavy-duty chopping and cutting. But it isn't seriously a hunk at all. Because hardwoods rarely come in the size needed for chopping blocks, they are made from many columns of wood fixed together, which is called laminate. There are two kinds of laminated chopping blocks: edge grain and end grain. Edge grain is made of long strips of wood. End grain blocks, from wood cut across the growth rings, resist nicks and chips better. And, because your knife edge goes between the wood grain instead of across it, end grain blocks tend to help your knives stay sharper longer.

Oak and maple are the most common woods used for chopping block construction, though any hardwood will work, and you can find blocks made from birch, cherry, and walnut. Here you'll learn to make a stand-alone, checkerboard-patterned, end grain chopping block, using the hardwood of your choice.

TOOLS:

Measuring tape • Pencil • Table saw • 3 or more bar clamps • Metal straightedge • Electric sander or sandpaper and large muscles • Rag

MATERIALS:

- **One 3-foot 2 × 6 light-colored hardwood board**
- **One 3-foot 2 × 6 dark-colored hardwood board**
- **Wood glue**
- **Coarse, medium, and fine sandpaper**
- **Mineral oil**

1 Before you start, measure the depth of your hardwood boards and make sure they are really 2". If not, let the width of your boards define the size of the cubes you will use throughout (i.e.,

if your board is 1¾" deep, you will make cubes of that size). Whatever the depth of the boards—let's assume it's exactly 2"—use your table saw to rip the hardwood boards into exactly square strips, the length of the board. Cut these strips in half. You should now have six 2" × 2" × 18" light strips and six 2" × 2" × 18" dark strips.

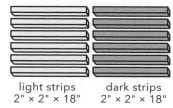

light strips   dark strips
2" × 2" × 18"   2" × 2" × 18"

2 On a flat surface, lay the strips next to each other, alternating light and dark. Apply a thin, squiggly strip of wood glue between each wood strip, making sure they lay square to one another. Clamp the strips together with at least three

bar clamps. Use a damp cloth to wipe away any excess glue that squeezes out. Let dry overnight.

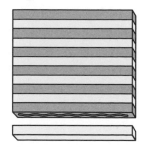

3 You just turned the strips into a sheet, and now you'll turn the sheet back into strips. The distance between cuts will be the width of your butcher block. For this project, we'll cut the 18"-long sheet crosswise into 12 new strips each 1½" thick. Use a tape measure to make marks every 1½" along the endmost light strip and then

(continued)

corresponding marks every 1½" along the endmost dark strip. Use a straightedge and a pencil to draw straight lines connecting the marks opposite each other—your new strips should alternate light and dark blocks (just as in Step 4 of How to Build a Chessboard, page 86). Now use your table saw to cut these strips. Cut directly in the center of the lines you drew. Because the finished thickness of your board needn't be precise, don't worry about how much wood you lose to the saw blade (this thickness is called the "kerf"). As long as you're consistent in the way you cut, your chopping block will turn out flat.

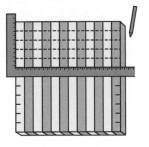

4 On a flat surface, lay the alternating-block strips next to each other to create a checkerboard pattern. As before, apply a thin layer of wood glue between strips, and clamp together what should now look like a finished, checkerboard-pattern chopping block. Wipe clean any excess glue. Let dry overnight.

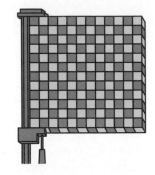

5 Use an electric sander or sandpaper and significant elbow grease to sand both faces and all corners of the block, first with coarse, then medium, and finally fine sandpaper, until smooth. Use a damp rag to wipe the block free of sawdust. Use a rag to wipe the block with mineral oil. Let the piece sit overnight, and then apply a second coat of oil. Wipe away any excess oil. Apply a new coat of oil every couple of months to keep your chopping block looking great.

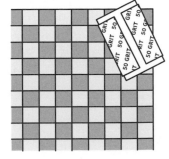

✕ ✕ ✕ ✕ ✕ ✕ ✕ ✕ ✕ ✕ ✕ ✕
Oiling a Butcher Block

Whether you make your own or have a store-bought block in need of some TLC, butcher blocks are perfect for experimenting with oil finishes (choose from the options listed on page 92). Here are some tips and tricks:

• Make sure the wood is clean—a little mild soap and a damp rag will do the trick.

• The oil works best if it's warm when you use it. You can place the bottle in a bowl of hot water for about 5 minutes to heat it.

• Use a rag or, better, an old sock, to apply the oil to the wood in multiple coats.

• Let the butcher block sit for 5 minutes or so between applications, until the block cannot absorb any more oil. (It should take 5 or 6 coats.) Wipe up any excess oil with a rag. ✕

Butcher block is great for countertops because its natural look matches almost any decor, and with proper care, it can last 20+ years.

#40 How to Stain Wood

Halfway between paint and varnish is stain, which brings its own pigment to the project but allows the look of the wood to remain dominant. Stains generally include a pigment or dye suspended in water or mineral oil as a solvent. You apply it wet, the solvent dries away, and you're left with a consistent coat of color. Oil-based stains dry slowly and don't raise the grain of the wood. Water-based stains dry more quickly, don't carry odor, and clean up with soap and water—however, they likely necessitate a final sanding. If you like the color of your wood as is, skip straight to a protective finish. If you want to darken or change the look of your wood, apply stain first, and then a protective topcoat of varnish or another finish (see How to Refinish Furniture, page 30).

Pick a Color

The color you apply isn't always the color you end up with—stains typically change hue as they dry. And because a stain's color is influenced by the underlying wood, even the samples at the store are only best guesses. If you need to match a target color, the only way to do it right is to try a stain on a scrap or an unseen corner of your piece.

TOOLS:

Fine sandpaper • Sanding block • Chemical-resistant rubber gloves • Rags • Old sock or disposable paintbrush

MATERIALS:

• Wood stain

1 Prepare the surface. Because stain rests in the pores of a piece, stain must be applied to bare, sanded wood. To start, unscrew any functional or decorative elements. With new wood, simply sand with fine-grit sandpaper to open the pores. With old wood, strip away any existing finish (see How to Strip Paint, page 28) and then sand.

2 Apply the stain. There are many ways to apply stain, but the best method depends on the size of the wood's pores. To ensure full saturation of the large pores of "open-grain" woods" (oak, ash, and mahogany), use an old sock wrapped around your gloved hand to work the stain into the wood, scrubbing across the grain in a swirling pattern. With closed-grain woods—like cherry, aspen, and birch—use a brush to apply stain in long, gentle strokes.

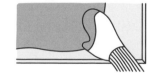

3 Wipe the stain. The longer you leave a stain to dry before wiping, the darker the finished color. However, pools or droplets of stain left on the surface will create an uneven finish. Ideally, you would apply only as much stain as would reasonably dry to a consistent, flat color. However, wood tends to have uneven absorption, so once your piece has dried, you'll need to wipe it free of excess stain with a dry rag. Wipe in straight lines with the grain of the wood. Repeat Steps 2 and 3 for a second and even a third coat.

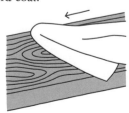

#41 How to Build a Bookcase
(or, How to Use Edge Banding)

At some point in your woodworking career, you'll probably want to build a bookcase. When you do, the easiest thing to build it with is plywood. But you'll have to do something about those raw plywood edges. That's where edge banding comes in. Edge banding is thin veneer with pre-applied glue that comes in rolls of various widths, most commonly ¾". In this project, you'll learn how to iron edge banding onto the exposed edges of a plywood shelf.

TOOLS:

Tape measure • Straightedge • Pencil • Table saw, circular saw, or jigsaw • Clamps • Electric sander (optional) • Utility or heavy craft knife • Clothes iron • Plane (optional) • Hammer • Drill, with a pilot bit • Safety goggles

MATERIALS:

- **One 4' × 8' sheet of ¾" grade A or A/B plywood**
- **One 3' × 6' sheet of ½" grade A or A/B plywood**
- **1 roll ¾" wood veneer edge banding to match the plywood**
- **Wood glue**
- **Coarse, medium, and fine sandpaper**
- **Fifty 1⅝" wood screws or finishing nails**
- **Four 3" wood screws**
- **14" × 70" × ¼" plywood or panel backing (optional)**
- **Paintbrush**
- **Wood stain**

1 Use a tape measure and straightedge to draw the following rectangles on the 4' × 8' sheet of ¾" plywood: two 12" × 70" strips; one 16" × 38" strip; and two 14" × 36" strips. Draw five 12" × 33½" strips and ten 1" × 12" strips on the 3' × 6' sheet of ½" plywood. Use a table saw, circular saw, or jigsaw to cut out these pieces.

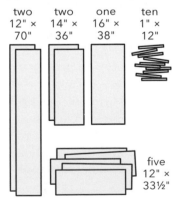

two 12" × 70"	two 14" × 36"	one 16" × 38"	ten 1" × 12"

five 12" × 33½"

2 Now you'll add edge banding to all the plywood edges that will be visible (consult the assembly instructions to determine which sides will be visible). Clamp each plywood piece to your workbench so that a

visible edge points up. Sand the edge clean and wipe away any sawdust, being careful not to round the edges of the plywood. With a utility knife, roughly cut the edge banding to be slightly longer than the raw edge.

3 Prepare the iron: Pour out any water and set the dial to cotton/hot. When it's hot, press the edge banding to the plywood edge and run the iron along the banding slowly enough to melt the glue but quickly enough to avoid scorching. If you make a mistake, strip the edge banding and try again with a new strip. Once the banding is successfully attached, use a scrap wood block to press it firmly to the edge

to secure it. Unclamp the plywood and lay it, banded-side-down, on a flat surface that is safe for cutting. Use a sharp utility knife to trim the edge banding to the exact dimensions of the plywood. Repeat for all plywood edges that will need to be covered.

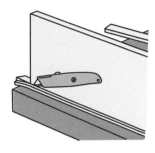

4 Make the stepped base of the bookcase: Lay the 16" × 38" piece on a flat surface. Center one of the 14" × 36" pieces on top of this base with a 1" margin on all sides. Glue the top piece to the bottom piece and press firmly in place. Let dry, preferably overnight. (Wood glue is dry to the touch in 30 minutes, but allow at least 12 hours to set completely.)

5 The 12" × 70" strips are the sides of the bookcase. Lay them side by side to check that their lengths are exactly equal. If necessary, shave with a planer to make them even, being careful not to chip the edge banding. With the sides of the bookcase still side by side, mark the heights of the five shelves, spaced every 14". (To hold taller books or knickknacks, adjust the heights of your shelves.) Measure and mark straight lines across both boards to indicate the tops of the shelves.

6 Attach 1" × 12" strips just under every line on what will be the insides of the bookcase sides (edge banding pointing out). Drill three evenly spaced 1⅝" wood

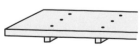

screws from the outside to attach the strips. They will support your shelves.

7 Assemble the sides and top of the bookcase. First, lay the sides of the shelf on their edges with the shelf supports facing each other and the edge banding pointing out, as they will appear in the finished bookcase. Because the two-sheet base is stepped by 1" and the 12" sides should be centered on the 14"-wide base, raise the sides of your shelf by 2" off the ground to match. Do this by resting the sides on stacked scraps of ¾" plywood. Position the sides of your bookcase facing each other across a 33½" gap.

8 Position the base on its side with the edge banding pointing out and rest it against the bottom of the bookcase's sides. Center the 12" sides on the 14" base. Use two 3" wood screws per side to screw up through the bottom of the base and into the ends of the sides.

9 Lay the 14" × 36" bookcase top on its side with the edge banding pointing toward the front

(continued)

and align it with the tops of the bookcase sides so that the sides are flush and the front and back overhang by 1". Use three evenly spaced 1⅝" wood screws driven through the top and into the sides to fix the top in place.

10 Carefully stand up the bookcase frame. Slide the 12" × 33½" shelves into place on their supports. Use finishing nails to hold

the shelves securely to their supports.

11 If the bookcase feels as if it needs additional support, consider adding panel or ¼" plywood backing. Lay the bookcase on its face, support the shelves with plywood scraps, and

use finishing nails to attach backing to the frame and shelves, being careful to drive thin nails into the center of the plywood sides so as not to split the wood. Sand the bookcase smooth and then apply stain to match the color of the edge banding.

Oil Finishes for Wood

Getting a beautiful oil finish on wood is an art as much as a science. It's also much more time-consuming than simply unleashing a can of polyurethane varnish on a project. This is partly because rather than sitting atop the wood or stain, an oil finish lives in the wood's grain itself—and it's your hard work that puts it there. The most common place to find an oil finish is on a butcher block or cutting board in your kitchen, but oil finishes offer a rich and natural look and are easy to apply, so consider them for your woodworking projects or to revitalize vintage furniture.

Linseed oil. Also known as flaxseed oil, this multipurpose liquid is not only used alone as an oil finish, but also as the solvent in some varnishes (before you add it to your smoothie, note that it is processed with petroleum—it's not the same as the flaxseed oil taken as a nutritional supplement). Linseed oil isn't the clearest finish—it's likely to slightly yellow your wood, and despite its long history of

use, it's not actually that protective. Consider any surface you use it on water-repellant, but not waterproof. It is the traditional finish of gun stocks, cricket bats, and the fret boards of stringed instruments like mandolins.

Mineral oil. As the name implies, mineral oil does not come from plant material. Instead it is distilled from petroleum. It's odorless, so you'd never know it's a cousin of gasoline. It has many uses, including in cosmetics and baby oils, as well as in an insulating fluid in electrical transformers. It is a food-safe finish that is much clearer and slightly more protective than linseed.

Tung oil. Tung oil, from the nut of the tung tree, dries to a golden finish somewhat similar to the look of wet wood. It is the most protective of the pure oils listed here and is arguably slightly more resistant to mildew than linseed oil. Commercial manufacturers of products labeled "tung oil" have sometimes freeloaded on the environmentally friendly cachet of the oil without including any actual tung oil in the product. When you buy any oil, and especially when you buy a tung oil finish, inspect the label closely to make sure that what you're buying is the real McCoy.

Danish oil. Danish oil is a somewhat imprecise term used by manufacturers to describe a few different formulas. Most oils labeling themselves "Danish" use a linseed or tung oil base and add resins that perform much

like a varnish. Danish oil is likely to be more protective than other oils, but due to inconsistent labeling, test it on scrap wood before applying it to your piece. That said, the classic recipe by Watco for Danish oil has been around for many years, and many woodworkers swear by its balance of an oil finish's shine with the protection of a varnish. If you need your oil finish to hold up in a high-traffic area, consider trying Danish.

#42 How to Build a Storage Chest

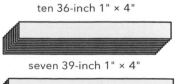

Whether family heirloom, bench seating, or organizational unit, a storage chest is an incredibly multi-purpose piece of furniture. By hand-crafting your own, you're making a useful and timeless object to pass down to future generations. Rather than plywood sheets, this chest uses 1-by boards to make elegant walls (use the wood of your choice—pine or oak will work well). Your finished chest will be 3 feet by 2 feet, but after previewing these instructions, you could easily adjust the size as you see fit.

TOOLS:

Measuring tape • Pencil • Miter saw or handsaw • Table saw or circular saw • Bar clamps (at least three) • Hammer • Electric sander • Drill • Countersink bit • Safety goggles

MATERIALS:

- Nine 6-foot 1 × 4 boards
- Seven 39-inch 1 × 4 boards (buy larger and cut to size)

- 36" × 24" piece of ½" plywood
- Fifty 1¾" wood screws
- Two hinges
- Polyurethane or tung oil (for finish)

1　Put on your safety goggles and use a miter or handsaw to cut five of the 6-foot 1 × 4 boards in half to create ten 36-inch 1 × 4 strips for the front and back. Measure, mark, and cut the remaining 6-foot 1 × 4 boards into even thirds to create ten

21½-inch 1 × 4 strips for the sides. Cut seven 39-inch 1 × 4 strips for the lid.

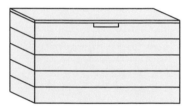

Cut down the 6-foot 1x4 boards to create:

ten 21½-inch 1" × 4"

ten 36-inch 1" × 4"

seven 39-inch 1" × 4"

(continued)

2　If the plywood is not already sized, use a table saw or circular saw to cut the ½" plywood into a 36" × 24" floor.

floor
36" × 24"

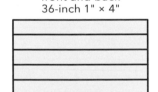

3　On a flat surface, line up five 36" 1 × 4 boards— these will be the front of the

front and back
36-inch 1" × 4"

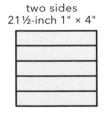

two sides
21½-inch 1" × 4"

lid
39-inch 1" × 4"

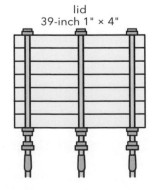

chest. Make sure the boards lie flush to each other and are perfectly flat against the work surface. Apply wood glue between the boards and use three bar clamps to hold them securely together. Place a flat piece of scrap wood over the boards and use a hammer to bang any uneven seams until the face of your newly joined boards is completely smooth. Use a damp rag to wipe away any excess wood glue and allow 4 to 6 hours to dry. Repeat this step for the five 36" 1 × 4 boards that will be the back, the five 21½" 1 × 4 boards for both sides, and the seven 39" 1 × 4 strips for the lid of your chest. Once the glue is dry, remove the clamps and sand the newly made boards with an electric sander until they are smooth and the seams disappear.

4　Measure, mark, and use a jigsaw to cut a notch 6" long and 1" deep in the top-center of your front panel. This will be the handhold under the lid seen in most storage chests.

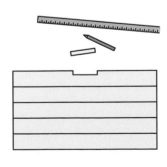

5　Assemble the walls and base of the chest. You will be screwing through the front and back of the boards. Countersink four evenly spaced holes through the vertical edges of the front and back boards. Then use 1¾" wood screws to attach the front and back walls to the sides of the chest. Use wood screws or tack nails to attach the base of the chest, screwing or nailing up from the bottom.

6　Use a table saw or circular saw to bevel the undersides of the front and sides of the lid to 45-degree angles. Set your saw blade to cut at a 45-degree angle and then run your lid across the blade so that it takes off a triangular strip from the undersides of these three edges. Screw hinges onto the (untouched) back underside of the lid and mount the lid to the back interior of the chest. Sand and finish as desired, with polyurethane or oil finish.

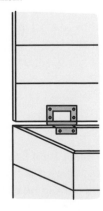

XX

Jigsaw Tips

Jigsaws are commonly thought of as curve-cutting machines, but in reality, they're a versatile tool that you can use for a variety of cuts, both straight and curved. Typically used for finishing work, jigsaws can be either corded or cordless (see page 67 for the distinction), and they come as handsaws or the table-mounted variety. The saw is made to fit different blades—teeth matter, depending on the density of your wood (the teeth face the front of the saw), as do length and width, so make sure you're choosing the right blade for the material you're using.

Typically, you'll need to use a clamped straightedge guide to make straight cuts. To cut a circle (as in How to Build a Birdhouse, page 72), you should first drill a ⅜" pilot hole at one edge of the circle to drop the blade in the hole. Circle-cutting jigs will help you make a perfect circle, if you need a little artificial guidance.

When cutting, be steady with your hands, start the blade before touching the wood so it can get going, and don't pivot the blade too quickly, at the risk of chipping the wood. And remember: Practice makes perfect! X

#43 How to Build a Table

Even basic woodworking can benefit from a little bling. In this project, you'll build a basic table and then choose how to decorate it—think inlay, stencils, fancy finishes. This simple design also lends itself well to stretching or squishing to fit your space. Simply consistently adjust the dimensions of all the materials to change its size.

TOOLS:

Measuring tape • Pencil • Miter saw or handsaw • Bar clamps (at least 3) • Hammer • Tools for decorative effects (see page 97)

MATERIALS:

- Three 6-foot 1 × 4 pine boards
- One 8-foot 1 × 4 pine board
- One 6-foot 1 × 1 pine board
- Four 2" × 2" table legs, cut to desired table height
- Brad nails
- Sandpaper
- Wood glue
- Materials for decorative effects as desired (see page 97)

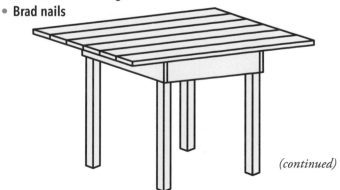

(continued)

1 Select and cut the three 6-foot 1 × 4 pine boards in half with a saw to make six 3-foot 1 × 4 strips.

2 Join these boards to form a 36" × 24" tabletop. Lay the six 3-foot boards side by side on a flat surface, glue between each board, adjust until flush and flat, and use at least three bar clamps to hold the boards together while they dry (at least 4 to 6 hours). Once dry, sand the tabletop until smooth.

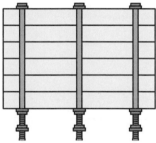

3 Measure, mark, and cut two 20½" lengths of 1 × 4 and two 22" lengths of 1 × 4. You will use these four pieces to make a boxlike frame for your tabletop to sit on. Center the four boards on their sides in a square on the

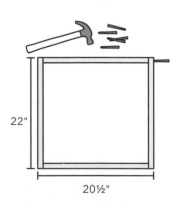

22"

20½"

underside of your tabletop, with the 22" pieces outside the 20½" pieces. With the frame perfectly square, drive two brad nails per side through the 22" pieces into the ends of the 20½" pieces to hold the frame together. Later, you'll attach this frame to the tabletop.

4 Saw four 2 × 2s to equal lengths for the legs. Kitchen or dining tables are usually about 29" tall, and end tables are usually about 24" tall. Place the four legs in the inside corners of the 1 × 4 frame you made in the previous step, flush to the top, and drive brad nails through the 1 × 4s to hold the legs in place.

5 Measure the four distances along the frame between the inside faces of your 2 × 2 legs. Cut four lengths of 1 × 1 to this measurement and fix them between the legs, against the frame and flush with its top. Drive brad nails through the

1 × 1s to attach them to the frame.

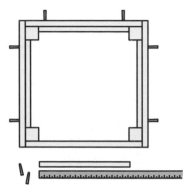

6 Add the tabletop. Center it on the frame and use brad nails spaced about every 6 inches, driven up through the 1 × 1s to hold it in place.

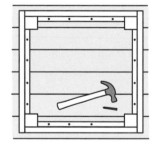

7 Slightly countersink all nails and cover the heads with a mixture of wood glue and sawdust (optional). Sand the table until smooth, then paint, stain, and decorate as desired (see Suggested Decorative Effects, facing page).

Suggested Decorative Effects

Inlay. A router, some wood veneer, and a little artistic moxie can turn a table into a treasure. Draw the shapes of your inlay on carbon tracing paper, then onto thin wood veneer. Once the inlays are drawn on the veneer, carefully cut them out with a sharp, fine-toothed jigsaw. Working with one piece at a time, use double-sided tape to hold the inlays on the tabletop and trace deep lines around them with a utility knife. Remove the taped inlays and switch to your router. Use a 1/16" bit set to the depth of your wood veneer to carefully rout your shapes into the wood. Glue the inlays in place and clamp until dry. Sand the tabletop smooth. End with a protective finish.

Mosaic. Any small, tilelike pieces can be used for mosaics: bits of Venetian glass, ceramic pieces, mirrors, small stones, sea glass, marbles, and so on. Use a hammer to make small shapes and tile nippers to further sculpt them. Plan your mosaic pattern and then outline it in pencil on your tabletop. Dab adhesive on the back of every piece—you'll need to match it to your mosaic materials. Try to leave less than 1/8" between pieces, using small tiles to fill spaces. Once the tiles are in place, use a rubber squeegee to spread grout across the entire surface of the project, being sure to fill all gaps. In this case, you'll want to use fine grout. Choose a grout color that complements your mosaic and table, and consider a polymer grout if you imagine heavy use. Let the grout set until firm, at least 15 to 20 minutes, and then wipe it from the tile with a cloth or wet sponge. Scrape sticky grout with a wooden or other non-scratch tool. If you use porous material, consider finishing with a sealant.

Distress. In order to distress a finish, you must first put one on. Either stain and then distress or distress and then stain—both work equally well. If you'll be staining as the final step, focus on adding dents to the wood. Try one of these destructive options: Flay the table with a chain, beat it with a sock filled with nuts and bolts, or throw an old tool at your table (it works!). If you will be distressing after finishing, use extremely coarse sandpaper—50- or 60-grit—to rough up the paint or finish, adding scratches and clouds.

METALWORKING TOOL KIT

Locking pliers

HAND TOOLS

Calipers

Fan of thickness gauges

Squares

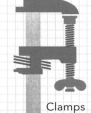
Measuring tape

Ball-peen hammer

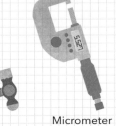
Micrometer

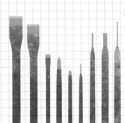
Clamps

Tin snips

Wire brush

Kevlar gloves

Metal files

Set of punches and chisels

Hacksaw

POWER TOOLS

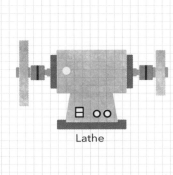
Lathe

Welding torch

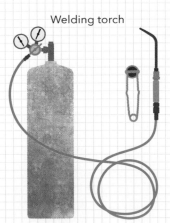

Angle grinder

Hand Tools

Even constructing the USS *Bismarck* starts with a single box of simple tools. Gather your measuring implements first. The main measuring tool for woodworking is a retractable measuring tape, but in metalworking, measuring is a new skill altogether. In addition to basic tools like a measuring tape and squares, you may need calipers, a micrometer, and a fan of thickness gauges. Another essential tool is a set of punches and chisels—make sure the set comes with pin, taper, and center punches, and with a set of cold chisels ranging from about ⅜ inch to 1 inch. You'll also need a hammer to drive these punches. Go with the basic ball-peen hammer—good for both metal- and woodworking. Rather than scissors, which are best for cutting paper, you'll need snips to cut metal—tin snips may be little more than burly scissors, whereas metal shears usually include an extra joint that increases your power and the thickness of the metal you can cut. Also get a set of metal files that includes a round and a flat rasp and a file. An adjustable wrench (or wrench set), pliers, hacksaw, clamps, and wire brush round out the necessary basics. You'll also need a very good pair of Kevlar gloves. Again, the tools for metalworking tend to be even more specific than the tools needed for woodworking, so evaluate your tool kit based on the project at hand.

Power Tools

The term *metalworking* applies to the tiniest jewelry, the biggest ocean liners and bridges, and everything metal in between. With the huge scope of projects comes a huge scope of techniques, including welding, soldering, turning, grinding, casting, machining, and many more. And depending on whether you want to make earrings, sculpt a steel buffalo for the front yard, or trick out your truck, you'll need drastically different power tools. Shoddy metalwork makes nothing but scrap. Metal requires mettle. The following tools are good to have, but it's likely you'll need to add power tools specific to your project.

Welding torch. There are two common kinds of handheld torches: air and oxyacetylene. An air torch uses a bottle of gas—like propane—and burns the oxygen found in air. An oxyacetylene torch combines gas with pure oxygen for a much hotter flame. You can weld with a torch, so if your budget is tight, get a torch before investing in a specific welder. But in an expert's shop, the torch is usually used for cutting. Expect to spend in the neighborhood of $250 for a quality unit.

Angle grinder. An angle grinder is the metalworking mash-up of two woodworking tools: a circular saw and a disc sander. With this handheld power tool, you can cut, grind, and polish metal, and it's a must in any metal shop. Angle grinders are driven by electricity or compressed air (pneumatic), and the latter is generally lighter and more maneuverable but less powerful. In addition to the power of your grinder, choose based on disc size, which generally runs from 4 to 7 inches or, in some cases, 12 inches. Most metalworkers start with a 4- to 4½-inch grinder and evaluate their needs from there.

Lathe. There are many kinds of lathes designed for many different uses, but the basic idea remains the same: a lathe spins your metal piece while stationary tools cut into it. As such, you can use a lathe for cutting, sanding, and, most important, shaping a piece of metal.

(continued)

Most shops will start with a lightweight bench engine lathe (a powered lathe that bolts to a workbench) and upgrade to a freestanding lathe (called a precision or gap lathe) if needed. It's important to make sure your cutting tools are compatible with your lathe and are right for your project. Your lathe may come with a set of cutting tools, or you might need to buy them separately. Start with a basic set of carbide-tipped cutting and turning tools. Expect to spend from $600 to more than $4,000 for a quality metal lathe. Metalworking is for the detail-oriented among us—a craft that depends on fractions of millimeters. That said, there are darn good tools available that make this precision possible, and a strong finished product tends to depend more on careful work than rocket science. By starting with easy projects and slowly upping the difficulty level (it helps to have a willingness to throw out a couple of failed attempts), you can learn to bend metal to your every desire.

Paul Revere was a highly regarded silversmith—after learning the craft from his father, he spent more than 40 years in the trade, and even used it to cross over into dentistry, wiring dentures made of ivory or animal teeth into the mouths of his patients.

#44 How to Make a Spoon Ring
(or, How to Cut and Bend Metal)

If you were an English servant in the seventeenth century, chances are you couldn't afford a pricey wedding band. But without a band, you couldn't wed! Many servants resorted to thievery, stealing silverware to fashion into elegant wedding bands. The practice became so common that in many places you could tell which house a servant worked for by the crest on his or her ring.

The so-called spoon ring—basically a cutlery handle bent into a circle—had a resurgence in the 1970s, when you couldn't really call yourself a hippie without a couple of lengths of sterling silver wrapped around your fingers. It's a classic that has stood the test of time; plus, this simple project is a great primer on how to cut and bend metal—skills that will serve you well in more complicated metalwork.

When you're choosing a utensil, keep in mind that you'll be using only the handle, so your spoon needn't be a spoon at all. A fork works just as well. But it's worth it to get a sterling silver rather than stainless steel utensil—stainless is much stronger and thus more difficult to work. Check thrift or antique stores, or even eBay, for sterling silver flatware—commonly stamped "sterling" or with the numbers 900 or 925. When you're buying, consider the aesthetics: Does the spoon have a decorative handle? Is the handle's width appropriate for a ring?

TOOLS:

Measuring tape • Hacksaw • Angle grinder, half-round metal file, or emery cloth • Safety goggles • Insulating gloves • Bench vise or clamp • Butane torch (optional) • Needle-nosed pliers • Rawhide or wood mallet or a hammer covered in cloth

MATERIALS:

- Sterling silver spoon or fork
- String or paper
- Finger-sized dowel or metal pipe, or ring mandrel
- Silver polish or polishing cloth (optional)

1 Measure the circumference of your finger. Wrap a length of paper or string around the digit on which you'll wear the ring. Mark your desired length and then straighten the paper or string to use it as your length measurement. A spoon ring can either wrap up your finger (a wrapped ring) or wrap around until one end touches the other (a closed ring). If you want a closed ring, add ¼" to your paper or string length measurement. If you want a wrapped ring, the length needn't be precise as long as it's longer than your finger circumference.

2 Cut the spoon to length. Remove the "bowl" of the spoon, and as much of the top of the handle to make it fit as desired. A sterling silver spoon is easily cut with a hacksaw, but if you have an angle grinder, here's an excuse to use it. Grinding metal is likely to create sparks, so first, be sure to protect both yourself and your work area. Wear long clothing, safety goggles, and insulating gloves, and remove flammable items from the space. Then, install a metal cutoff wheel on your angle grinder. Secure the spoon with either a bench vise or a clamp, exposing the line on the neck of the handle where you'll make your cut. Start the angle grinder and drop it smoothly through the spoon, letting the weight of the grinder do the work.

3 Smooth the cut end of the spoon. Cutting with a hacksaw or grinder is likely to leave a viciously sharp edge. If you have an angle grinder, switch to a sanding or polishing pad, secure the metal again, and polish the spoon's cut end until smooth. If you used the center length of a spoon's handle, not the decorative end, you can also use the grinder to grind one or both ends to equalize their shape. Be careful not to remove too much—you can always take more, but adding metal back is impossible! If you don't have a grinder, you can perform the same smoothing (but not necessarily shaping) with a metal half-round file or emery cloth.

4 Shape the ring. Because you won't be soldering the ring closed, you can always adjust the diameter of the ring once you try it on. Still, it's worth trying to get close with your first attempt. There are a couple of methods you can try to shape the spoon into a ring. First, try using finger power to bend the spoon around a finger-sized dowel. If that doesn't work, hold the metal with needle-nose pliers and tap it carefully with a mallet to curl the spoon handle around the dowel into the desired shape. You shouldn't need to heat the metal unless you're

(continued)

using a stainless steel spoon, but if you do, use a butane torch (and the proper safety precautions). First, grip the metal with needle-nose pliers and heat it with the butane torch until pliable (but not glowing). Then, hammer it around the dowel or mandrel with the mallet.

5 Adjust as needed. Once the ring has cooled, try it on your finger. If the size is drastically wrong, reshape the spoon using a different-sized dowel or another width of ring mandrel. In most cases, though, you'll be able to shape the ring to size with just a couple of taps. Use silver polish or a polishing cloth to buff the ring until it shines.

#45 How to Make Earrings
(or, How to Beat Metal)

Ear piercing has been around since ancient times, as many of the mummies of Africa, Europe, and the Americas can attest. Even 5,000-year-old Ötzi the Iceman, found poking out of a glacier in the Austrian Alps, had pierced ears. One of the first designs used with pierced ears was the hoop earring, first as bent metal wire and then as beaten metal. Hoops were found in the graves of Persepolis in Iran, dating to about 2500 BCE, as well as in graves of the ancient cultures of Babylonia, Assyria, Egypt, and India. One reason for the ancient ubiquity of hoop earrings is the ease of making them. Once you roll wire into a circle, you're most of the way there. This project goes a step further than a simple circle, and with that step you'll learn the skill of beating metal, which is applicable to many other metalworking projects.

The hoop is one of the classic earring shapes—pirates wore them as a superstition, believing that the precious metals carried magical powers.

⌗⌗

Picking Wire Gauge

Simple wire earrings in which the wire passes completely through the ear are usually 21-gauge or thinner. For this project, you'll taper the ends and beat the middle, and so a thicker gauge—which means a smaller number—works better. Approximately 12-gauge wire is ideal, though you could choose to make a thicker earring from 10-gauge wire or a slightly thinner earring from 14-gauge wire. ⌗

TOOLS:

Wire cutter • Coarse sandpaper • Rolling mill or file • Round form (mandrel or appropriately sized dowel) • Wooden or rawhide mallet • Planishing or ball-peen hammer • Needle-nose pliers

MATERIALS:

• At least a 14" length of 12-gauge metal wire (copper, silver, and brass are common metals that have the advantage of being soft enough to work)

1 The length of the wire depends on what size you'd like the earrings to be—longer wire means bigger earrings. Consider buying extra wire so you can wrap a test earring and evaluate the size in the mirror. Once you have a test earring that looks about the right size, unroll it and use it as a measuring template when cutting the wire. Leave an extra ½" to be bent for the earring closures. Hoop earrings range from tiny to huge, but a 7" length of wire each is a good starting point. Cut the desired length with wire cutters and use emery cloth or coarse sandpaper to sand the cut ends until smooth.

2 Use a file to taper one end of each earring, 1½" per end. This tapered wire will be bent into clasps and one of these sides will pass through your ear, so file the end until you are comfortable with the result. Sand until smooth.

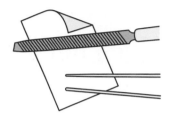

3 Hoop earrings are round, as their name implies, though they can be shaped like teardrops. To make a teardrop shape, simply bend the two ends together and the wire should naturally form a loop with a wide arc on the bottom coming to a point at the top. A hoop takes a little more work. Wrap the earring wire around a mandrel or a round form like a dowel, overlapping the ends by about ¼" for the clasps. Use the mallet to hammer the wire around the form until the wire holds its round shape.

4 There are many styles of hoop earrings, but for this project, you'll beat the lower arc to make it flat vertically. Lay a bent earring flat on a pounding surface, preferably a metal plate or at least a flat, hardwood work surface. Use

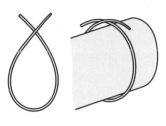

a wooden ball-peen hammer to work the earring. (If the hammer has a ridged face, consider filing and sanding the hammer until the face is smooth so that it doesn't mar the surface of the earrings.) Start with gentle taps and focus on slightly flattening the lowest point in the center of the metal wire, not the edges. Remember: You can always hit harder, but it's difficult to un-dent your work. Flip the earring frequently. Some metal jewelry intentionally has a pockmarked, beaten look, but for this project it's worth learning how to smooth the metal, using many smaller strokes rather than a few more forceful ones. Work up the sides from the lower arc, flattening less and less as you go so that the upper widths of the earrings narrow toward the tapered ends.

(continued)

5 Use needle-nose pliers to form the clasp. Bend about ¼" of wire out at a right angle from one end. Grab the end and bend it back on itself to form a tiny circle. Then bend a short length (about ¼") of the other end to about 45 degrees. The bent wire hooks inside the circle to form the clasp. The earring should be wide enough that the clasp is held together by the spring of the metal. If it's not, you can slightly adjust the earring size.

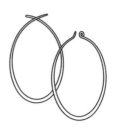

#46 How to Make a Decorative Metal Plate
(or, an Introduction to Perforating)

When working to transform sheet metal into something decorative, you'll hear the terms "blanking" and "piercing." In blanking, the shaped piece is punched from the plate; in piercing, a design is left behind when pieces are punched from the plate. In this project you'll learn about piercing, and more specifically about the piercing technique known as perforating. Basically, perforating is just what it sounds like: the process of punching holes in metal. These holes could be the result of a nail used to decorate a thin sheet of copper or of complex punch and die sets that help metalworkers mass-produce intricate designs. Here you'll use simple holes to perforate a piece of metal (think of your kitchen colander), either to let light shine through or simply for the pattern of the holes themselves.

TOOLS:

Pencil • Paper • Scissors • Straightedge • Drill • Small cobalt or titanium bit, ⅛" to ¼" • Emery cloth • Hacksaw (optional) • Angle grinder • Bench vise

MATERIALS:

• Any length and width "hobby" sheet of metal (0.024" or 0.048")

⌘ ⌘

What Can You Do with Decorative Metal Plates?

The project detailed here results in, literally, a simple plate with a design on it. But as you become more experienced in the technique, there are many items on which you can use this method.

• The perforations let light shine though, making it ideal for a small metal lampshade, whether for an electric light or a candleholder or sconce.

• Use it to decorate a metal picture frame or to frame a mirror.

• Make a design on a metal garden pot, such as an ornamental copper pot in which a ceramic or terra cotta plant holder sits.

• Put a design on kitchen items or wall hangings, such as the rim of a metal serving platter, a metal spoon rest, or a wall-mounted row of hooks. ⌘

1 Search, copy, and print a stencil from the internet, then cut it out and trace it on the piece of metal with a pencil. Or, use your creativity to draw the outline of a picture on the metal.

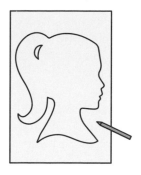

2 Using a straightedge, draw perpendicular gridlines inside the outline. For a larger picture, you might draw vertical and horizontal lines every inch. For a small, perforated design, your gridlines might be every couple of millimeters. You'll be tracing a grid that looks like graph paper inside your picture outline.

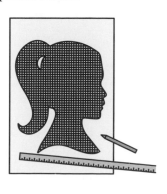

3 Use a drill with an appropriately sized cobalt or titanium drill bit to make a hole at every place inside the outline where gridlines cross. For small designs with tight gridlines, you will want an equally small drill bit, such as a ⅛"; for larger pieces with more widely spaced gridlines, you could choose a larger drill bit, such as a ¼". Size your bit based on aesthetics. Smooth away excess metal shavings with an emery cloth. You should end with an organized pattern of dots that define your picture.

4 Remove the paper stencil from the metal surface to reveal a series of dots arranged in the shape of the image you selected.

In other materials, like paper, perforations are used to efficiently separate portions of paper (like the postcards, paper dolls, and original perforated stamps) from a larger piece, without the use of scissors.

#47 How to Make Wind Chimes

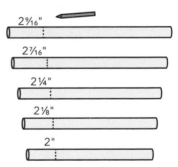

The ancient Romans hung their porticoes with bronze wind chimes to ward off evil spirits, while metal, wood, and even glass chimes have hung for centuries in temples and homes from around the world. Today, wind chimes are made from materials including seashells, glass, ceramic, and even flatware. Here you'll learn to make pipe chimes—drilling, hanging, and tuning a set of copper or other metal wind chimes.

Only certain combinations of musical notes are pleasing when sounded together. One of the most pleasing is the pentatonic scale, a group of five notes that can be played on a piano's black keys. It takes some fairly involved calculations to determine the pipe lengths that make the desired tones. Deviating from these measurements may result in some odd sounds.

TOOLS:

Measuring tape • Pencil • Hacksaw • Fine sandpaper • Bench vise • Center punch • Hammer • Safety goggles • Leather work gloves • Drill with ⁵⁄₃₂" metal bit and small wood drill bit, such as ¹⁄₁₆" • Cutting and tapping fluid • Hacksaw • Wood saw (any type)

MATERIALS:

- 5 feet of ¾" copper or stainless steel tubing
- 5 no. 6 machine screws with nuts
- Locking nut or threadlocker compound (optional)
- 7 small wood eyelets
- 1 larger wood eyelet
- Nylon twine, string, or fishing line
- Scrap wood for mount, clapper, and scoop
- Wood glue

1 With a hacksaw, cut the following lengths of ¾" copper or steel tubing: 11½", 10⅞", 10", 9⁷⁄₁₆", and 8⅞". These should produce the tones C-sharp, D-sharp, F-sharp, G-sharp, and A-sharp. If you have a piano (or a piano app) match the bell tones to these notes, using sandpaper to shave tube ends slightly to make higher pitches. It's impossible to add back removed material, so don't take too much!

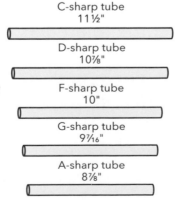

C-sharp tube
11½"

D-sharp tube
10⅞"

F-sharp tube
10"

G-sharp tube
9⁷⁄₁₆"

A-sharp tube
8⅞"

2 Measure and mark mounting holes at the following distances on one end of each tube (from the longest to the shortest tube): 2⁹⁄₁₆", 2⁷⁄₁₆", 2¼", 2⅛", 2". Hanging pipes at these measurements allows for the best resonance.

2⁹⁄₁₆"

2⁷⁄₁₆"

2¼"

2⅛"

2"

3 Secure a section of tubing in a bench vise (tighten it enough to hold the tube, but not enough to dent the pipe). Use a center punch and a hammer to make a small depression on one side of each tube that will keep the drill bit from wandering. Carefully align the center punch

with the desired mounting hole position and strike the punch once, firmly, with the hammer.

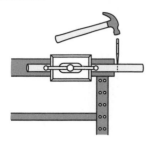

4 Put on your safety glasses and leather work gloves. A drill press is necessary for many metal projects, but for this thin tube, you can get away with a handheld electric drill. Because you will drill directly down through the top wall and also through the bottom wall of the tube, be sure to turn the pipe in your vise so the center punch depression is directly on top of the tube. Secure a ⁵⁄₃₂" metal bit in your drill and coat the bit with cutting and tapping fluid, which is a coolant and lubricant that will help to ensure clean holes. Hold the drill perfectly vertical while drilling a hole through both tube walls.

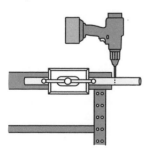

When finished, use a rag to wipe away excess fluid and shavings. Repeat with the remaining tubes.

5 Insert machine screws through the mounting holes and secure them with nuts. Because the wind chimes will be in motion, the nuts will have a tendency to loosen. Consider using a locking nut or painting the machine screws with threadlocker compound.

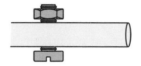

6 Make the mount from scrap lumber, using any wood saw. One successful design is a 5½" diameter circle of 1-by pine, but feel free to be creative with the shape. Draw a 4½" diameter circle on the bottom of the larger pine circle and make five equally spaced marks around the circle, which will be the hanging locations of the five bells. Screw a small wood eyelet into each of these five marks. Screw another wood eyelet into the center of the circle, to hang the wind-powered clapper.

7 Tie 6 to 8 inches of twine, string, or fishing line to the machine screws drilled through the bells, and tie the other ends to the five evenly spaced eyelets.

8 Use any type of wood saw to make a 2½" diameter circle of 1-by pine for the clapper—or a design of your choice. Round the edges by sanding or routing. Use a small wood drill bit to drill a small hole in the center.

9 Cut a small paddle of scrap wood to use as a wind scoop. Shape and smooth into an oval or the shape of your choice. Screw an eyelet into the top of the wind scoop and attach twine. Tie a knot or knots in the twine at about the midpoint of the chimes to support the clapper. Feed the twine through the hole in the clapper and then tie the top of the twine to the mount's center eyelet.

(continued)

10 For an optional decorative finish, stack and glue additional wood circles on top of your mount to make a pyramid-like shape. Let the glue dry for 4 to 6 hours. Mark the top-center of your mount and screw in a large wood eyelet. Use twine or chain to hang the wind chime from a secure beam or tree branch in a breezy spot.

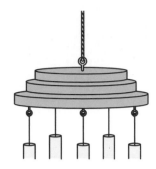

Creating Patina

An old copper roof, like that on Chartres Cathedral, will have a pale green tint—the result of copper oxidizing over the centuries—called the patina. But you can also apply patina to your metal projects to create an aged look.

Because patina work is meant to distress metal, it generally involves chemicals you don't want on your skin or in your eyes. Always wear proper safety equipment, including chemical-resistant gloves and safety goggles, and protect your arms and legs with appropriate work clothes. Patina also requires clean metal. If you'll be using old metal, be sure to strip away any existing finish. Depending on the project, stripping may require chemical paint stripper, an orbital sander with metal paper, elbow grease—or a combination of all three. (If you're not sure which is most appropriate for your piece, ask a professional at your local hardware store.) Once the metal is clean, and even if you're working with new metal, be sure to degrease it with rubbing alcohol and a lint-free rag prior to applying the patina, and make sure no dirt or other grime remains on the surface of the piece. Once you've degreased a piece, avoid touching it with your bare hands, which can leave oil fingerprints in your patina.

Rust patina. Most of what you need to make a basic rust patina probably lives under your kitchen sink. Fill a spray bottle with distilled white vinegar. Spray the metal with the vinegar and then let it dry. Repeat this step a couple of times, and then mix hydrogen peroxide with a little white vinegar and salt, using the ratio 8:1:1. Put the ingredients in another spray bottle and shake vigorously to dissolve the salt. Spray the solution on the metal. It should soon start foaming. Let dry and repeat.

Green patina. This green patina recipe is most appropriate for copper or bronze, but will work on iron or steel as well. In a plastic spray bottle, combine white vinegar, non-detergent ammonia, and noniodized salt in the ratio 4:4:1. Shake until mixed. Put on your chemical-resistant gloves and safety goggles, then spray the solution on your prepared metal and let dry. Repeat as needed.

Faux patinas. Patina paints are meant to create a patina-like visual effect on metal. One useful technique is to lightly sponge turquoise paint over bronze primer. No paint will give the full effect of a real metal patina, but it's always good to have a nontoxic paint alternative.

Finishing the patina. Most patinas on outdoor pieces, like garden furniture or decorative metalwork, will actually help the metal resist further corrosion. However, if you find that your patina runs or streaks with moisture or stains surrounding areas, consider finishing the patina with sealant. Use an acrylic or solvent-based sealer, not urethane or polyurethane.

PLUMBING

C logs, leaks, and parts-replacement are the staples of home plumbing repair. But to unplug, seal up, and troubleshoot, you'll need a fairly specialized set of tools in addition to those in your basic domestic repair tool kit (see page 2). Not only can having these tools on hand help avoid the cost of a plumber, but (because a massive water leak waits for no one) having the ability to triage a disaster can also keep the Niagara Falls in your basement, bathroom, or kitchen from doing more damage than it has to.

PLUMBING REPAIR TOOL KIT

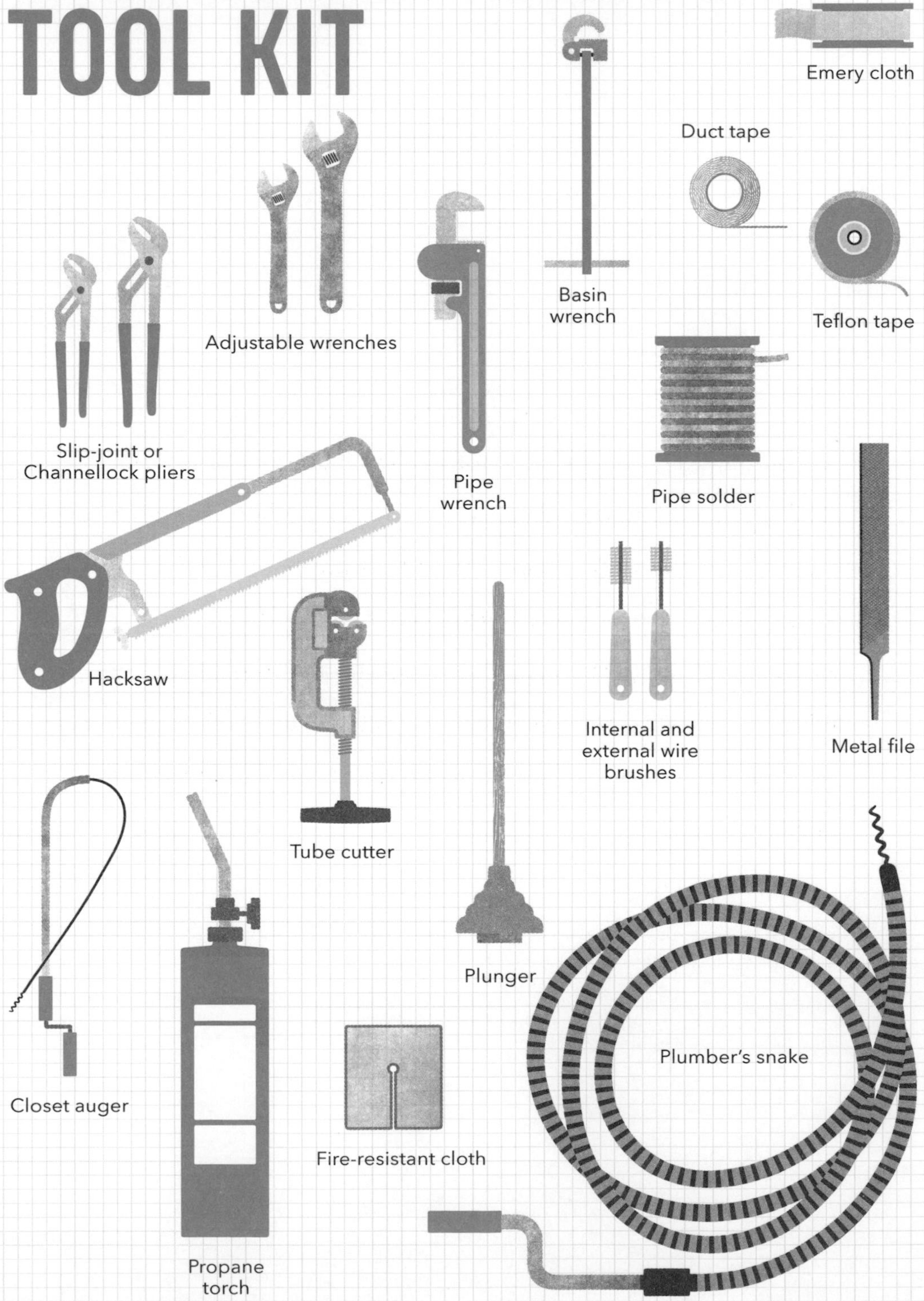

Emery cloth

Duct tape

Basin wrench

Teflon tape

Adjustable wrenches

Slip-joint or Channellock pliers

Pipe wrench

Pipe solder

Hacksaw

Internal and external wire brushes

Metal file

Tube cutter

Plunger

Closet auger

Propane torch

Fire-resistant cloth

Plumber's snake

Tongue-and-groove pliers. Tongue-and-groove pliers will grab and twist most pipes and pipe fittings. Expect to pay about $15 for 10-inch and about $30 for 12-inch—and keep both on hand.

Adjustable wrenches. Adjustable wrenches (keep a 6-inch and a 10-inch in your tool kit) will help you turn the hexagonal nuts of supply lines and compression fittings. They fill the middle ground between tongue-and-groove pliers and proper pipe wrenches.

Pipe wrench. A pipe wrench is a serious hunk of metal. Its ingenious design allows it to lock on to round surfaces, tightening and loosening its teeth into soft iron fittings. Some repairs will require you to twist in opposite directions at once, so it's useful to have two or more pipe wrenches. A basic quiver should include one 10-inch, two 14-inch, and one 18-inch.

Basin wrench. The other pliers and wrenches may do double-duty on other household projects, but a basin wrench is for one use and one use only: reaching hard-to-get fasteners that you can't get a wrench on any other way. The specialized head of a basin wrench is designed to lock on to fasteners with pressure, and the very long handle allows you to get the head onto the nuts that hold faucets and other fixtures in place deep in the recesses of your sink. This is a tool that you don't need until you need it, and then there's nothing else that'll do.

Propane torch. "Sweating" is the process of joining copper pipe in a watertight joint, which you'll need to do if you're replacing cracked or old water pipes. To do it you'll need a small, handheld flame torch. Propane is standard for most basic home repairs, though you may also consider methylacetylene-propadiene (MAPP), which heats joints a little faster. Get a torch kit for about $50, and consider investing in a model with a self-lighting head, which is much easier than using a striker, lighter, or matches.

Hacksaw. A hacksaw is the go-to blade for cutting both metal and plastic pipe, as well as screws, nuts, and bolts. Ten- or 12-inch saws are standard and either will complement your kit. In addition to the saw, consider getting three blades—one with 18 teeth-per-inch (TPI), one with 24 TPI, and another with 32 TPI. The more tightly spaced the teeth, the thicker the material it will cut.

Tube cutter. The tube (or pipe) cutter is a specialized cousin of the hacksaw. It's not as versatile, but it does the job of cutting copper pipe so much more efficiently that it's worth adding to your kit. A tube cutter can look like a wrench with a pizza-cutter-like tooth, or it can be a clamp with the same round blade. Either way, the tube cutter fits around a pipe and you spin it, making a clean slice. Expect to pay about $20.

Metal file. Once you cut copper pipe, you'll want to smooth the rough edges with a metal file. It's worth having two files on hand: a half-round file, with a flat and a round side, for de-burring metal; and a rat-tail file (it's round and tapered, as its name implies) for filing concave surfaces and enlarging holes.

Plumber's snake. Technically called an auger and also known as an electric eel, the plumber's snake is a hand-cranked drain-cleaning tool. Twenty-five feet is a fairly standard length, and a ¼-inch cable can be used in drains up to 2 inches wide.

Closet auger. For any drain more than 2 inches wide—especially the toilet—you'll need the thicker version of the plumber's snake known as the closet auger. This short, hand-cranked auger usually includes a plastic stem that protects the finish on the porcelain basin and is just long enough to reach the trap under the toilet, which is home to most clogs.

(continued)

Plunger. Before you reach for a snake, give your toilet clog the old college try with a plunger. A toilet plunger is slightly different from a sink plunger, with a second sleeve of rubber (called a "flange") that extends just below the cup and helps to form a seal with the tubular constriction at the base of most toilets. Buy one of each kind. Buying a good plunger can help you avoid other, less pleasant interventions.

Miscellaneous supplies. In addition to duct tape and sheer moxie, you'll also need fire-resistant cloth for guarding wood from flames while working on pipe, emery cloth for sanding metal, Teflon tape for protecting pipe threads, internal and external wire brushes, and pipe solder. Unlike the assortment of generic nails, screws, and bolts that will see you through most non-plumbing fix-its, most of your plumbing replacement parts require hardware specific to the job. Evaluate the needs of your plumbing project and then plan on going to the hardware store for the job-specific parts you need.

#48 How to Stop a Drip
(or, Understanding Your Water Supply)

According to the US Geological Survey, it takes 15,140 drips to make a gallon of water. If you have one faucet leaking a drip every two seconds, that's just over 1,000 gallons a year. (Never mind that a running toilet can waste up to 73,000 gallons of water in a year!) Not only does a drip waste water, but it can very easily lay waste to your sanity as well. So fix it! Usually turning off the drip is a simple fix requiring 15 minutes and only a few common tools. But this first foray into the world of plumbing can also teach you the basics of working with water—for starters, shut off the water supply before taking apart that faucet.

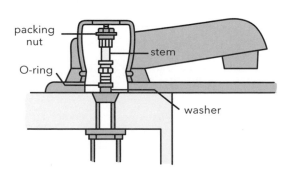

packing nut

stem

O-ring

washer

Why a Faucet Drips

From the water treatment facility, water enters pipes that branch off into your home's water main, which in turn divert to all the taps and faucets and spigots in your house. The thing is, all of this water is pressurized—faucets don't suck water, they block it. This requires a pressure-proof seal, which is usually created by screwing a washer down tight against the top of a pipe. When the washer or its seat decays or cracks or simply comes loose, water from the pressurized pipes can leak out.

TOOLS:

Utility knife (if needed) •
Screwdriver • **WD-40 (if
needed)** • **Slip-joint pliers**

MATERIALS:

- **Rubber O-ring**
- **Washer**

1 Shut off the water supply. Most sinks and toilets have obvious local shutoff valves located near where the pipes enter the wall. With tubs and showers, shutoffs can be a little trickier to find. Look for a nearby access panel in the wall or check your basement or crawl space for a hidden shutoff. If all else fails, shut off the water main to the house. There should be shutoff mains on either side of your water meter, one for shutting off the supply side and one for shutting off the house side. Turn off the supply side (the pipe that comes from the street).

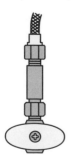

2 Most faucet handles are attached by one screw on the top or back, which may be hidden underneath a plastic button. Cover the drain with a stopper or towel before removing the faucet handle(s). Pop out the button with a flat blade, if necessary, and remove the screw. If it's tight, use WD-40 or another all-purpose oil to help loosen it, rather than cranking on it with the screwdriver alone and risking gouging out the screw head. Once unscrewed, remove the handle (the specifics will vary depending on your faucet).

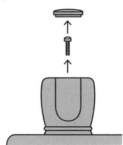

3 Underneath the handle, a packing nut guards the faucet's inner workings. Use slip-joint pliers to twist off the packing nut. Lubricate with WD-40 if needed.

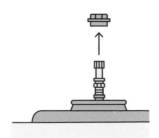

4 The packing nut limits the distance the faucet's stem can travel when you turn the handle. With the packing nut removed, you can use the handle itself as a wrench to remove the stem. Reseat the handle and turn it in the "on" direction to unscrew the stem.

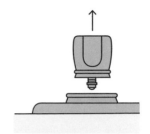

5 On the bottom of the stem is a small rubber washer. Remove the screw that holds the washer in place. The stem is likely to also have a rubber O-ring, which keeps water from sneaking up alongside the stem. Take the O-ring off, too. Examine the stem for any imperfections in the metal (and try to avoid making new imperfections!). If you see chips or cracks, it may be the metal and not the rubber pieces of your faucet that is causing the leak. Bring the washer and O-ring with you to the hardware store, along with the stem, if it looks damaged, so that

(continued)

you can match them to exact replacements. Because these pieces are cheap (and because when one fails the other can't be far behind), it's worth replacing both.

6 On the stem, replace the washer and O-ring and reassemble everything you took apart. First insert the stem and its new parts into the faucet tube. Then replace the packing nut, the handle, the handle screw, and any plastic button. Remove the rag that was blocking your drain and turn the faucet to the *off* position.

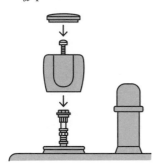

7 Turn the water back on from the wall or the main. Steps 2 to 6 should fix 99 percent of leaky faucets, but if yours continues to drip even after properly replacing the washer and O-ring, it's a good bet the stem or other metal parts are damaged. If needed, revisit these parts with a more critical eye and replace anything that looks suspect.

#49 How to Unclog a Drain

The purpose of a drain is to get rid of things you don't want. But sometimes these things don't want to go. That's called a clog. Your job is to be stronger than the clog. It can be trickier than it sounds. Unlike the water that comes into your house, water that goes out is pressurized only by gravity and the force of the water pushing down from above. It's inevitable that at some point accumulated gunk will overpower the strength of a little bit of water. First the sink just seems a little slow. Then it takes 20 minutes to clear. Then it's an hour. And finally you wake up to find last night's toothpaste still in the basin. It's time to unclog the drain.

Unclogging a drain is a little like solving a mystery. You want to eliminate potential culprits before calling in the big guns. For instance, before taking apart your sink, try a snake; before resorting to tools, try a solvent; before using commercial solvents, try a mixture of vinegar and baking soda. You can always escalate your efforts, but it's gentler on your pipes to start small and ramp up as needed.

TOOLS (DEPENDING ON THE CLOG):

Sink plunger • Plumber's snake • Slip-joint pliers • Bucket • Long screwdriver or wire coat hanger

MATERIALS:

• **Baking soda**
• **Distilled white vinegar**

1 Try a solvent. Liquid solvents that eat away at the clog can clear away some slow drains without doing too much damage to your pipes. Try baking soda and white vinegar first. Dump at least a half-cup of baking soda into the drain and then chase it with a half-cup of distilled white vinegar. The action should be immediate, bubbling out into the sink. But even once the volcanic spurt is over, the concoction continues to work. Let it sit for a few hours before rinsing with very hot water.

If needed, escalate to Drano or Liquid-Plumr. (Make sure the pipes in your home aren't old metal, since strong chemical formulas can corrode the pipes.)

2 Try a plunger. A sink plunger is shaped slightly differently than a toilet plunger. Toilet plungers usually have a rubber sleeve ("flange") that extends below the base of the plunger bell to make a seal with the pipe leading from the base of a commode. Drain plungers have no skirt and instead are usually just a rubber bell on a handle.

The trick to plunging a drain is to plug any openings other than the one you're plunging; otherwise they act as pressure releasers. Start by jamming a wet rag into a sink's overflow drain. If another sink shares the same pipe (as in double basins or back-to-back bathrooms), plug all other drains and overflow openings with drain plugs and wet rags.

Place the plunger bell over the clogged drain. Fill the clogged basin with water to reach at least halfway up the plunger's bell.

Form a seal over the drain and start working the plunger up and down—both the pushing and pulling actions help to loosen the clog.

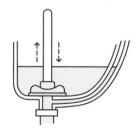

After about a dozen pushes and pulls, remove the plunger and see what happens. If water rushes out, problem solved. If not, give it a couple more tries before escalating your interventions.

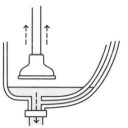

3 Try a snake. Plumber's snake, hand auger, sink auger—whatever you call it, it's a twisty head on a long wire that you push into a clog and crank until the clog is clear. Start the easy way, by trying to auger the clog down through the drain itself—if the clog is high enough in the pipe, a couple of cranks should clear it.

That said, many clogs will be lower in the pipe—too low to reach from the top. Instead, you'll have to auger the sink from below. If you think you'll bump the faucet or your cat or child will delight in turning it on while

(continued)

you're working, turn off the water supply at the wall. Then place a bucket beneath the curved pipe under the sink, known as a P-trap.

The P-trap is held in place by friction washers and slip nuts, which may only be hand-tight. If they're too tight, give the nuts a firm crank with slip-joint pliers.

Remove the P-trap and use the bucket to catch the water that drains from the pipe ends.

Check to see if the clog is in the P-trap. If so, you should be able to clear it with a long screwdriver or with a wire coat hanger.

4 Try digging deeper. If the clog isn't high in the pipe and it's not in the P-trap, it's farther down the pipe. Feed the auger wire down the pipe. The pipe that leaves your drain eventually reaches a T-joint, at which point one pipe leads farther into the drain (possibly toward the clog) and the other pipe leads up to the outside (and away from the clog). To tell the difference, listen as you feed the wire for whether the auger head is climbing (which you don't want) or descending. Once you feel resistance, tighten the set screw at the front of the snake and turn the handle while pushing into the clog. Work the auger back and forth until the clog clears. If the clog proves difficult, try pushing the auger past the clog and then pulling it back through while cranking. Enough passes should clear it. Gently extract the snake, trying not to make a horrible mess. Reassemble the P-trap and run a substantial amount of hot water down the drain

to wash away any material you scraped loose before it initiates a new clog.

5 Clear the house trap. Hopefully one of the previous steps cleared your clogged drain. If not, the clog must be even farther down. If you can follow the path of your pipes underneath the house, from either a basement or a crawl space, do it. Ideally your plumbing includes screw-off, clear-out plugs at periodic intervals, allowing you to check for clogs without removing sections of pipe. Eventually you'll reach the house trap—a U-shaped pipe probably buried in the basement floor and marked by clear-out plugs at the tops of the U. Unscrew these plugs and try the auger. If the clog remains, it's time to call a professional.

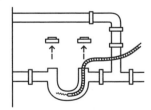

It may be common enough to see rings fall down drains, but plumbers have reported finding all kinds of living and nonliving items in them—from false teeth to electronic devices to live badgers!

#50 How to Fix a Burst Pipe

As water turns to ice, it expands. This expansion can be so powerful that ice pushing against pipe walls can burst the metal. Unfortunately, you're not likely to notice the problem while the water is still in its solid form. You notice a burst pipe when the ice *melts*—and the cracked pipe starts spewing water into your basement. The first step to fixing a burst pipe is actually prevention: learning to recognize the conditions likely to create it and watching like a hawk as a frigid night turns into a tepid day. The second step is being able to lay a quick hand on your house's water main, despite possible pitch-darkness and hemorrhaging plumbing. Where is your water main? Practice now. Really. Put down this book and go find your water main. Practice turning it off and then back on. The last thing you want is water rising around your ankles as you search desperately for the main. Now, with the crisis under control, it's time to think about a fix.

Replacing a Pipe Section

If you're lucky, you're dealing with a trickling leak and preparing for a patch situation (see How to Patch a Pipe, page 119), but a more serious leak requires a more serious fix: replacing the affected section of pipe with a new section. Again, due to the combination of the desperation you're likely to feel while staring at a burst pipe and Murphy's Law, which dictates that said burst pipe be inaccessible to anyone but a contortionist, you'll likely want to practice pipe repair with scrap pipe in the comfort of your garage on some warm evening. No matter the conditions surrounding pipe replacement, however, the procedure remains the same.

TOOLS:

Tube cutter or hacksaw • Torch (propane, MAPP, or other) • Measuring tape • Pencil • Wire brush • Safety goggles • Safety gloves

MATERIALS:

- Type L copper pipe, diameter ½" or ¾" (to match the damaged pipe)
- Couplings (to fit pipe)
- Plumbing flux
- Lead-free solder

1 Gather your materials. Before you start cutting, make sure you have the pieces needed to replace what you remove. Modern plumbing should exclusively use type L copper pipe, diameter ½" or ¾". Keep extra lengths of both in your plumbing tool kit, along with couplings of appropriate size to cover the joints between sections of pipe. Rarely, you might need to replace a fixture, which can require a trip to the hardware store.

2 Cut out the broken section. Use the tube cutter to cut the copper pipe on either side of the leak to remove the broken section. If the broken section is near a valve, joint, or coupling, you may be able to heat the section with your blowtorch, grip it with pliers, and twist it free instead of cutting it. Pulling pipe from an existing joint is slightly preferable, as it removes the need to add

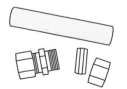

(continued)

a new joint or coupling on that side (one fewer fitting to solder).

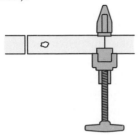

3 Cut new pipe. Measure the section of pipe you removed and cut a section of the same length from new, matching pipe with the tube cutter.

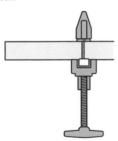

4 Prepare the surface. Before you slide sleeve-like couplings over the joints between the new and old pipes, clean all sections thoroughly. Use a wire brush to remove any rust from the old pipe, and do the same with the new pipe, until both sparkle. A little preparation goes a long way toward a successful repair.

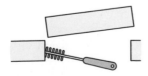

5 Attach the pipes. Slide two couplings onto the new section of pipe. Eventually, one coupling will cover the left seam and the other will cover the right seam. Paint plumbing flux onto the sanded ends of both the old and the new pipe. Slide the couplings to cover both joints.

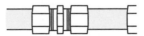

6 Sweat the pipes. An inexpensive propane torch—or, really, any modern blowtorch—works well to sweat copper pipe. Put on safety goggles and gloves, and then light the torch and adjust the flame until the inner cone—the hottest part of the flame—is a little more than an inch long. Hold the tip of this cone to one joint at a time, moving the flame evenly over the coupling. Plumbing can be tight work, so be careful not to bring the flame too close to ceiling joists or any other wooden or flammable material.

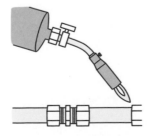

7 Solder the pipes. When the flux sizzles, put down the torch and apply solder (with experience, you can torch with one hand while soldering with the other, but, for now, use caution). Lead-free plumber's solder is usually sold as silver alloy wire on rolls. There's no need to cut from the roll; just work with the roll's loose end. Touch solder to one side of the coupling, where the sleeve ends and the pipe starts. The hot joint will suck solder. As solder melts into the joint, run the loose end around the pipe until the joint looks full. Repeat this step four times— once for each side of the two couplings.

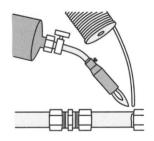

8 Test the pipe. Solder hardens as it cools, so after a minute or so the joint should be ready for use. Turn the water main back on and check the repaired pipe for drips. If it still drips, try again. This may include adding more solder to the joint, or heating and twisting the section free and replacing it with a new section of pipe.

#51 How to Patch a Pipe

I f the leak isn't catastrophic but instead is anywhere from a slow drip to a very moderate trickle, you may be able to patch the leaking pipe instead of replacing the section. There are many styles of plumbing patches—consider talking to employees at your local home improvement store about which kind is best for your needs.

In order to get most kinds of patches to stick to smooth pipe, you'll need to rough it up a bit. Use 80- to 100-grit sandpaper to both clean and texturize the pipe surface, sanding at least an inch in every direction beyond the location of the leak. Plumbing patches are generally made to bond once wet and do so pretty quickly, so dry-fit the patch before moistening it. If needed, cut the patch to size so that it doesn't overlap itself but still covers the sanded area.

If you're the gambling type, simply wet the patch, wrap it tightly over the affected area and let dry. If you're a little more careful, secure the patch with screw-together C-clamps or hose clamps. Tighten down the clamps and allow ample time to dry before testing the pipe.

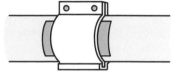

Due to the slightly imperfect nature of patches, check for leaks until you're confident the fix is permanent.

In the United States and Canada alone, there are approximately one million miles of water pipeline and aqueducts, enough to crisscross the continent about 300 times.

✕ ✕
Emergency Repair

If under extreme duress, you can make a temporary pipe patch with a length of garden hose or a bike's inner tube. Cut a section of hose or tube longer than the split in the pipe. Slit the hose or tube lengthwise and wrap the sheath around the pipe. Hold the temporary patch in place with either hose rings or C-clamps. ✕

#52 How to Stop Your Pipes from Freezing
(or, Lagging and Winterizing)

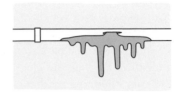

The best way to fix a pipe is to keep it from breaking in the first place, and the best way to keep it from breaking is to keep it from freezing. Because plumbing runs from the outside of your house to the inside, this can be easier said than done in climates where it gets below freezing. Plumbing also tends to run through the less insulated parts of your house, such as the basement, crawl space, and even garage. Because these pipes are a pain in the neck to access, it's worth spending a warm summer afternoon winterizing your pipes to avoid having to perform emergency repairs in the middle of some cold, dark winter night.

The process involves two steps. Step one is insulation, or lagging—stopping cold air from hitting the pipes so it can't freeze the water inside them. Air has a way of sneaking in through gaps, and so in order to be effective, pipe insulation has to be complete. Leave even a little gap, and inevitably that inch or two will be the part to freeze and burst. The second step is winterizing, or draining and closing vulnerable spigots.

Before You Go on Vacation . . .

When you escape northern Minnesota for a midwinter trip to the Bahamas, your worst nightmare will be coming home to a swimming pool in your basement—or worse, an ice-skating rink. If it's just an overnight trip, and assuming your pipes are properly insulated, you should be fine with your heat set to about 40 degrees. For a longer trip, simply turn off the water main and open all your faucets (double-check them to make sure no water is sneaking past the shutoff). Opening your faucets allows water the room it needs to expand as it freezes, without pushing against the pipes. If you're expecting a solid freeze while you're away, consider also draining the water from your pipes.

In the Cold, Cold Night

If a pipe starts to gurgle and spit on a freezing-cold night, there's a good chance it's the beginning of ice taking hold. If you can locate the exact trouble spot either by the sound of gurgling or by your considered opinion of where cold air is contacting the pipe, consider hitting it with your propane torch or, in a pinch, a hair dryer. Then, if possible, wrap the pipe with electric heating tape and leave the power on through the night. If you hit an unexpected cold snap before you've winterized your pipes, or if you know a certain line is prone to freezing despite your best efforts, you can leave a tap trickling overnight. Even a slight flow should move water through the system before it can freeze in the pipes.

TOOLS:

Measuring tape • Pencil • Flashlight (optional) • Duct tape • Utility knife • Pliers • Bucket

MATERIALS:

• **Fiberglass, foil, or foam pipe insulation**

1 Check your insulation. First, determine which areas of your home are likely to experience below-freezing temps. Pay special attention to pipes running along outside walls or underneath the house where the foundation meets the walls. In the northern hemisphere, the north side of your house is likely to see little winter sun and so may be especially prone to freezing pipes. (There should be ample fiberglass batting insulation to keep the outside from coming in. If not, fix your wall insulation after you insulate your pipes.)

2 Insulate the vulnerable pipes. There are two options: sleeve-like foam insulation that sandwiches the pipe like a hot dog bun, or tape-like fiberglass or foil insulation that wraps around the pipe. For most applications, it's easier to slip on a sleeve than wrap the tape. Measure the pipes and cut foam sleeves to length with a utility knife. Slip the sleeves over the pipe and close the slit with duct tape.

3 Seal around bends in the pipe. Where a pipe turns at a 90-degree angle, use a utility knife to cut insulation ends to 45 degrees, then push the cut ends together over the pipe to make a clean right angle. Do likewise for any joint: Evaluate how to best cut the insulation to fit, and then close all open slits with duct tape.

4 Winterize the spigots. First, disconnect any outside garden hoses or other attachments to your outside spigots.

If you have "frost-proof" or "freeze-proof" spigots, when you turn the handle you're actually shutting off the water two or three feet down the pipe, where it's likely to be insulated anyway. (Most of these types of spigot have a plastic vacuum breaker cap on the top of the spigot—so a spigot with extra parts or bulk may be "frost-proof.") As long as the attached pipes are properly insulated and installed at a slight downward tilt that allows water to drain when the tap is off, they shouldn't require further work.

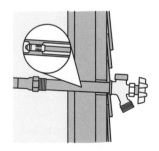

5 Shut off the supply. A regular spigot requires shutoff and draining, and the procedure is similar to any pipe that's likely to freeze. First locate the shutoff valve. (All outside spigots and most pipes in general have shutoff valves far enough inside the house's insulated

(continued)

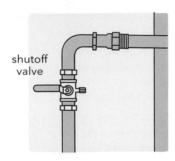

shutoff
valve

areas to firewall the rest of
your plumbing from a burst.)

Crank the valve closed, then
open the spigot. Check the
shutoff—there should not be
any water leaking from the
spigot.

6 Drain the spigot. With
the supply shut off, many
homeowners make it through
the winter with the spigot
open. Any water remaining in
the pipe has room to expand.

For added security, or in
especially cold climates, drain
this excess water from the
pipe. At the shutoff, find the
drain cap and open it with
locking pliers. Hold a bucket
under the drain, and open the
cap. Now, without water in
the pipe, you can turn off the
outside spigot.

#53 How to Install a Sump Pump

B efore you find yourself pumping water out of your basement, do everything you can to keep
it from coming in. That means draining water *away* from your house. Make sure that gutters
are running freely and all spouts extend at least four feet past the house's foundation. Check
that soil doesn't slope toward the house, which can funnel water into your basement. Still, some
soils are simply wet, and if that's the case, you may need to pump water out.

First, Try a Drain

If water is localized, and your house was built
atop a layer of gravel, you may be able to drain
the water into the gravel and soil below the
house. In that case, simply install a drain at the
lowest point in the basement floor. This will
require cutting a small hole with a concrete

saw, inserting a store-bought drain or grill,
and then pouring a concrete patch around the
drain. However, without a full gravel sub-
layer, water may continue to pool up through
the drain. In that case, you'll want a pit and a
pump.

TOOLS:

Measuring tape • Concrete
saw (plan to rent) •
Sledgehammer • Large
bucket (for mixing concrete)
• Wooden float • Trowel •
Hacksaw • Drill with bit size
matched to PVC (if needed) •
Caulking gun

MATERIALS:

- Plastic sump pit liner
- Gravel
- Concrete mix
- Sump pump
- PVC pipe connectors
- PVC pipe
- One-way (check) valve
- Two 90-degree PVC elbows
- Splash plate

1 Dig the sump pit. Staying
at least 8 inches from
foundation walls, use a
concrete saw to cut a hole
in the lowest section of the
basement floor, where water
accumulates. The shape
doesn't matter as long as the
section is greater than about
2 square feet. Break up the
concrete in the panel to be
removed by hitting it with

a sledgehammer. Remove and dispose of the broken concrete. Dig a pit deep enough to accommodate the plastic sump pit liner, with the lip of the liner level with the floor.

2 Fill the pit. Insert the sump pit liner and pack gravel into the hole around the liner to hold it in place. Spread and level gravel on the dirt around the sump liner until the level of the gravel is about an inch lower than the surface of the basement floor.

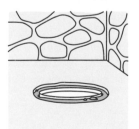

3 Pour the concrete. Following the package instructions, mix enough concrete to fill the area around the sump pit liner. Pour the wet concrete on top of the gravel layer outside the sump pit liner. Use a wooden float to make sure the poured

concrete pushes tightly against the existing basement concrete and also against the outside edge of the sump pit liner. Once the concrete is dry enough to hold its form but still wet enough to sculpt, use a trowel to finish the face of the patch in your basement floor. Let the concrete cure for a couple of days.

4 Sink the sump pump. Like toilets, sump pumps generally use a float that activates a pump once the water in the sump pit reaches a certain level. Start by screwing the appropriately sized PVC pipe connector into the sump pump discharge. With a handsaw, cut a length of PVC pipe to be just long enough to rise past the top of the pit liner with the pump in place (length of PVC will depend on the depth of your sump pump liner and how your pump sits inside the liner) and attach it. If you like, duct tape the pump's electrical cords to the vertical PVC pipe and then carefully lower the pump into the sump pit

liner so that the pump float is away from the wall and able to move without obstruction. Install the liner lid, cutting a hole in the top of the lid if necessary to accommodate the vertical PVC pipe.

5 Add a check valve. Capping the PVC that runs to the pump, install a one-way valve, sometimes called a check valve. This keeps water from flowing back down into the pump once the pump shuts off. The check valve should come with its own plumbing connections, including couplings and clamps. Be sure the arrow on the valve points up, indicating the direction you want water to flow.

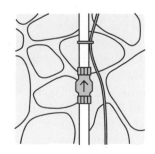

(continued)

6 Extend the PVC. From the top of the check valve, add enough vertical PVC to bring discharged water up past the foundation to just below the ceiling joists. Attach a 90-degree PVC elbow.

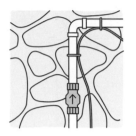

7 Drain the discharge. Pumped water should drain outdoors. To get the water outside, you'll need

to cut a hole in the wooden rim joist that caps the house's concrete foundation. Drill a hole wide enough for the PVC to pass through. Feed PVC from the outside through the hole and connect the PVC to the elbow inside. Outside, use a handsaw to cut the PVC so that only about ½" of the tube protrudes past the joist. Attach another 90-degree PVC elbow to the outside pipe, pointing down. Use a caulking gun to run a line of caulk around the PVC on both sides of the wooden joist. If your landscaping slopes away from the foundation, you

can discharge water directly from the down-pointing PVC onto a splash plate (like you would a hose spigot or gutter downspout). If discharged water has the potential to run back toward the house, forego the second 90-degree joint and use additional PVC to extend the drain away from the foundation.

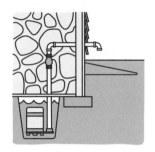

#54 How to Fix a Leaky Washing Machine

W hether you notice a slight dampening on the floor around the washing machine or a tsunami surges from the laundry room, don't delay fixing that washing machine leak. Like working on a car, working on a washing machine used to be easy—they were all roughly the same design, used roughly the same parts, and were prone to roughly the same leaks. However, with new direct-drive (as opposed to belt-driven) designs and the prevalence of computerized gadgetry, the one-size-fits-all approach to washing machine repair is no longer viable. There remain a few common leak locations, however, and thus common fixes for those leaks, but you may need to do some adapting to your specific machine. Before

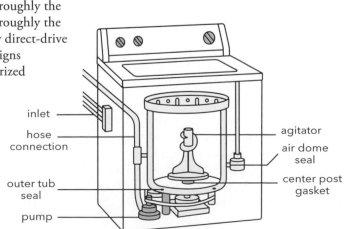

you start, check that repairs won't void your machine's warranty. Then, make sure the standing water near the machine isn't due to a plugged drain. It's not worth ripping apart the washing machine only to find the fix is as easy as grabbing a clump of hair.

TOOLS (DEPENDING ON THE FIX):

Putty knife • Adjustable pliers • Screwdrivers • Ratchet and socket

MATERIALS:

- Hose washers
- Supply hoses
- Worm-drive clamps
- Pump hoses

1 Remove the washing machine lid. There are holes punched in the tub, and any one of them is capable of leaking. Noting the exact location of a tub leak can help pinpoint the cause and the cure. Match the leak location to the washing machine specs. If you no longer have the paper plans that came with the washer, check online

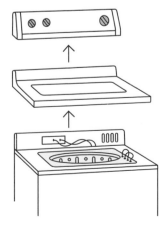

(most companies list their specs electronically). As with a car, start by looking "under the hood." Most lids are held on with a spring catch. Work a flat blade, like a putty knife, under the front seam between the lid and the cabinet. Release the spring catch and lift the lid (some lids also require unscrewing).

2 Check the four tub seals. These mount the tub to the cabinet, and each should consist of a bolt passing through a rubber washer. Bolts can rust and rubber can crack—if either is the case, replace them. If the tub itself is at fault—for example, its integrity is compromised

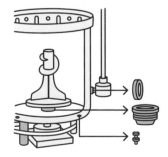

by rust—it's time for a new washing machine. While you have the tub seals removed, it's worth lifting out the tub to check the center post gasket, which should form a seal at the base of the tub. In most washing machines, an air dome measures the

internal pressure and acts as a switch, turning water on and off as needed. It can also leak. Most air domes have a slotted rubber seal. Replace it if needed.

3 Check the supply hoses. Supply hoses connect your plumbing to the machine. They are almost always flexible rubber hoses tipped with metal connectors that screw onto inlets on the washing machine. After years behind the machine, these metal connectors may be corroded into what looks like little lumps of rust. Set the washing machine to the fill cycle and check here to see if water is leaking between the supply hoses and the inlet ports. If it is, turn off the machine and close the water-supply valve—it's perfectly possible to break a rusty supply hose off the inlet, which can quickly result in Niagara Falls. You can try simply tightening the supply hose connectors a

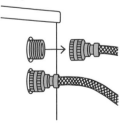

(continued)

good half turn with adjustable pliers and see if that fixes the problem, but a better solution is to disconnect the hoses and replace the hose washers. As these rubber circles age, they get brittle and eventually wear to the point of allowing leaks. Use a flathead screwdriver or other type of pry to pop a washer free of the supply hose and bring it with you to the hardware store to match it. While you're at the store, if the supply hoses or their connectors are in bad enough shape, consider replacing the lot.

4 Check the pump hoses. The supply hoses aren't the only water-conduits prone to leaks. There are hoses inside the machine, too, and to get at them you'll need to pull off the access panel, likely by unscrewing and/or unclipping it from the back of the machine. Once you can see underneath, start the washing machine's fill cycle and look for leaks. You should be able to trace the path from the supply hoses through a pump hose, to the pump, and then out through another pump hose. Check these pump hose

joints first, looking for clues like rust and calcium deposits in addition to leaking water. Hoses should be attached to the pump with either spring clamps or worm-drive clamps. Loose or rusted clamps are a common cause of leaks. If you replace the clamps, go with worm-drive rather than spring. You may also need to replace the hoses, which is easy to do with the access panel and clamps removed.

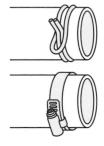

5 Check the pump. Unfortunately, pumps don't last forever. If you see water leaking from the pump itself, it's time for a new one. Grab a helper or two, unhook the washer, and tip it on its side to access the pump through the open bottom. Note the pump specs and buy or order a new one. Also notice the amount of wear on the drive belt—if

it looks worn, this is a good time to replace it. Just slip off the old belt and replace it with a new one. Then note the location of the pump's mounting bolts. Disconnect the in and out hoses and use a ratchet and socket to remove the mounting bolts. Slide the pump away from the drive belt and slip it free. Put in the replacement pump, seating the drive wheel in the belt and reconnecting the hoses. You'll need to adjust the position of the pump to tighten the belt, so after loose-fitting the mounting bolts, pull the pump tight against the belt with one hand while tightening the rear mounting bolt with the other. If needed, tighten the belt more and tighten the front mounting bolt.

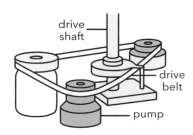

#55 How to Replace a Sink Faucet

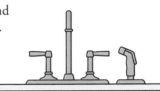

Sinks are easy: Open up the cabinet underneath the sink, and you will find all the pipes you need to plumb a new faucet. (Bathtubs are trickier—the faucets are generally mounted flush to the wall, so just getting to the pipes is its own challenge.) Here you will learn how to replace a sink faucet, whether it's broken, leaky, or just plain unstylish.

TOOLS:

Rag • Basin wrench • Slip-joint pliers

MATERIALS:

- **New faucet**
- **Supply lines (if needed)**
- **Teflon tape**
- **Plumber's putty or silicone caulk**
- **Friction washer and screw (for sprayer)**

1 Turn off the water supply, either at the shutoff valve in the bathroom or kitchen, at a shutoff valve farther upstream in the plumbing, or at the house's water main. Clear the area of soaps, sponges, and toiletries and make sure you have a bucket

and towel on hand, just in case. Shove a rag into the drain to avoid losing hardware down the pipes.

2 Access and remove the old faucet. In most older sinks and even many newer ones, having a long-handled basin wrench greatly eases the process of loosening the nuts that hold faucets in place. If not, it's useful to have long arms and patience. Reach up behind the sink and unscrew the tailpiece nuts that lock the faucets to the sink. Remove and dispose of the old faucet.

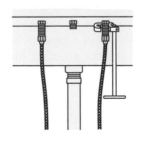

3 Evaluate your plumbing. While under the sink, check the integrity of your water supply line and shutoff valves. If you see rust or slime in excess of what can be cleaned, you'll need to replace those parts. Replacing the shutoff valves will likely require sweating new valves to the copper pipe (see page 118). Replacing the flexible

supply lines should be as easy as unscrewing them from the shutoff valves and screwing on new ones. Don't forget to wrap the threads with Teflon tape. The standard for under-sink use is braided stainless steel, which can be snaked around the myriad obstructions typical under any sink.

4 Connect the tailpieces. Faucet tailpieces bring water from the supply lines to the faucet itself. Whether you attach the tailpieces to the faucet and feed them down through the mounting holes in the sink, or attach the tailpieces to the supply lines and feed them up through the holes, depends in large part on the style of faucet. The faucet manufacturer should have provided pre-assembly instructions. Follow these

(continued)

instructions to determine how much of the faucet you should build from the top and how much should be fed from the bottom.

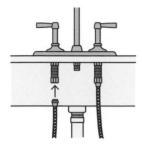

5 Seal the faucet plate. The line where the faucet plate meets the sink is a common place for water to seep underneath the sink, where it can create mold and rot. Guard against this by running a ¼" bead of plumber's putty around the base of the faucet before mounting it on the sink (if you have a marble sink, use silicone caulk instead). Be generous with the caulk or putty and then wipe away any excess.

6 Mount the faucet. After caulking the plate, set the faucet on top of the mounting hole, making sure it's pointing in the right direction. (Don't laugh. It happens.) Press down on the mounting plate to squeeze the putty or caulk

until the plate is tight to the sink. Use a basin wrench or a wrench supplied by the faucet manufacturer to tighten the mounting nut from below. To either side of a single faucet should be flange nuts that push down through open holes in the sink. Tighten these nuts now, too.

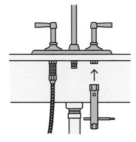

7 Attach the supply lines. Under the sink, attach the braided stainless steel supply lines to the faucet tailpieces, screwing them tight with slip-joint pliers. Connect the other ends of the supply lines to the shutoff valves. Use two wrenches to tighten the lines into the valves.

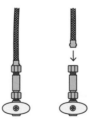

8 Attach the sprayer, if needed. Many sinks and newer faucet systems also include a sprayer. Attaching a sprayer is very similar to attaching a faucet. Run a ¼" bead of plumber's putty along

the bottom of the sprayer base. (The base should sit on top of long, screw-like threads.) Push these threads down through the appropriate hole in the sink and press the base in place. From below the sink, add a friction washer and screw on the mounting nut (which likely came with the sprayer). Tightening the nut will further pull the base of the sprayer against the sink. Wipe away any excess putty. With most sprayers, it will be easiest to feed the hose up through the hole in the base and attach it to the sprayer above the sink before setting the sprayer back into the base. Some sprayers include a length of attached hose, meant to attach to an extension hose under the sink. If that's the case, feed the hose down through the sprayer base and connect it as appropriate.

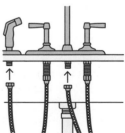

9 Let the putty dry and make sure the faucet is off before turning the water supply back on. If you have to leave the room to turn on the water, it's useful to have

a second set of eyes watching for leaks so that you can immediately turn the water back off if needed. Even a tiny drip will cause problems, so watch with eagle eyes for any sign of misplaced moisture, and if it's leaking at all, scrape off the putty and start again, reapplying it carefully.

#56 How to Replace a Drain Basket

You don't want gunk in your pipes, and that's why in many sinks, there's a drain basket to guard the entrance. The basket also forms the watertight funnel that directs water from the sink down the pipes. Because it's the gunk filter, and also a heavily used funnel, the basket will almost certainly wear out before the sink itself does. When that time comes, or when you deem it simply too disgusting to remain in the household, it's time to replace the basket. Here's how:

TOOLS:

Slip-joint pliers • Locknut wrench (optional) • Pliers • Screwdriver • Hacksaw (if needed) • Plastic or wooden scraper • Rag

MATERIALS:

- Plumber's putty or silicone caulk
- New drain basket
- Tailpiece washer (if needed)

1 Close the water shutoff valve. Look for it under or near your sink. Because you're working with the drain instead of the water supply, it's not technically necessary to turn off the water while completing this repair. That

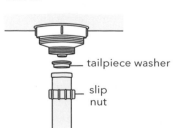

said, it's at least possible to loosen or unscrew something on the supply side that can quickly soak your kitchen or bathroom. Err on the side of caution.

2 Remove the tailpiece washer. Under the sink, use slip-joint pliers to loosen the plastic slip nut that holds the PVC tailpipe to the base of the strainer. Spin the slip nut completely off its threads so that it falls onto the plastic pipe. There's likely a plastic washer set in the top of the tailpiece—remove it now and put it someplace you won't lose it.

tailpiece washer

slip nut

3 Evaluate your pipes. If you find that you need to replace any of the PVC pipes leading from the drain basket to the wall (including the tailpiece, waste arm, trap, or any other under-sink plumbing leading from the basket), now is a good time to do it (see Step 7). Before ripping anything out, draw a diagram or take a picture of the existing plumbing so you can replicate it later. If you plan on keeping the old pipes, simply spin the tailpiece out of the way in order to complete the remaining steps of basket replacement.

(continued)

4 Loosen the drain basket. The locknut—the large-diameter ring that holds the bottom of the basket snug to the sink—is your number-one challenge in removing the basket. Give it a good twist with a locknut wrench or slip-joint pliers set at their widest extension. In many cases you may find that when you crank with the wrench or pliers, the entire basket spins rather than the locknut. After years of sitting in the same position under the sink, rust may be contributing to the locknut's locking power. In order to twist the locknut, you'll have to hold the basket steady. From the top of the sink, look down into the basket. At the bottom should be two or more holes. Shove the handles of a standard set of pliers into the two holes and have a

helper stick a long screwdriver between the handles of the pliers and hold the screwdriver tight to resist the turn of the locknut wrench. In some cases, turning the locknut may prove impossible, in which case you'll have to cut it off with a hacksaw. Fortunately, because you're replacing the sink

basket anyway, you needn't worry about cutting into it—just don't slice the sink itself. All that should be required is one cut completely through the width of the locknut, which you should be able to make (uncomfortably) with a flexible-bladed hacksaw.

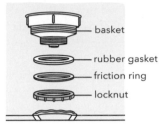

basket
rubber gasket
friction ring
locknut

5 Remove the basket. With the locknut removed, access the other under-sink parts of the basket, namely the friction ring and gasket. The friction ring is a strong cardboard circle that should make it possible to turn the locknut independently of the rest of the system. The rubber gasket presses tight to the bottom of the sink to block any water from sneaking through—both should slip free fairly easily. With these pieces pulled free, the basket should be held to the sink only by the power of the dried putty under the top rim. Pull the basket free and scrape away the old putty with a plastic or wooden tool to avoid scratching the basin.

6 Install the new drain basket. Run a ¼" bead of plumber's putty around the

top of the drain in the sink basin. If putty won't adhere to your sink, use silicone caulk instead. Press the new basket down onto this layer of putty or caulk. Under the sink, slip the new rubber gasket and friction ring in place and then tighten the locknut with slip-joint pliers to hold the new basket in place. Wipe away any excess putty squeezed from underneath the top lip of the basket with a damp rag.

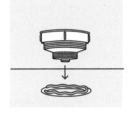

7 Plumb the new basket. If you kept the old PVC, spin the tailpiece back into position, reinsert the tailpiece washer (or a new one), and tighten the plastic slip nut onto the base of the basket. If you're replacing pipes, refer to the notes or picture you took in Step 3. Many home improvement stores sell outlet assembly kits that will have most everything you need to make the replacement. Installation should require cutting PVC to length, assembling with cone washers at all PVC joints, and tightening slip nuts. Between the tailpiece and the system's waste tee, make sure the PVC waste arm slopes gently downward

so that wastewater flows down through the system. Sink options vary, however, sometimes including a garbage disposal, so refer to your diagram or notes to ensure that everything goes back together the same as it was.

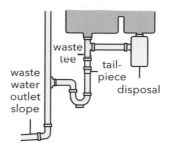

8 Turn the water supply back on and inspect the system thoroughly for leaks. If you see any, remove the basket, scrape out the putty and reapply carefully.

#57 How to Replace a Toilet

Water-efficient toilets typically use around half the water of a standard model. But that's not the only reason to replace your old commode. Maybe it's cracked. Maybe it's leaking. Maybe it's an eyesore. Whatever the reason, if it's time for a new toilet, here's how to install it. The following instructions will take you from the pipe, known as the closet bend, all the way up.

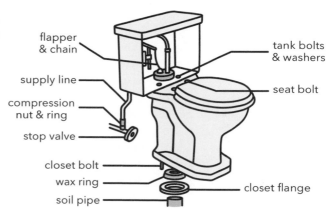

TOOLS:

Bucket • Tube cutter • Rags • Propane torch (if needed) • 4-foot level • Two socket or adjustable wrenches • Hacksaw • Screwdriver

MATERIALS:

- Flange (if needed)
- Four 3½" closet bolts

- Shutoff valve (if needed)
- Flux and solder (if needed)
- Thread tape or Teflon paste (if needed)
- Wax ring
- Toilet shims (if needed)
- Replacement toilet
- Braided stainless steel supply pipe that fits the space between your toilet and the water shutoff valve on the wall (if not included with toilet)

1 Turn off the water supply. Make sure it's turned off! The importance of this step can't be overstated.

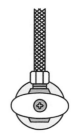

2 Cut the supply line. Place a bucket beneath the supply line that runs from the wall to the toilet tank and then use a tube cutter to cut the supply line near the

(continued)

shutoff valve. Catch any water that drains from the line. Flush the toilet to get rid of any remaining water.

3 Remove the toilet. The mounting bolts are likely underneath small caps on the toilet's base. Remove the caps, use a wrench to unscrew the nuts and washers, and then, with help, lift the old toilet out of the way.

4 Evaluate the plumbing to decide how much of the old material you want to keep. The flange is the circular piece that screws to the floor. If it's not in good condition, you can likely replace it without replacing the soil pipe it's connected to. Whether or not you replace the flange, plug the soil pipe with old rags to prevent sewer gas from escaping into the house and to prevent your tools and hardware from escaping into the sewer. Then, replace the 3½" closet bolts that point up from the flange.

5 Replace the shutoff valve. If necessary, now is the time to swap out the shutoff valve behind the toilet. The old shutoff valve may unscrew from the wall or you may need to pull the valve slightly away from the wall and use a propane torch to heat the soldered joint until the old valve slips free. Replace with a new valve, either by screwing it in place or by sweating a new joint with flux and solder. If screwing on a new valve, use one wrench to hold the valve steady and another to tighten the nut. Wrap it with thread tape to prevent corrosion.

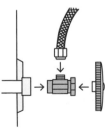

6 Place the wax ring. Correctly installing the wax ring that seals the toilet base can prevent water from seeping from underneath the toilet. Be sure to purchase a wax ring correctly sized to your flange, likely 3 or 4 inches. If your toilet is too big for the flange, buy a 4-to-3

reducer. If the flange sits below floor level, get a thicker wax ring to plug the empty space. Place the wax ring on top of the flange.

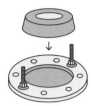

7 Place the new toilet. Toilets are heavy, so if you're not built like an offensive lineman, get help. Slip the holes over the bolts and set the toilet down gently on top of the wax ring. Sit on the toilet to press it into the wax ring until the toilet sits flush (no pun intended) on the floor. If the toilet rocks or the floor is uneven, use toilet shims to make it level and then use a utility knife or short handsaw to trim the shims until you can't see them.

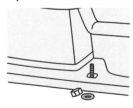

8 Place the washers and nuts over the closet bolts. Make the nuts hand-tight and then use a socket or adjustable wrench to further tighten the nuts, alternating sides with every turn. Don't over-tighten the nuts, or the porcelain toilet will crack. Once the nuts are tight, use a hacksaw to cut the closet bolts so they

extend about ½" past the nut. Cover the closet bolts with the caps that came with the toilet.

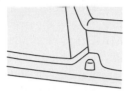

9 Now install the tank. Push the bolts that anchor the tank to the toilet down through the included rubber washer and then down through the holes in the bottom of the tank. Line up these bolts with the mounting holes in the toilet and set the tank in position. Below the tank and toilet, place a metal washer and then a nut onto a tank anchor bolt (which should have been included with the new toilet). Hand-tighten and then use a wrench and screwdriver to tighten further.

10 Connect the tank's handle to the flapper chain inside the tank and look

to be sure the float and chain aren't being held down by bands or wire.

11 Plumb the supply tube. Water flows from your plumbing through the shutoff valve, through a short length of supply pipe, and into the toilet's tank. In this step, you'll add the short length of pipe that goes between the shutoff valve and the tank. Hand-tighten the supply pipe to the tank using the provided tank nut. The supply pipe should point down toward the shutoff valve in the wall. If needed, sculpt the shape of the supply tube until it runs from the tank to the shutoff valve. When choosing the size, err on the side of leaving the pipe

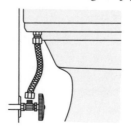

a little too long. The supply pipe should be able to insert easily into the shutoff valve.

12 Slide the included compression nut over the supply pipe end and then seat the pipe end into the shutoff valve. Use thread tape or Teflon paste to coat the screw threads. As you use a wrench to gently tighten the compression nut over the shutoff valve, the nut will squeeze the pipe to form a watertight seal. Your toilet should now be functional.

13 Turn the water to the toilet back on, either from the shutoff valve or from the main water supply. Flush the toilet a couple of times and inspect the unit closely for leaks. If it does leak, remove the thread tape or Teflon paste and start again, using a little more tape or paste.

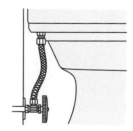

Though pitch is said to be affected by water volume and velocity, most American toilets flush in the key of E-flat.

Common Toilet Repairs

What other fixture bears full human weight multiple times per day and holds a reservoir of water in a tank that must be repeatedly emptied and filled? The toilet has too many moving parts, too many water transfers, and too much use to survive without problems. Here's what to do when the inevitable occurs.

A broken seat. The seat is meant to be sat upon. The lid is not. When you sit on the lid, it inevitably slides this way and that, stressing the hinges and their connections to the seat. And when either the hinges or the seat breaks, there's nothing to do but replace it. Hopefully you can find a seat that matches your toilet. At the very least, make sure your replacement seat and lid set is the correct size (there are two standard sizes). Then simply unscrew the nuts and washers from below the seat mount and install the new seat. With bolts and nuts near water, the probability of rust is fairly high. If you suspect that you have a corroded nut, it's worth taking the time to fit the right size wrench socket to ensure turns without slippage.

Water runs constantly. Inside the toilet tank, a floating ball is attached to the switch arm. It essentially functions like a light switch: When the water reaches a certain height, the arm turns off the switch and water stops flowing into the tank. There are two common reasons why the switch might not turn off the water. Either the switch is incorrectly gauging the amount of water in the tank, allowing water to continue flowing in through the supply pipe and straight back out through the overflow drain, or the tank is accidentally draining into the toilet bowl and the switch is correctly

welcoming in new water. You may need to fiddle with fixes for both possibilities. First, work with the floating ball and the switch arm. Check the float to make sure it's not full of water. If it is, replace it. Then check that the float rod is positioned correctly to shut off the water once it reaches the desired level. You should be able to turn a screw near the anchored end of the float arm to adjust its height. If not, you can carefully bend the metal float arm to adjust it. Bend the arm and its float slightly down toward the water to make the water trip the switch earlier. If the switch isn't the problem, water is likely leaking out the bottom of the tank into the bowl. First check the length of the wire or light chain connected to the drain plug. If the chain is too short, it may be preventing the plug from forming a good seal. The chain may also simply be hooked around something—make sure it's clear of obstructions. If that doesn't work, turn off the water to the toilet, flush to drain the tank, and check the integrity of the tank drain itself. Is there corrosion? If so, thoroughly sand it away. If the plug looks torn or worn, replace it so that it forms a perfect seal with the drain. Reassemble, turn the water back on, and check that the water now flows as desired.

Toilet won't flush. Is the flushing mechanism not letting water into the toilet bowl or is water from the bowl failing to make its way down the pipe? If water is pooling in the bowl or even (heaven forbid!) overflowing, chances are you have a clog. First, see How to Unclog a Drain on page 114. If the flushing mechanism isn't working, check that the handle hasn't simply become detached from the tank's flushing mechanism. Another common cause of failure to flush is not enough pressure from the tank. In a toilet, pressure is created by gravity pulling water down from above—if there's not enough water, there's not enough push. Check the tank. If the water level is low, try adjusting the float ball to allow more water into the tank, either by turning the adjustment screw or by gently bending the metal float arm to let the ball ride higher in the tank.

Squealing noise when filling. When water flow is restricted, pipes can whistle. First check that the water shutoff valve that connects the supply line to the wall is fully open. Restricted flow may also be due to pipe corrosion creating a partial blockage. Check the shutoff valve for signs of corrosion, and also check the entrance of the supply line into the tank. If you find corrosion, either use a wire brush to clear it or replace the affected part.

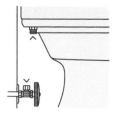

Water leaks from the base. By far the most common cause of a leaking toilet is a cracked

wax seal. And the most common cause of a cracked wax seal is a toilet with too much wiggle. So first check the integrity of the toilet itself. If the nuts holding the toilet base to the flange have come loose, tighten them, pulling the toilet more firmly down into the wax ring. (Don't crank the nuts too tight, though, or you'll crack the porcelain!) A loose toilet can also be caused by a cracked base. If that's the case, you'll need to replace the toilet. If everything looks structurally solid, try replacing the wax ring itself. See How to Replace a Toilet, page 131 for how to trade in the old ring for a new one.

Other leaks. Where is the water coming from? If not the base (see above), check that a little moisture isn't due to condensation around the underside rim of the tank. Most toilet tanks include a foam ridge to block moisture from condensing—yours might need to be replaced. Also check the connection where water flows from the tank to the bowl. If needed, gently tighten the connecting nuts until you re-form a seal. Cracks can be surprisingly tricky to spot, so if everything else seems to be working properly, it's time to take a very close look at the porcelain itself. Look for hairline fractures—if you find one, it's time to replace the fixture.

#58 How to Troubleshoot a Showerhead

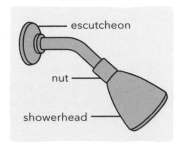

S howering lends itself to contemplation. There you are, standing in the hot water . . . fixating on the showerhead that seems stuck in time somewhere in the late 1970s, or on the trickle of water leaking out from between the head and the supply pipe. Time in the shower, in fact, is an important information-gathering period. What exactly is wrong with your showerhead?

1 *Showerhead leak.* It's usually easier to simply replace a head than search for the source of the leak. First try unscrewing the old showerhead by hand. Hold the supply pipe so that it doesn't wiggle free and then give the old head a good counterclockwise crank with your other hand. If it comes off, great. Wrap the pipe threads with Teflon tape and screw on the new head. If the old head refuses to twist, it's time for wrenches. Use strap wrenches or wrap the teeth of slip-joint pliers with electrical tape to avoid scratching the finish on the supply pipe. Grab the pipe with one set of pliers and the fixture with the other and give it a forceful twist.

2 *Joint leak.* If the joint where the showerhead meets the supply pipe is leaking, give the head another half a turn to tighten it. If it still leaks, unscrew the head completely (see above) and check for corrosion or other irregularities. Wrap the screw threads with Teflon tape and reapply the head. If that

still doesn't work, test the showerhead to see if water passes through it. Over a sink, pour water in the back of the head and see if it trickles out the front. The increased pressure caused by a partial obstruction could be causing the leak around the screw threads. Fixing an internal obstruction requires taking the head apart (see below).

3 *Interior leak.* Remove the showerhead from the supply pipe (see above). All showerheads are different, but almost all swivel, and most swivels are made watertight by a rubber O-ring. If the head is leaking, the O-ring is a good place to check first. Disassemble the showerhead—if you're worried about reassembly, take notes or pictures. On your way to the O-ring, you may find grit, grime, or other deposits. Pay special attention to the swivel ball—if there's sediment or mineral deposits, soak the ball in distilled white vinegar. Thoroughly scrub all dirty or gritty parts and look for small, embedded objects that might create channels

for the passage of water. Once you reach the O-ring or a similar gasket, inspect it for grime or imperfections. Unless it looks perfectly new, replace it. There are a number of gasket types and sizes, so make sure you match the old gasket exactly. If you've replaced the O-ring, scrubbed the showerhead until it shines, used Teflon tape on the threads, screwed it as tight as you can, and the shower still leaks, admit defeat and get a new showerhead.

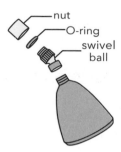

4   *Pipe leak.* In some cases, the leak might not be in the showerhead at all, and you'll need to explore farther up the pipes. Is there a visible crack in the pipe? Is the leak coming from inside the wall? If so, you'll have to go in and fix it. First check to see if the shower's supply pipe is accessible from the back,

perhaps from a closet. If not, you'll have to cut a hole in the wall. When cutting around pipes and water, consider using a hand-powered keyhole saw. The leak may be upstream, downstream, or in the middle of the elbow joint that connects the pipe running vertically up the wall to the pipe that sticks out into the shower. Once you find the leak, you'll know what section of pipe needs to be replaced. If the leak is downstream of the elbow joint, use a propane torch to heat the joint until the solder loosens and then use two pairs of pliers to pull apart the joint. Cut new copper pipe to match the removed sections and sweat the joints as described in How to Fix a Burst Pipe, page 117.

ELECTRICAL

All electrical jobs have the potential to be dangerous if done carelessly or without the right tools. For obvious reasons, DIY electrical work is the most dangerous thing you're likely to do around your house. A leaky pipe can make a wet room, but a "leaky" electrical wire can cause a fire or potential for electrocution. But it's good to have a basic understanding of how your house is wired, both for emergencies, and basic repairs. Anything electrical that is not connected to the main supply is a much safer job and is well worth knowing how to do yourself if you're careful and thorough.

ELECTRICAL REPAIR TOOL KIT

Wire nuts

Wire strippers

Voltage tester

Electrical tape

Wire strippers. Most wire strippers also include a wire cutter and end with tips that will do many of the jobs of a pair of needle-nose pliers.

Electrical tape. Insulated tape holds things together while helping the electricity stay where you want it.

Wire nuts. These are the screw-on "caps" that are used to hold two wires together. Get a range of sizes to keep in your tool kit.

Voltage tester. Even once you've turned off the electricity feeding whatever it is you're working on, you'll want to test at the source for juice. A voltage tester is a quick and easy way to confirm that what you *think* has no electricity, in fact, has no electricity.

AC/DC: An Introduction to Electricity

The genius of modern society is that any power source that can turn a turbine (and even some that can't) can be transformed into electricity. Turbines turn loops of wire within a magnetic field. As British scientist Michael Faraday showed in the 1830s, this turning action effectively pumps electrons through the wire. It is the force of these electrons that we call electricity. Typically, electricity is generated in hydroelectric, coal-fueled, wind-turbine, and other types of power stations, after which it's concentrated for long-distance delivery in what are called step-up transformers. It then travels through transmission lines to step-down stations, which then distribute the electricity to customers. Electricity enters most neighborhoods at any level up to 34,500 volts.

From there, step-down transformers (located on power poles) cut down the power to 120 or 240 volts, suitable for residential use. Here are the basics of how your residential electricity works.

AC current. You've probably heard of the electricity-producing piece in your car called an alternator. The reason for the name is that it produces alternating current, or AC, the same way that power stations do: by turning a metal coil within a magnetic field. In this configuration, the coil first pushes and then pulls electrons through the system, resulting in a current that travels both directions through conductive wire. Alternating current is the standard for power generation around the world. It's easy to transform AC to higher

(continued)

or lower voltages (using, yes, transformers), and transmission of extremely high voltages is much more efficient than transmission of lower voltages—over many miles of cable, less power is lost as heat. Early power companies realized they could concentrate AC into its efficient high-voltage form, then transmit it, then transform it back to lower voltages for use in houses and businesses.

DC current. DC stands for direct current, and as the name implies, electrons flow down a conductive wire in one direction. DC was Edison's great vision, but it doesn't fare well over long distances, quickly losing its punch. It's also hard to transform the voltage of a DC current, and so generally what is produced must be the same as what's used by a device. This makes DC well-suited to batteries—you can buy a battery with the exact voltage you need, and the juice needn't flow far before being used. DC is also used in some industrial applications and in some urban rail systems.

#59 How to Slash Your Electricity Bill

Almost everything we do at home relies on electricity. Turning on the lights requires power. So does heat in the winter and cool air in the summer. Want to turn on the coffeemaker or make a smoothie? Yep, it takes power. Any form of electricity costs money, and the most common sources also cause environmental damage. There are few things in this world as unambiguously good as saving power. Here are a couple of ways to do it.

1 Swap your bulbs. One 120-watt incandescent lightbulb left on for four hours a day costs about $50 per year in electricity. A comparable compact fluorescent bulb costs just $13 in electricity (not to mention the savings in polar bears). The United States and other countries are on the road to mandating the replacement of incandescent bulbs, but even without the power of law, there's really no reason not to. Fluorescent bulbs are a direct switch in terms of lighting quality, and with a few tweaks to your lighting design, halogen and LED lights can also add layers of light with a fraction of the cost.

2 Winterize your home. Aggressive weather stripping and additional insulation will help keep the winter outside where it belongs. Start with insulation, which works like magic to keep the house warm in winter and cool in summer. There should be at least six inches of insulation in the attic. Older homes may not have any insulation at all in walls and floors—if that's the case in your home, add it, both for energy savings and comfort. It should be easy to roll batts of insulation into any open-topped walls. Insulating closed walls is more difficult and may require a contractor's assistance. To locate drafts where air enters your house, close all windows and the fireplace flue and

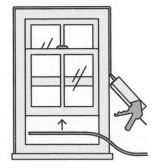

then do the candle test on page 44. When you find a leak, consider insulating, caulking, weather stripping, or otherwise plugging the draft, as appropriate. (See How to Weather-Strip Windows and Doors, page 44.) If you find a larger crack, use ozone-safe expanding foam sealant.

3 Program your thermostat in winter. Set heating to automatically lower at night and during weekdays when you're gone. Also make sure the furnace is blowing freely by replacing furnace filters and clearing dust and debris from ducts. Most homes don't have insulated heat ducts—make your home an exception and you may qualify for rebates or tax incentives. And insulate those windows! Check a window's labeled U-value to discover its efficiency. If possible, install more energy-efficient models or add drapes or heavy blinds for another layer of defense against the elements.

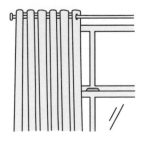

4 Reprogram your thermostat in summer. Forget about setting the thermostat low as you did in Step 3—in the summer, set it as high as you can stand. And consider alternatives to running the AC, including fans and evaporative cooling. Trees can help keep homes cool, too. Planting deciduous trees on the southwest and southeast corners of your house blocks morning and evening sun in the summer but allows the sun to warm the home in the winter.

5 Kill vampires. Most electronics continue to suck power even when they are switched off—hence the name "vampires." The power-suckers in your home might include TVs, game consoles, stereos, and microwaves. To kill these vampires, plug them into a power strip and then flip off the strip's power switch when not in use.

6 Avoid kitchen waste. Do you have a heating vent behind your refrigerator? Seems a little counterproductive, doesn't it? Likewise, keep the fridge away from that southern-facing window. If your refrigerator isn't an Energy Star model, consider replacing it (Don't forget to recycle the old one!). Also, strive to avoid oven or refrigerator overkill—a yogurt and a gallon of milk don't require a 22-cubic-foot refrigerator/freezer to keep cool, and a baked potato doesn't require an oven big enough for a Thanksgiving feast. Match your appliances to your lifestyle to avoid shelling out for unnecessary

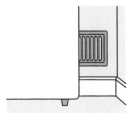

(continued)

"Vampire" energy costs the United States approximately $3 billion per year in energy costs.

heating and cooling. Just as you mastered thermostat technology, learn to properly use the dishwasher's themed cycles to avoid overkill. You don't need to wash tea cups with the same ferocity as you wash roasting pans.

7 Be laundry-savvy. Most loads of laundry will be appropriately cleaned with cold water, especially if you use detergent designed for cold-water washing. Heating the water for a load of wash costs about 20 cents. And like the dishwasher, try to run the washing machine when it's full but not overfull, to use the most efficient amount of water. In terms of power usage, though, the washer can't compete with the dryer. A dryer can use about 5,000 watts per load, for a cost of about 30 cents. If you're going to take extra steps to save electricity somewhere in the housecleaning cycle, make it with the dryer. Who doesn't love the smell and feel of clothes dried in the sun?

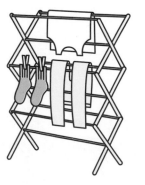

8 Wash dishes at night. Many modern dishwashers and even some clothes-washing machines have timers and delays so that you can run them long after you've gone to bed. The benefit is that energy costs are reduced at night when demand is lower, so, for example, if your dishwasher has a four-hour delay, push that button when you load your dinner dishes, and let the machine run as late at night as possible.

9 Take advantage of smart appliances. "Smart" or connected appliances are a major growth area in the home appliance industry. Whether or not your home system is connected to your smartphone—allowing you to cool, heat, light, or monitor your house via your phone or computer—a range of interconnected home appliances are increasingly available to give consumers far more remote control over running the home, and thus far more potential to save or conserve energy.

10 Take advantage of programs and incentives. Not only are your efficiency upgrades likely to pay for themselves over time in lowered utility costs, but they may even pay for themselves up front in the form of government subsidies and other incentives. Tax credits or subsidized loans are offered for replacing windows with energy-efficient models, installing a solar water heater, and insulating exterior walls (or even for buying a hybrid car). Some state programs offer additional incentives for projects like solar panel installation, and others offer tax rebates based on meter ratings for increased electrical efficiency. Visit the Database of State Incentives for Renewables and Efficiency (dsireusa.org) for information about incentives in your state.

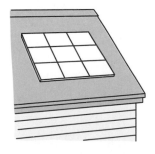

If a person yelled for 8 years, 7 months, and 6 days, they would produce enough energy to heat one cup of coffee.

#60 How to Make a DC Circuit
(or, the Basics of Circuit Soldering)

Soldering is a skill you'll use nearly anytime you do circuit work. To get started, you will first solder wires to a 9-volt battery, both demonstrating the principles of the electrical circuits that you'll be applying later when fixing lights and switches, and employing the technique of electrical soldering. You will then wire those nine volts of DC power directly into a load—it can be a small lightbulb, electric motor, buzzer, or other little electrical tchotchke. The important part is to find a tchotchke or other gizmo rated to just above nine volts—voltage should always be as close as possible to the rating without going over it.

TOOLS:

Soldering iron • Safety goggles • Wet sponge • Wire strippers

MATERIALS:

- **0.025" lead-free solder**
- **9v battery**
- **2 pieces copper electrical wire (6" each, one red and one black)**
- **Small item to power**
- **Single-pull-single-throw (SPST) switch**

SAFETY TIPS:

- **NEVER touch the heating element of the iron.**
- **Some solder contains lead. Always wash your hands after use.**
- **NEVER put the iron down on you workbench–it should remain in its stand when not in use.**

1 Check your work area to make sure it's free of potential fire hazards. Plug in the soldering iron and let it get hot. While it's heating, cut 6" lengths of red and black copper wire and then use the wire stripper to strip about ½" of the plastic sheath from both ends of both wires. As you strip the plastic, you will see that the wire tips are made of many strands. At the end of each wire, twist each cluster of bare strands together (don't twist the two wires together!).

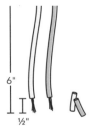

2 Don your safety goggles and wipe the tip of your hot soldering iron on a wet sponge to clean it. You should hear it sizzle. The basic idea is to use solder to connect the wire to a battery terminal and use the iron to heat the solder until it holds fast. Red wire always goes to the positive terminal on the battery and black always goes to the negative. Drip a bead of solder onto a terminal and then push the wire into it as you reheat the solder with the iron as needed. Hold the wire steady until the solder is done drying. Give the wire a gentle tug to test the joint.

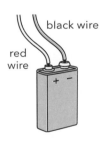

red wire
black wire

3 Use the battery and wires you soldered to make a simple DC circuit. First, solder a small single-pull-single-throw (SPST) switch to the red wire using the same soldering technique you used

(continued)

to fix the wire to the battery in Step 2. Once the switch is soldered, solder another section of stripped red wire from the switch's other terminal to one terminal of the load. Finally, solder the black wire to the load's other terminal. You should now have a completed circuit: The battery's positive terminal should be connected to the first switch terminal, the second switch terminal to the first load terminal, and the

second load terminal to the second battery terminal.

4 Use the switch to turn on the device. If it doesn't work, check your connections. If you find a loose connection, apply more solder. If it still doesn't work, try replacing the switch or load—and check that the 9v battery works!

Although electricity was discovered by the ancient Greeks when they observed that rubbing fur against amber led to a mutual attraction between the two materials, Alessandro Volta produced the first steady electrical current in 1800.

Always Turn Off the Power!

If you fail to properly turn off the water when making plumbing repairs, you will get soaked. Fail to turn off electricity when making electrical repairs, and you risk fire and severe injury. This isn't to scare you off—it should be simple to turn off the electricity to appropriate areas of the house while making repairs, and a wire without electricity running through it is harmless. Just make sure you do it right—and then double-check.

First, locate your home's circuit breaker box. Inside the box are voltage-controlled switches that automatically turn off the power if fixtures and appliances overdraw the board. In other words, rather than frying the system, the breaker box turns it off. You can also use these circuit breakers to manually shut off power to different parts of the house. The breakers should be labeled according to the areas they protect. If not, think about the things that draw electricity in your house— would it be harmful to momentarily turn any

of these things off? If it wouldn't, experiment: Flip the breakers until power goes off in the desired area of the house.

Circuit breakers are little levers that toggle between on and off, though they sometimes take a firm push to activate. If you don't have an assistant to monitor room lights for you, plug in a loud stereo or other noisy appliance in the room you are trying to power down and flip circuit breakers until you kill the sound. Next, double-check that you've turned off the correct power by testing the switch or outlet you'll be working on, flipping it on and off. Nothing should happen. For added security, use a voltage tester to ensure that the outlet is no longer live—you can buy a tester or plug in any device that you're absolutely certain works. If it doesn't work in this case, there's no power and you may proceed with repairs.

This should go without saying, but if you can't access the circuit breaker box, don't do the repair yourself—call in the experts.

#61 How to Install a Dimmer
(or, Working with Switches)

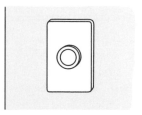

A basic on-and-off light switch doesn't allow for a whole lot of *mood*. But never fear: If your mojo needs modification, it's pretty simple to install a dimmer. In fact, the procedure you'll use here to install a dimmer is the same needed to replace most common switches.

TOOLS:

Screwdriver • Wire cutter

MATERIALS:

- Electrical tape
- Wire nuts
- Dimmer switch
- Dimmer plate

1 Turn off the power. Make sure you've killed electricity to the fixture by flipping the switch on and off—nothing should happen.

2 Remove the old switch. Most switches are covered by cosmetic switch plates. Remove the old plate; your dimmer will have its own new plate. In most light switches, wires connect at terminal screws. The terminals may be covered by a layer of electrical tape—if so, remove the tape. Loosen these screws and unhook the wires, which are most likely wrapped around the screws themselves. You may also encounter push-in terminals in which the wires

enter a hole in the switch. To loosen these wires, push a small screwdriver into the hole and then pull the wire free. If wires are permanent to the switch, it's likely the switch wires are connected to the house wires and capped with wire nuts. If needed, twist off the wire nuts and separate the wires. Because switch specifics vary, it's worth taking notes, or taking a picture of how the original switch was installed, for reference.

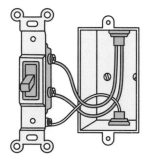

3 Check the condition of the switch box. If the wires inside the box look at all suspect, replace them (or, at this point, call an electrician to do it for you). If the box is dirty, clean it. Check that the switch box is firmly mounted to a 2 × 4 stud in your wall.

The box shouldn't wiggle—if it does, check that the mounting nails near the top and the bottom of the switch box are driven flush to the box wall. If needed, replace these nails, and if the nail holes have widened to the point of losing their friction, consider replacing them with screws. Finally, make sure that the ends of the house wires are pointing accessibly out of the box.

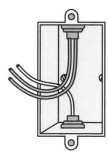

4 Prep the wires. With the old switch removed, check the condition of the wire ends, which may be weakened—look for nicks, dings, or irregular bends. Likewise, check the connections under the wire nuts, if your switch has them. You should see no copper

(continued)

sticking out from under the nuts, and the connection within the nut should resist a gentle tug. If in doubt, use a wire cutter to snip back the wires past the weak points and strip about ½" of the sheath from the new wire ends.

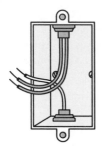

5 Install the dimmer. Look for the house wires—there should be two black wires and a ground, which is sometimes bare copper and sometimes wrapped in green. The dimmer should be fitted with wires of the same colors, and so your job is to attach like-colored wires. First, if needed, strip the sheath from about ½" of the ends of the dimmer wires and wall wires,

leaving exposed copper. Twist the exposed copper ends of the black-to-black, the second black-to-black, and then green-to-green (or bare) wires together. Cap the joints by screwing wire nuts over them and tightening until they won't turn anymore. Make sure the wire ends are tidy and not exposed and then cover the terminals with strips of electrical tape to insulate them.

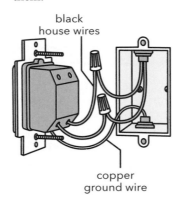

black house wires

copper ground wire

6 Attach the dimmer switch. Gently pack the wiring back into the box, making sure all joints and connections keep their

integrity as you manipulate the wires. Push the back of the dimmer into the box on top of the wires. Use screws to attach the dimmer switch to the switch box. Replace the plate, using the new plate that came with the dimmer switch.

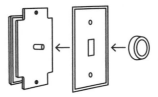

7 At the circuit breaker box, flip the one breaker that is in the "off" position back to the "on" position to resend electricity to the room. Test the dimmer switch. Enjoy the newly enhanced mood.

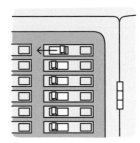

Dimmers are not only used in homes. Electric lighting technicians (ELTs) in the theater industry use dimmers for more deliberate control over stage lights. The ability to subtly influence lighting helps create different moods to complement the emotions of the actors and actresses.

#62 How to Install a Light Fixture
(or Ceiling Fan)

A bare, swinging lightbulb may be appropriate for a dramatic police interrogation, but it's probably not doing much for your living room. You'll be shocked to learn how easy it is to replace it with a chandelier. However, shocked is the last thing you want to be and so, before you go any further, make sure you turn off the electricity to the fixture (see Always Turn Off the Power!, page 144). It's tempting to simply switch off the light or fan at the wall switch, but this method could cause serious injury. Instead, go to the source: Shut off the power at the breaker box before you start and, once you can access the bare wires, use a voltage tester to double-check that they carry no power.

Ladder Up

Replacing a light fixture or ceiling fan requires significant work at ceiling level, so it's worth taking the time to ensure a stable perch. For example, using a stepladder rather than a stepstool or chair means you have handholds throughout the project and aren't simply teetering above the ground while holding on to your new, 50-pound fixture. It's likely that some debris may be sifting down from the hole in your ceiling, so either cover the area below the old fixture with a tarp or sheet, or expect to do some vacuuming when you're done.

TOOLS:

Stepladder • Tarp or sheet • Screwdriver

MATERIALS:

- **New fixture**
- **Patching plaster and paint (if needed)**

1 Evaluate the old fixture. If it's a bare bulb on a plate, all you'll need to do is unscrew it. If it's a larger fixture or fan, support the fixture as you remove it to avoid the heavy object pulling free catastrophically, ripping down wires, likely a chunk of your ceiling, and possibly taking you with it. If needed, recruit a helper with a second ladder. Notice how the old fixture is attached to the ceiling—in the case of a ceiling fan, it will likely have a central mounting nut, and maybe other screws as well. While supporting the fixture, remove these screws. Let the

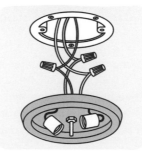

fixture drop just enough to access the wires behind it. Most fixtures will be attached to your house wiring with wire-to-wire connections capped by wire nuts. Remove the wire nuts and untwist the wires before fully removing the old lighting fixture or fan.

2 Troubleshoot the fastening location. Hopefully your old fixture included a ceiling box attached firmly to a ceiling joist or support brace (if so, skip to the next step). But if not, see "Mounting a Ceiling Box," page 148.

(continued)

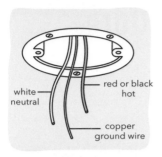

Fixture with a ceiling box

Fixture without a ceiling box

3 Attach and wire the new fixture. Heavy fixtures and fans generally come with their own mounting brackets. These brackets should attach to the ceiling box—follow the manufacturer's instructions for hanging the mounting bracket and for positioning the fixture itself. The weight of a new fixture can make attaching wiring tricky. Most fixtures allow rough attachment to the ceiling to hold their weight while you attach the wires. If not, recruit a helper to hold the fixture in place while you attach the wires. Attach like-colored wires: Twist black to black and cap with a wire nut, then do the same with white and any copper or green wires. If attaching a more technologically advanced fixture—for example, a remote fan or light control—there may be additional wires. Follow the manufacturer's instructions to properly wire these components.

4 Assemble and finish. Many fixtures will require further assembly after wiring, perhaps adding fan blades, bulbs, or shades. Assemble these parts now. You may also need to install a fixture-specific wall switch. Double-check that the power to this switch remains off and then see How to Install a Dimmer on page 145 for detailed instructions for replacing a switch.

5 Once you've completed all wiring and properly closed all junctions with wire nuts, turn the switch to the "off" position and restore power to the room and fixture by flipping the appropriate circuit breaker back to the "on" position. Switch the fixture on to test it. If needed, patch and paint the ceiling or wall.

Mounting a Ceiling Box

Murphy's Law holds that a fixture without a ceiling box is floating on drywall. To comply with building codes, your new fixture needs to mount to a junction box (a container for electrical wires and cables), and if the fixture is more than about 30 pounds—especially with ceiling fans that tend to wobble a bit against their mount—it's best to mount to wood instead of drywall. First, take a look at the joists. Use a stud finder or other sleuthing tool (see What a Stud!, page 7) to discover the location of the ceiling joists. If a joist exists

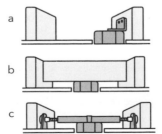

at the desired hanging location, great—use a keyhole saw or jigsaw to cut a hole in the ceiling the size of the new junction box. Discover where the wires that fed the old fixture pass nearest the joist and feed them into the box. Then screw the box into the ceiling joist (figure A).

If there's no ceiling joist at the desired hanging location, you may need to add a brace between joists to which you can mount the junction box. If you can access the ceiling through an attic, do so. Nail a 2 × 4 between ceiling joists, flush to the ceiling drywall (figure B). If you can't access the joists from the top, you can feed an expandable metal brace (figure C) up through the hole left by the removed fixture. Any of these options—

attaching a new junction box and fixture to a joist, wooden brace, or expandable metal brace—would be preferable to hanging a heavy light fixture or ceiling fan in drywall alone.

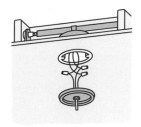

Problems in the Breaker Box

Former Soviet leader Boris Yeltsin once noted that, like air, you don't notice freedom until it's gone. For the most part, the same is true of electricity. You flip a switch and you expect light. You push a button on the blender and you expect blending. You open the fridge and you expect it to be chilly. If a circuit breaker goes bad in your breaker box, however, you will have an immediate appreciation for electricity. Hopefully that appreciation isn't accompanied by absolute darkness, an unblended smoothie or spoiled food. If the problem is in fact just a bad circuit breaker or a blown fuse, and you have a replacement on hand (always keep replacements on hand!), the problem will take only a couple of minutes to fix. But it might be more complicated—if so, here's how to diagnose the problem and get the electricity flowing again.

Evaluating the breaker. Be very careful: If a circuit breaker is tripping continuously, the breaker is likely doing its job properly and tripping in the presence of a constant problem like a short or an overload. When a breaker trips and seems unable to reset, first make sure you're resetting it properly. Force the handle firmly to the "off" position and then firmly to the "on" position. If the breaker won't stay on, observe what happens as it trips—do you hear a hum or buzz as it pops? If so, the breaker

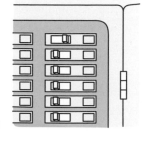

is likely good, closing the circuit in the presence of a problem. Use a screwdriver to remove a wire from the breaker and see if it now stays in the on position. Without the possibility of current, the breaker should stay on. If it doesn't, replace the breaker. If a different breaker functions where the first did not, it's a good bet the problem was a bad breaker. The opposite may also be true: A breaker may appear stuck in the "on" position, despite appliances in the relevant room remaining without power. Again, switch the breaker for a new one.

Diagnosing a short. If a breaker that constantly trips turns out to be functioning properly, or if you replace it and the problem continues, you'll have to look for the source of the problem. Hopefully the problem is a simple overload. Try unplugging appliances from the affected room to decrease the load. If you decrease the load and the circuit breaker stays on, experiment with the combination

(continued)

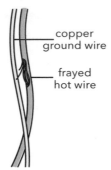

copper
ground wire

frayed
hot wire

of appliances, electronics, fixtures, etc., to see if any particular component is drawing an overly large load. If so, move or replace that component to avoid overloading the circuit.

If reducing the load doesn't do the trick, you may have a more serious problem—a short circuit commonly occurs when exposed wires touch, either a hot wire to another hot, or to a neutral wire or a ground. A short circuit lets electricity bypass anything that offers resistance—an appliance or other electrical component—and allows the circuit to draw infinite amperage. This is bad—wires asked to carry an overly large load can melt through their coatings and start fires. That's the reason for a circuit breaker in the first place. But finding the exact location of the short can be tricky. The most important question is whether the problem is in your walls or in a device or appliance. Try unplugging appliances and flipping switches each in turn to narrow

in on the source of the problem—if the short is in the interior of an appliance, it's almost certainly a goner. Next, check junction boxes, fixtures, switches, or outlets where the wires connect to other wires or terminals and look for imperfections, including bare wire or wire protruding from beneath tape or wire nuts. Consider, too, that the problem may have occurred when you smacked a big nail into the wall—it's possible to drive a nail into a bundle of wires, creating an accidental connection through the nail. Find the problem spike. If your searching has yielded no results, it is time to call an electrician.

Replacing fuses. If you need to replace a fuse, turn off the main power (not just a single breaker) in the circuit breaker box. This is important! Remove the faceplate from the box; typically you'll have to remove a few screws that hold the face in place. Each breaker should have two wires connected to it, one bringing electricity into the breaker and one leading out. Loosen the screws that hold these wires and bend the wires out of the way. The circuit breaker itself should now pop from its slot with finger power or with the use of a screwdriver to pry the breaker loose. Pop the new breaker into place and connect the wires to their appropriate terminals. Screw the faceplate onto the breaker box and restart the power.

Four Rules for Safety in Electrical Repairs

Much of the safety information listed here is common sense, but it's worth repeating—when it comes to electricity, it's better to be safe than sorry. (And always keep in mind that sometimes the safest thing to do is to call a professional.)

Turn off the mains and/or unplug the item. Yes, the most obvious starting point, but don't get so interested in what you're doing ("Hey, I know how to fix that!") that you forget the

most basic safety rule when making electrical or electronic repairs.

Take off metal jewelry and wear rubber gloves. Accidentally brushing a ring or watch against a metal circuit may cause an unpleasant shock while you're working. Slip off any jewelry, and you might consider wearing rubber work gloves if possible, since rubber is an excellent insulator against electricity.

Be sure everything is totally dry. Don't stand on a damp basement floor while you work. Be sure your hands are completely dry. Don't have on a damp shirt, cuffs or sleeves, either from sweat or rain or anything else. Electricity and damp combined are a serious safety hazard.

Don't close the circuit. If it's at all practical, work with one hand to prevent possibly making yourself part of an electrical circuit.

✕ ✕

Types of Fuses

Before you remove a broken circuit breaker ("fuse"), you'll want a replacement on hand. The most common breakers in your box take a single slot and are rated to either 15 or 20 amps—when the amperage exceeds these amounts, the breaker trips. Generally, these single breakers are 1 inch wide. The other common breaker in your box is a double-pole breaker, which looks like two single breakers hooked together with a bar. Single breakers typically monitor the power to a room or area of the house. Double-pole breakers typically monitor the power supply to large appliances, like clothes dryers or water heaters. When in

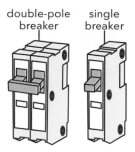

double-pole breaker / single breaker

doubt, bring a busted breaker with you to the hardware store to ensure a proper match. It's best to replace a breaker with one of identical amperage from the manufacturer of the breaker box. ✕

Next time your fuse blows, thank it for its sacrifice in its sleepless quest for fire safety: A fuse blows when too much electricity passes through the circuit. The flow of electricity is interrupted by the breaker so that the sudden energy surge does not overheat the circuit and possibly cause a fire.

#63 How to Rewire a Lamp

Whether it's a new-to-you lamp that's actually very old or a lamp you love whose wires have frayed, learning to rewire a lamp is an easy way to give your decor new life. First, evaluate the wiring: Check the sheathing for cracks or exposed wire. Check the switch and the plug prongs—they should be strong and free of rust. Any fails on this list and you'll need to get a new cord in addition to new wiring.

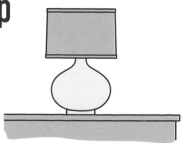

(continued)

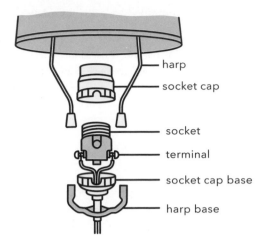

harp
socket cap

socket
terminal
socket cap base
harp base

TOOLS:

Wire cutter • Screwdriver

MATERIALS:

- **Electrical cord and two-pronged plug**
- **Two-way switch and/or socket (if needed)**

1 Buy new wiring. If the lamp is easy enough to transport, take it with you to the hardware store to shop for wiring, or bring along a photo that includes the lamp's old wiring. Most modern appliances use a flat electrical cord, and for a lamp, a two-pronged plug is adequate. You will need enough cord to run from the desired wall outlet up through the entire height of your lamp. You may want to add a switch along the length of the cord, or perhaps swap out the existing switch on the lamp. Evaluate the

integrity of the lamp's socket, socket cap, and terminals, too, replacing anything if it is at all in doubt.

2 Disassemble the lamp. First, make sure it's unplugged. The base of a modern floor lamp is almost certainly held together by a nut that attaches to a tube. The cord runs inside this tube. Beyond that generality, you'll have to explore your lamp to learn its specifics. Old lamps may run the cord along the outside directly to the socket, and handmade lamps may have no base at all or run the cord in an unexpected way. In any case, note how the old cord enters the lamp and its path through or along the lamp body. Remove the shade and, if one exists, the top of the wire harp that supports it. In one piece, unscrew the socket and its cap, and remove the wire harp base, if applicable. Use a wire cutter to cut the plug

from the old wire. Use the socket still connected to the cord to pull a length of slack cord up through the system—but don't pull it completely through yet!

3 Thread the wire. Once you've cut off the old plug, attach the new wire to the bottom end of the old wire with a wire cap and then pull the socket from above to thread the new wire up through the lamp. If the lamp includes a built-in switch, you'll need to run wire to the switch and then again from the switch to the socket terminals. In that case, attach new wire to the switch and run the wire along the path of the old wire so you end with new wire poking out the top of the lamp.

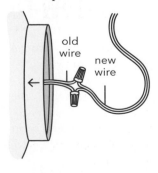

old wire

new wire

4 Knot the wire. Slide the harp base (if used) and socket cap base over the new wire. Cut between the wires to separate about 3" of the end of the two-threaded wire. Strip about ½" of insulation from each end. Because you don't want the weight of the wire pulling down against the connections, tie a knot in the wires that will be supported by the socket cap—this is called an underwriter's knot. Make a loop in each wire and then pass the end of each opposite strand through each loop. You should end with a high-profile knot that won't pull through the base of the socket cap.

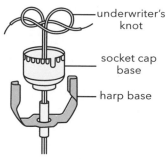

underwriter's knot

socket cap base

harp base

5 Wire the socket. The hot wire is encased in the smooth sheath, and the neutral wire is encased in ridged sheath. The socket itself will have a brass terminal for the hot wire and a silver terminal for the neutral wire. Loosen the terminal screws and wrap the stripped lengths of wire around the appropriate terminals so the insulation is fairly flush with the terminals and very little if any exposed copper wire is visible. Tighten the screws to hold the wire in place (if additional stripped wire bulges from beneath screw terminals, shorten the stripped wire and reattach it). Slip the socket down into the socket cap and screw or otherwise seat the wire sandwich down into the lamp.

6 Attach a plug and switch. Most simple electrical cord switches include a removable cover that hides in and out terminals—the only tricky part is keeping track of the smooth and ridged sides of the cord, to ensure that you match the hot in with the hot out, and the neutral in with the neutral out (the kind of wire that went in should be the same as the wire that comes out). Once you have carefully matched the wires, wrap them around the screws on the correct terminals as determined by the way the switch is made. Plugs also include a removable cover—for two-pronged plugs, try

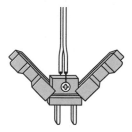

squeezing the prongs together to release the core from the cover. Inside the core are two screws: again, brass for hot and silver for neutral. Hook the appropriate wire over the appropriate screw, turn to tighten, and replace the cap.

7 Put the lamp back together. Ensure that all connections are secure and all protective caps and covers are reinstalled. Completely reassemble the lamp, including the base, bulb, and any other pieces removed during rewiring. Turn the switch to the "off" position and then plug in the lamp. Flip the switch to test.

Lighting a Room Like a Pro

In Hollywood, a lighting director is no minor job, because good lighting can help make someone a star. And while you may not intend to star in your own personal show every time you walk in the living room, properly lighting a room takes more skill than screwing in a bulb and flipping the switch. There are many types of lights and bulbs, each with its own best use. Combine these resources to create lighting that makes you feel good when you walk in the room:

Ambient lighting. A room's ambient light source is the base around which you'll build additional lighting. In the daytime, ambient lighting may come

from sunlight. In the absence of sunlight, a room's ambient light is typically provided by ceiling or wall-mounted fixtures like a central chandelier or track lighting.

Task lighting. As the name implies, task lighting is placed to aid specific activities in various areas of the house. For example, you might place a lamp near the couch for reading or over-counter lighting for preparing food. Where ambient lighting keeps you from tripping over things, task lighting highlights the things you really need to see.

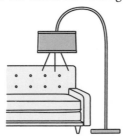

Accent lighting. Do you want to make sure visitors notice the Picasso sketch you've placed in a glass case? Use accent lighting to call attention to it. As a rule of thumb, the lights you use to accent your home's best features should be three times

as bright as the surrounding ambient and task lighting. To accomplish this ratio, use brighter bulbs, use more bulbs, or focus a bulb's light on areas to be highlighted.

Types of bulbs. Most lighting designers recommend staying away from fluorescent tubes because they cast a slightly pale glow that makes skin look sickly. That said, the best type of bulb depends on the function of a room—fluorescent

tubes may be just fine for the basement or garage (as long as you can avoid hitting them with a ladder). Incandescent bulbs are the historical standby—however, these inefficient bulbs are on the outs—they're banned in some states—for environmental reasons. Halogen bulbs, compact fluorescent lightbulbs (CFLs), and light-emitting diodes (LEDs) are primarily replacing these electricity suckers.

Halogen bulbs are common and relatively inexpensive when you consider their increased efficiency and lifespan compared to incandescent bulbs. They do require that you take a couple of precautions—touching the glass during installation can leave a film of oil that shortens the life of the bulb, and because they reach temperatures of 300 degrees Fahrenheit, take care not to touch the bulb when lit or to install a halogen bulb near flammable materials. Fluorescent bulbs burn nearly without heat and are extremely efficient. CFLs are becoming the standard replacement for incandescent bulbs, although they may not be available in all sizes and wattages. On the plus side, CFLs can last about 10,000 hours. Most lighting designers consider LED an up-and-coming technology—it's extremely efficient but currently doesn't pack the punch of lumens offered by other kinds of bulbs. Consider LEDs for lighting very small, defined areas, but leave the heavy lifting to halogens and CFLs.

Room-specific lighting. Again, your lighting design must match the function of the room. The kitchen is a functional place—light it accordingly, with task lights pointed at the various prepping and cooking areas, and of course the sink. Because the focus of a dining room is almost always the table, this is a good room for a strong centralized light source, such as a chandelier. The opposite is true of a study or home office—a strong overhead light should be replaced by task lights pointed at reading and work spaces. Bedrooms are similar to studies—install reading lights by the bed and desk, perhaps a floor lamp for dressing, and consider an overhead light with a dimmer for ambient use. For your primary bathroom,

you'll likely want an especially bright light by the mirror. For guest bathrooms, consider the softer touch of sconces with dimmers.

The living room is where your creative lighting sense should shine. In the living room, more so than anywhere else in the house, lighting is part of the decor. Think of lighting in layers—rather than a single overly bright source, incorporate a range of fixtures, including table and floor lamps and recessed or track lighting. Use accent lighting to draw attention to the room's best features, be they architectural aspects or design elements, like art or plants. Consider not only the types of fixtures and bulbs and the directions in which they point, but also how you can diffuse the light with shades. A lamp can go from being a harsh eyesore to warmly glowing with the addition of an elegant shade.

✕ ✕

Which Fixture Where?

Figure that you need 200 watts for every 50 square feet of a room, then divide those 200 watts among a few styles of lighting fixtures.

• **Chandeliers** are commonly used as a source of ambient light in dining rooms, but can be fitted with down-pointing sockets for task lighting or a dimmer for bedroom use.

• **Pendants** hang from the ceiling and—with a shade and dimmer—provide ambient light or, if more focused, provide task lighting.

• **Track or rail lighting** provides design flexibility and the ability to point small, individual lights as needed for accenting features or specific areas of a room.

• **Recessed lighting** adds brightness without being visible and is a subtle choice that can be used for ambient, accent, or task lighting.

• **Wall sconces** connect to our torch-lit, castle-dwelling pasts and can liven a dead wall or hallway, or even be paired with a headboard for bedtime reading. ✕

Pendant lighting

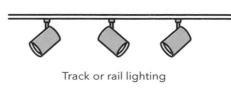

Track or rail lighting

Recessed lighting

Wall sconces

Holiday Lights 101

At the end of the year, when the days darken early, there's nothing more festive than some holiday lights. And there are few things more frustrating than putting up a string of good, solid, expensive lights that you've used successfully the last several seasons . . . and finding that they won't turn on. Or the red ones are burnt out, or only half the string will light up.

If you're using super-cheap lights that you grabbed from a bargain bin at the front of a big-box store, well, they may not be fixable and may simply have to be replaced. But those cheapie lights that break with ease tend to be shorter strings of lights. You may have invested a fair amount in the longer strings of lights that you use to decorate the Christmas tree or hang along the eaves of your front porch, and those lights are worth a little effort. With some care and attention, you can get the festive lights back on and earn your cup of eggnog as you sit back and survey the scene.

Change the fuses. Longer strings of lights often have a fuse in the plug. If the plug is big, or has a box slightly up the string from it, your string most likely has fuses. With the string unplugged, slide back the plastic plate on the surface (there may be a small

To create the first functional lightbulb, Thomas Edison used a strip of paper coated in carbon, attached it to a battery with wire, and put it inside a vacuum-sealed glass globe.

screw holding it in place—don't lose it!) and replace the one or two fuses you find inside. These are usually simple small fuses, and some spares may have come with your lights. Otherwise, replacement fuses are easily found where holiday lights are sold. If this doesn't get your bulbs blinking . . .

Test all the bulbs. This sounds like an onerous job, but the testers for holiday lights (probably sold right next to those replacement fuses) are inexpensive and easy to use. Read the packaging and try to buy the kind that only requires you to touch the bulb, not remove each bulb from its socket. As you work, tighten each bulb. Make sure none are loose or partially disconnected. You may have a loose bulb rather than a blown one, and you don't want to pass the whole string of lights through your hands a

second time if you don't find one that's burnt out.

Continue to the end. If you do come across a blown bulb, stop and replace it, but don't lose your spot on the string. There could be additional burnt-out lights farther along, and any one of them could be blocking your holiday cheer. Continue testing to the end of the line, replacing as necessary, and including any additional strings you may have plugged together on the entire chain of lights.

Don't let it happen next year. If the lights came in the sort of packaging where every individual light has a slot, it's probably worth the time to pack them away with care to prevent them loosening in their sockets or breaking. If you don't have the original package, try wrapping them gently, not tightly, around a sturdy piece of cardboard to prevent them from flapping around and the bulbs banging off one another during those ten months when the lights are stored in the garage. Do not wrap your light strings in a loop around your forearm, like a rock band roadie might wrap an extension cord. That's just asking for them to break. Instead, coil them loosely and store them in a box, perhaps in a bed of all that crumpled tissue paper left over from your holiday unwrapping spree.

MECHANICAL

E ven if you think you're not a mechanic, you'll likely face an issue with one or all of your modes of transportation, whether that be bicycle, car, or motorcycle. Luckily, there are a lot of repair jobs that can be accomplished with only a few basic tools. Some auto repairs are so simple that there's absolutely no reason to take your car to a garage—other than your own!—to fix it. And anyone who rides a bike should be able to repair a flat. With these tools on hand, you can.

GARAGE TOOL KIT

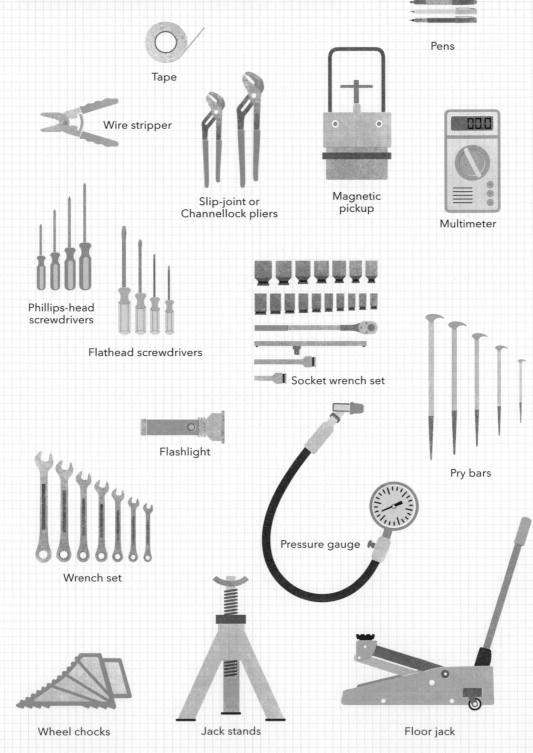

Pens

Tape

Wire stripper

Slip-joint or
Channellock pliers

Magnetic
pickup

Multimeter

Phillips-head
screwdrivers

Flathead screwdrivers

Socket wrench set

Pry bars

Flashlight

Wrench set

Pressure gauge

Wheel chocks

Jack stands

Floor jack

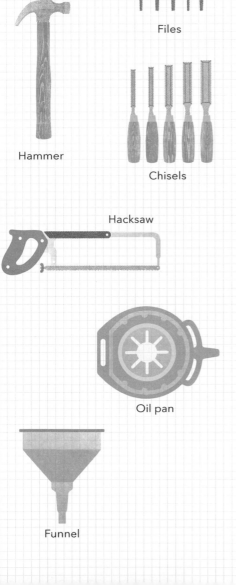

Wire brush

Rags

Set of punches

Files

Hammer

Chisels

Hacksaw

Oil pan

Funnel

Garage Tools

The crux of auto work is diagnosing the problem and having the right tool to fix it. As you'll discover, almost all car work can be done with just a handful of tool types. Here are the essential tools to keep in the garage.

Screwdriver set. Yes, most Phillips-head screwdrivers will fit most cross-head screws (+) and most flathead screwdrivers will fit most slot screws (–), but matching size as well as shape can help ensure a clean turn without stripping the head or dulling the driver. Because auto work might require turning screws in tough-to-reach places, make sure at least one of each type of screwdriver is magnetic so that you can work one-handed without having to hold the screw in place. In addition to a set of standard screwdrivers that includes a range of diameters and lengths, consider adding a set of hex drivers, commonly called Allen wrenches, which you'll need to turn bolts with hexagonal holes in their heads.

Socket wrench set. It used to be that Japanese and European cars used exclusively metric nuts and bolts, whereas American cars used inches. Now parts are sourced from everywhere and you'll need a socket wrench set for each system of measurement. It's worth making a precise match. Also look for a set with a couple of wrench extensions, which can increase your torque for pulling on an especially sticky or welded nut or improve your precision when working in tight spaces. And add a DIY cheater pipe: a length of spare, hollow pipe that you slip around a ratchet to increase your torque. A socket wrench set that comes with a spark plug socket is a bonus.

Wrench set. You already have a socket wrench set, but there's nothing like just the right wrench to reach tight spots. Like your sockets, you'll

(continued)

want wrenches from about 8 to 22 millimeters or ¼ to ⅞ inch. It's useful to buy wrenches that are open on one side and "box" on the other, allowing you to slot the box side completely over a bolt or slip the open end around a bolt if it's tough to get at. Augment with a couple of sizes of adjustable wrenches: 8- and 12-inch wrenches are a good place to start. These adjustables aren't nearly as good for aggressive tightening or loosening, but there's nothing like the ability to adjust by a millimeter or two instead of sliding all the way out from under your car to retrieve the next size fixed wrench. You'll also want a specialized oil filter wrench, a lug wrench sized to your tires (to be kept in the trunk of your cars), and maybe a torque wrench, used to tighten bolts to a specific pressure.

Pliers. You can never have too many pliers, and you'd be sorry to be caught without at least the basics of large and small sizes of slip-joint pliers (the kind with the sliding adjustment groove): Channellock (the eponymous tongue-and-groove slip-lock plier), needle-nose, and large and small locking wrenches, like a 7-inch Vise-Grip. You can't use Vise-Grip pliers in place of a socket or box wrench, but they're darn useful for grabbing things that don't otherwise want to be grabbed, like rounded nuts and headless screws.

Hammer. Most automotive work is best done with a ball-peen hammer—the one with a flat face on one side and a curved head on the other. (In the garage, use pry bars for prying, not a hammer's claw.) You'll want a couple of hammer weights, ranging from 8 ounces on the tiny side to 32 ounces on the huge side. If you're working with older cars or imagine needing to do extensive work, add a small sledge, which you can use to knock rusty bits that need extra oomph.

Floor jack, jack stands, wheel chocks. Much of the garage work on your car will take place underneath it, so you'll need tools to raise it safely. The basic process is to pull the emergency brake, use wheel chocks to ensure that the car can't roll forward or backward, use a floor jack to raise the car off the ground, and use jack stands to keep it up. First, the floor jack: A 2-ton floor jack might be more than your car needs, but it should run only about $10 more than a 1.5-ton jack and even with smaller cars is easier to use, requiring less power and fewer strokes to raise the car. Start with two adjustable-height floor jacks. (No matter what kind you get, make sure the jack weight capacity exceeds the weight of your car.) And wheel chocks work better than bricks—by placing these curved wheel-stoppers against tires that aren't jacked up, you can help ensure that your car doesn't slide off the jacks and on to you.

Miscellaneous tools. Pressure gauge, magnetic pickup tool, multimeter (to test voltage, resistance, and amperage), punches, chisels, files, pens, tape, pry bars of various sizes, wire stripper, wire brush, oil pan, funnel, hacksaw, rags, and a couple of good flashlights (because one will inevitably be broken . . .).

TRUNK TOOL KIT

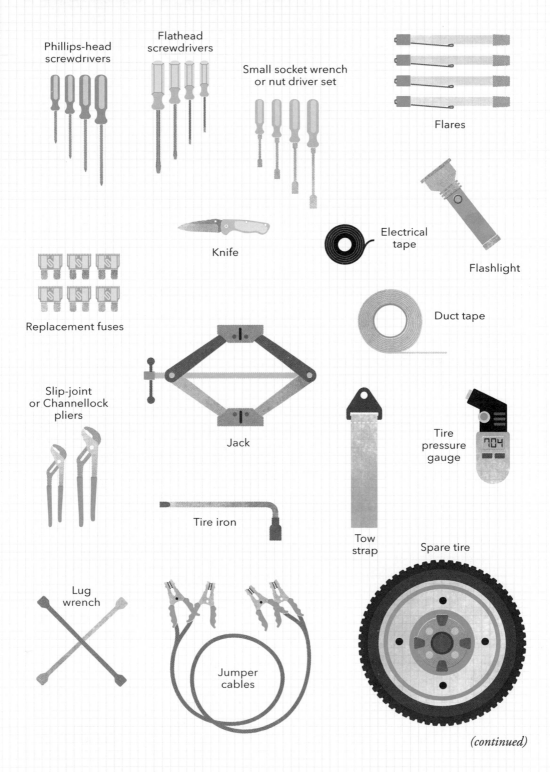

Phillips-head screwdrivers

Flathead screwdrivers

Small socket wrench or nut driver set

Flares

Knife

Electrical tape

Flashlight

Replacement fuses

Duct tape

Slip-joint or Channellock pliers

Jack

Tire pressure gauge

Tire iron

Tow strap

Spare tire

Lug wrench

Jumper cables

(continued)

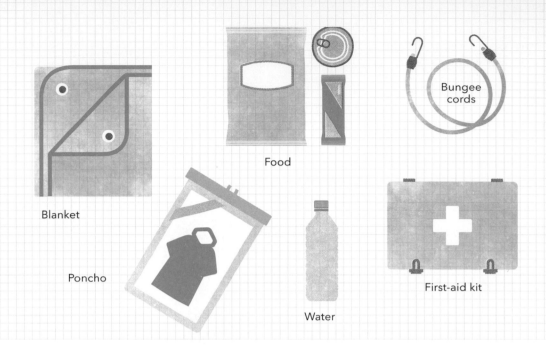

Blanket

Food

Bungee cords

Poncho

Water

First-aid kit

First-aid kits came into being in the late 19th century—a time when doctors would have been summoned on foot. Precious minutes or even hours could be lost before an injured person received treatment.

Here's what to keep in your trunk for emergency repairs on the road. As with a first-aid kit, the goal here is to be able to patch everything up just enough to get to better care.

You should carry much more than tools in your car's emergency kit, including but not limited to flares, water, food, a blanket, poncho, first-aid kit, and flashlight. These things keep you safe while you're futzing with the tools on this list in the attempt to get back on the road. Basically, you should carry a pared-down version of your garage kit and a couple of other items specific to emergency repairs. You can buy these kits ready-made or piece together your own. Here are the components of a strong roadside repair kit: large and small Phillips and flathead screwdrivers, slip-joint pliers, tire pressure gauge, electrical tape, duct tape, small (10-piece) socket wrench or nut driver set, replacement fuses, jumper cables, 2-ton tow

strap, basic pocket knife, and bungee cords. Of course, you should also have tire-changing equipment in the trunk, including a jack, lug wrench (aka tire iron), and spare tire.

Engines, gears, and moving parts. These sound complicated, and they are. In this section, and especially when working with cars and motorcycles (as opposed to bicycles), there's a hair trigger on giving up and taking it to the experts. That said, there are absolutely things you can do at home without fancy lifts and expensive pneumatic tools. Some of these things are faster and easier than scheduling an appointment at the garage and figuring out how you're going to get around without a car for the day.

Life-saving stuff. Poncho, blanket, water, food (such as sealed energy bars), flares, a knife, and a first-aid kit are things that automobile drivers would really prefer never to use as they journey safely from Point A to Point B. But if you ever needed those items—and plenty of drivers have—you'd be very glad to have such a well-stocked trunk.

Tire changing tools. Make sure your spare always has air, and don't take the lug wrench out and forget to put it back. The jack never leaves the trunk, either, unless you're using it on the car.

Quick-fix stuff. A bungee cord, duct and electrical tape, pliers, socket and screwdriver sets, a tire pressure gauge, and jumper cables can all get you out of a tight spot in a hurry.

Tow strap. When all else fails. If you have a tow strap, someone can get your vehicle to help. Or you can tow someone else to help.

#64 How to Wash a Car

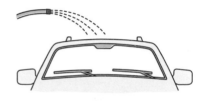

It takes some elbow grease, and attention to detail, to get a gleaming, spotless car (just ask the people down at the car wash). But it's an easy car maintenance task to DIY, and on a warm summer day, it's even kind of fun. Don't use kitchen soap—it may strip your car's wax. Instead, use soap specially designed for cars.

TOOLS:

Rags • 2 buckets • Garden hose • Large sponge or wash mitt • Long-bristled brush and short, stiff-bristled brush (optional)

MATERIALS:

• Car wash soap
• Car wax
• Glass cleaner

1 Park the car in the shade. If you leave a very wet car in the sun, it will get spots similar to those on an improperly washed wineglass. You will need to be parked within reaching distance of a garden hose. And don't forget to close the windows! When your car is situated, mix the car wash soap in a bucket as instructed on the wash bottle. Fill another bucket with plain water.

2 Hose down the car. Rinse it clean of major debris. Stay away from high-pressure jets of water, which can drive grit across the car's finish, potentially scratching it. Likewise, angle the spray

down near the windows, as water pressure can blast through loose window molding and leak into the car.

3 Soap the car. Pull the windshield wipers up and then scrub the car with soapy water, using a large sponge or wash mitt. Start at the top and spiral your way down, soaping up one small

(continued)

area at a time. This is like sweeping your house from the corners first—starting at the top ensures that dirt rains down and away from cleaned areas. When the sponge or mitt looks gray, rinse it in the bucket of plain water (don't squeeze it into the soapy water). Once you've scrubbed an area of the car from top to bottom, rinse it with the hose before going on to the next section. Don't let the soap dry on any area, and periodically spray the entire car with the hose to keep it from drying (again, to prevent the spotty wineglass effect).

4 Clean the wheels and lower panels. Use an old wash mitt or sponge to scrub the lowest parts of the car last. These are the grimiest parts of the car and there's no need to sully a good sponge with the worst of the dirt. You might consider using a long-bristled

brush to clean the hubcap spokes, then a short, stiff-bristled brush to clean the tires' sidewalls.

5 Rinse again. Once more, rinse the car from the top down, spraying underneath to loosen road grime. This is especially important in the winter to make sure salt deposits from icy or snowy roads don't eat away at your undercarriage.

6 Before the water has time to evaporate, use towels to dry the car thoroughly, again from the top down. Use Windex or another glass cleaning product on the windows to avoid streaking. If you want to apply wax, now is the time. (See Wax On, Wax Off, for details.)

✕ ✕ ✕ ✕ ✕ ✕ ✕ ✕ ✕ ✕ ✕ ✕

Wax On, Wax Off

Wax should be applied with your right hand in clockwise strokes and removed with your left hand in counterclockwise strokes—that is, if you're Ralph Macchio in *The Karate Kid*. For the rest of us, the exact strokes don't matter so much, as long as you use a clean, soft, lint-free cloth. A liquid or soft wax is fine for most washings. If it's been a while, consider a hard or paste wax, which will protect your car longer but will also be more difficult to apply and remove. For the most durable care, go with a polymer preservative. With a soft or liquid wax, apply to the whole car according to the package instructions and then use a lint-free cloth to polish the car clean. With a hard wax, apply to only a small section at a time and then polish clean before the wax sets into an impenetrable veneer. ✕

No time to wash? Live in a drought zone? Using glass cleaner to wipe down windows and windshields can make a **big difference in appearance and water conservation.**

#65 How to Detail the Interior of a Car

C leaning your car is like cleaning your house—it's all about work flow. There's a certain order of doing things when detailing a car, mostly to avoid dirtying surfaces you've already cleaned. Also, as with housecleaning, standardizing the way you clean your car assures that you don't miss any hard-to-reach or hard-to-remember spots. Follow these instructions from start to finish and your car will shine inside.

TOOLS:

Vacuum cleaner • Rags

MATERIALS:

- **Foaming car upholstery cleaner**
- **Compressed air**
- **Cotton swabs**
- **Glass cleaner**
- **Surface cleaner**

1 Clean the floor mats. Remove all mats, front and back, and beat them free of debris. A heavy shoe works well, or a broom handle. Outside the car, coat the floor mats with a foaming cleaner designed for car upholstery. Work the cleaner into the mats with a rag and continue adding cleaner until the mats are saturated. Let them sit while you work on the rest of the interior. When they're dry, vacuum them and put them back into the floorboards.

2 Vacuum the interior. Use a coin-operated car-wash vacuum, a wet-dry vacuum, or, as a last resort, your household vacuum to clean the car's upholstery. Use the smallest nozzle attachment to vacuum hard-to-reach places like the insides of door panel pockets, around the gearshift, and along the front dash and rear window ledge. Push the front seats all the way forward and then vacuum behind and underneath them. Push the seats all the way backward and vacuum underneath from the front. Don't forget the trunk and in between the backseats, where crumbs tend to accumulate.

3 Shampoo the upholstery. Use the foaming cleaner on the interior, this time stopping short of saturating it so you don't get mildew. If you have a vinyl or leather interior be sure to use a cleaner specific to the material (not foaming upholstery cleaner!).

Quick Fix for Upholstery Holes

If you have a small hole or stain in your car's upholstery, consider using a razor blade to cut a patch just bigger than the unsightly hole from an unseen area, like the underside of a seat. Then use the razor blade to clean the edges of the hole or cut around the stain. Use a small amount of epoxy or other water-resistant adhesive to carefully glue the patch in place. Holes in vinyl or leather upholstery can be patched with kits made for those materials. ✕

(continued)

4 Clean the nooks and crannies. Use a can of compressed air to blow dirt, dust, and grime from crevices and areas around buttons and dials. Use cotton swabs to clean air vents.

5 Wipe down interior surfaces like the dashboard, parking brake, plastic interior panels, console, and steering wheel with an interior cleaner.

6 Clean the glass. Use a glass cleaner (such as Windex) and a lint-free rag or paper towels to clean the insides of all windows, as well as the rearview and vanity mirrors.

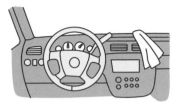

Ray Harroun won the 1911 Indianapolis 500 after he attached a mirror to see behind his car instead of using a lookout (a crewman positioned to watch competing cars). It was thus that the rearview mirror was born.

✕ ✕

For Brighter Headlights . . .

The difference between hazy and clear headlights can be the difference between seeing and not seeing the deer in the road ahead of you. If your lights are looking dim, it might be time to polish the headlight covers. After you've washed your car, cover the area around your headlights with painter's tape and use a drill-mounted polisher and plastic polish to de-haze the plastic covers. (If they're really dirty, consider removing the covers and cleaning the inside as well.) One common drill-mounted polishing tool is called Mothers PowerBall, which can be found at most auto supply stores. ✕

#66 How to Bang Out a Dent

B odywork used to be easy—you got a dent? Just bang it out. However, banging on a plastic or fiberglass body panel is likely to do nothing but make the dent worse or even punch through the panel. So basic auto bodywork depends in large part on what your car's made of—find out the material of your panels before going any further.

If your car's panels are made of metal, which is pliable, you can bend small dents back into shape. Either an indentation will pop back to its convex form, or you can rework the shape of the metal. If you have plastic panels, duct tape your dents together as best you can and head for the nearest auto body shop. If you are feeling ambitious, consider ordering and installing your own replacement plastic panels from the dealer. Many plastic panels on modern cars simply click into place.

TOOLS:

Auto body or planishing hammer • Wheel chocks • Metal dolly

1 Level the dent. Starting on the outside of the panel, use an auto body hammer to lightly pound the ridge of raised metal around the dent. You don't need to flatten it completely, but do your best to return this ridge to the level of the surrounding panel. Be aware that this will likely hurt the paint, and so if you're reworking a dent, you might also have to repaint.

2 Hammer the back of the dent. With the car on a flat surface, in gear or in park, block the tires with wheel chocks and put the parking brake on. Reach under the wheel well to access the back of the dent. You may be able to access a dent in the front fenders by raising the hood or in the back fender by opening the trunk and removing panels. If you hammer straight into the back of a dent, you will almost certainly end up punching through the metal. Instead, reach around to the front of the dent and hold a metal dolly (which looks like a metal bar of soap) against the outside of the dent while you hammer against the inside. If your arms aren't long enough to reach both sides of the dent, you'll need a helper to hold the dolly while you hammer. Hammer the dent, from the front and back if necessary, braced against the dolly, until it smooths out.

✕ ✕

Sanding a Scratch

If you see a scratch in your car's paint, make sure that it isn't just something stuck to the outside of the panel—run your fingernail over the mark to see if it has depth. If your fingernail doesn't catch on the scratch, that means you have a scratch in your car's clear coat that doesn't extend down through the paint. Instead of filling the scratch, you can simply hide it by sanding down the surrounding finish to the level of the base of the scratch. Start by rubbing something into the scratch that contrasts with the car's paint color—shoe polish or Wite-Out works well. Now you'll gently sand the scratched area with very fine, 2,000-grit wet sandpaper until the shoe polish or other material disappears, at which point you'll know you've reached the base of the scratch. While sanding, pour ample water over the scratched area. Polish with rubbing compound and then finish with wax. ✕

#67 How to Fill a Ding or Scratch with Putty

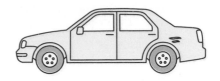

If you have a small ding or scratch, or if you've hammered a larger dent back into a reasonable approximation of its original shape, it's time to smooth over the affected section with putty. You will end up with a somewhat unsightly patch—see How to Repaint Your Repair, opposite, to get your paint job back in tip-top shape.

TOOLS:

Wire brush, orbital sander, or sanding disk attached to a drill • Rags • 2-inch putty knife • Smooth-grain sandpaper

MATERIALS:

- Rubbing alcohol
- Auto body putty (such as Bondo)
- Scrap cardboard

1 Clean the surface. Start by removing any rust around the ding or scratch with a wire brush, orbital sander, or sanding disk in a drill, then clean the area with alcohol.

2 Apply putty. The brand name Bondo is synonymous with auto body dent repair, though other kinds of putty exist (and Bondo's parent company, 3M, sells a nice dent-repair kit that includes putty and all other needed supplies). To use Bondo, mix the putty with the bonding catalyst (following package instructions) on a piece of scrap cardboard. Make sure no leaves or dog hair have floated into your clean dent while you weren't looking, and then use a putty knife to spread Bondo over the dent. If you're repairing a rusted-out section of panel, apply the putty to the front and back of the panel until you've built an appropriate base. The more the putty overflows the dimensions of the dent,

the more sanding you'll have to do later—but better too much than too little.

3 Dry the patch. If it's a sunny day, park the car with the repair in the sun to dry. If not, consider pointing a heat lamp or hair dryer at the patch. Dry for at least 30 minutes and run your hand over the patch to check that it's not still tacky. Sand the patch with smooth-grain sandpaper until it's smooth with the body panel, then repaint as needed (see How to Repaint Your Repair, opposite).

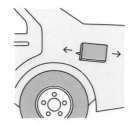

#68 How to Repaint Your Repair

Once you've repaired a ding, scratch, or dent, it's time to paint over the repair. The layers of auto body paint go from steel panel, to primer, to color, to clear coat. If you're looking to repaint a scratch, first check the depth of the scratch. What color is it? If you see the car's color, follow the sanding instructions on page 167 and then just apply a layer of clear coat. If you see primer that is different from the car's color, apply color and clear coat. If you see bare steel (or very discolored plastic), you'll have to apply all three. Unless you have an unusual car, your auto shop should have the matching paint.

TOOLS:

Rags • 80-grit sandpaper • Thin paintbrush

MATERIALS:

- Automotive body prep solvent
- Auto body primer
- Auto body paint
- Clear coat
- Car wash soap
- Car wax

1 Use a colorless solvent specific to auto painting to meticulously clean the surface to be painted.

2 Apply primer. When repainting a car completely, an auto shop will use spray primer. Ask your local auto shop for primer recommendations to use with your car and the size of your repair.

3 If the area to be painted is larger than, say, a quarter, sand the primer with fine-grain sandpaper while pouring water over the area. Let dry, add a second coat, and dry according to the primer instructions.

4 Use a thin paintbrush to apply at least three coats of color paint, letting each coat dry thoroughly before applying the next.

5 After the last coat of paint has thoroughly dried, apply the clear coat. Again, talk to your auto-parts store about which clear coat to use.

6 Finally, wash and wax the repaired area.

#69 How to Change a Windshield Wiper Blade

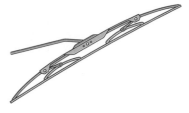

Agood windshield with good wiper blades goes a long way toward avoiding accidents—better visibility means lower risk. If the rubber blade is cracked or weathered, is screeching against the glass, or is leaving streaks or areas of the windshield untouched, it's time to change the blade. Even if yours seem fine, the National Highway Transportation Board recommends changing wiper blades at least every year and ideally every six months. It's much easier to install new blades on a sunny afternoon than it is to do the same on the side of the road some icy night. Take a couple of minutes to ensure your car-sight is everything that it should be.

TOOLS:

Screwdriver

MATERIALS:

- **Replacement blades**
- **Replacement clips**

1 Pull the old wiper assembly away from the windshield. There are three common types of windshield wiper blade attachments: hook-slot, pin arm, and straight-end connectors. Hook-slots are the easiest to work with—look for a small tab on the underside of the wiper that holds the blade in place. Press the tab and slide the wiper clean of the blade.

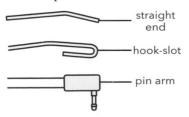

straight end

hook-slot

pin arm

Pin arms are similar to hook-slots—either push the pin or remove it to free the old blade from its mount. Straight-end connectors usually require a screwdriver to release the old blade. Once you have the blade removed, avoid letting the metal arm slam back against the glass windshield. If need be, the exposed metal arm can rest gently in the "down" position against the windshield.

2 Evaluate the wiper. Determine whether you need to replace the plastic wiper clip or just the rubber blade. If replacing the clip, examine the connection of clip to arm to discover how to free it. Commonly, wiper arms will include a U-shaped metal end that slots around the wiper clip. Discover how to free the clip and then take notes or a picture to remember how to put it back

later. If needed, remove the old wiper clips and replace with new ones, being sure to orient the new clips correctly. The new wiper clip should click into place with its mount inside the U-shaped curve at the end of the wiper arm.

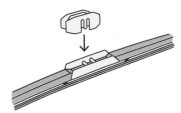

3 Install new rubber blades the same way you removed the old ones. Gently lower the assembly back to the window.

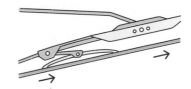

#70 How to Fix a Chipped Windshield

There are a number of ways to repair windshield dings, including taking the car to a repair shop, where it should take a technician five minutes to fill the nick, and your insurance company is likely to cover the repair pre-deductible (it would rather pay a little for a repair now than a lot for a replacement later). If you decide to do it yourself, buy a windshield repair kit at a car-parts store or online. Kit specifics will differ, but it should include a doughnut-shaped adhesive to surround the ding, a syringe or similar tool to pull air bubbles from the crack, and resin to fill it.

TOOLS:

Razor blade

MATERIALS:

- **Rubbing alcohol**
- **Windshield repair kit**
- **Paper towels**

1 Prepare the windshield. Clean the affected area and a couple of inches around it with rubbing alcohol, making sure to remove all windshield gunk from the area and any small chips of glass from within the crack itself.

2 Create a seal. Remove the backing from the adhesive doughnut that came in your kit, and place the center directly on the chip—you want to make an airtight seal around the damage.

3 Remove the air from the crack. Peel the second backing off the ring to reveal the adhesive and press the syringe-like tool into the ring. Use the syringe to draw air bubbles out of the crack. If the kit allows, lock the syringe in the "up" position and leave it for about 10 minutes.

4 Fill the crack. Now reverse the process, using the syringe to slowly add resin to the vacuum you created in the crack. Before the resin dries, have paper towels at the ready and use a razor blade to scrape free the adhesive ring. Dab the adhesive that oozes out with the paper towels.

5 Finish the repair. If your kit includes one, use the small plastic square to smooth the adhesive. Let dry in the sun.

#71 How to Change a Flat Tire

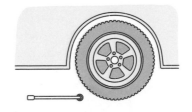

Though modern tire technology makes flats less common than they used to be, there remains no skill more central to car ownership than changing a flat. At some point in your life, you'll get a flat tire, and when you do, it might be on a dirt road without cell coverage, many miles from civilization or the graces of a good Samaritan. In that case, you'll need to know how to fix the flat yourself, with naught but moxie and a couple of tools that should be stashed in your trunk (see Trunk Tool Kit, page 161).

TOOLS:

Jack • Lug wrench • Wheel chock

MATERIALS:

• Spare tire

1 Put the car in park and apply the parking brake. Turn the engine off, and ensure that the car is on a level surface, far enough away from traffic. If moving the car to level ground is impossible, consider calling for help. Changing a tire on a slant is not worth the risk.

2 If you have a wheel chock or can find a substitute, such as a heavy stone, place it behind the wheel that is diagonally opposite the one

you're changing. So if you're changing the right rear tire, place a block behind the left front.

3 Retrieve your spare tire and tools. Your car's spare tire is likely hiding under the floor mat in the trunk. On an SUV, it may be held underneath the vehicle by a wire or attached to the back gate. Look for the jack and lug wrench inside trunk panels or in recessed hatches in the back. Your car may also come equipped with wheel chocks, which make changing a tire slightly safer. If your spare tire is flat, you are out of luck, so check it first.

4 Loosen the wheel lugs with the lug wrench. This is the crux of the whole operation. If the lugs are rusted past the point of turning, you won't be able to get the wheel off. To maximize your chances of a successful turn, seat the

wrench completely and snugly over the lug. Then crank counterclockwise with all your might. Don't remove the lugs, just loosen them each a couple of turns. If your hub cap is covering the lug nuts, remove it first. Your hubcap may have clips that pop off with a flat screwdriver, or your hubcap may have lugs of its own that screw to the lug posts of your wheel (in that case, unscrew them).

5 Jack up the car. Your owner's manual should indicate the proper jack points—the places on your car's frame strong enough to withstand the pressure of the jack. If not, look underneath the car to locate the vehicle's

frame (do not jack the siding!). Generally, the proper place to set a jack is along this frame, on a seam fairly close to the tire being raised. When the car is held firmly in place by its gear, parking brake, and wheel chock, insert the provided handle into the jack and turn the handle to expand the jack itself. The jack should scissor together, pushing the head upward into the jack point. Even after the car's weight is supported by the jack, refrain from putting any part of yourself underneath the vehicle. Despite your best preparation, cars can and do roll off jacks, and you don't want any part of yourself underneath any part of your car. Keep raising the car until the wheel to be changed is completely off the ground.

6 Remove the lug nuts. Use the lug wrench to remove the lug nuts completely and place them in a safe place—inside the hubcap, for example.

7 Pull off the flat tire and then seat the spare onto the wheel studs, lining up the holes in the spare with these metal posts. Expect to get dirty. Tires are heavy and it can be a surprising pain in the neck to get them lined up just right. Stick with it! Fit the spare flush against the brake hub by pushing the tire firmly onto the posts as far as it will go.

8 Hand-tighten the lug nuts. These should slip on fairly smoothly, though rust may necessitate a slightly firmer hand. Don't immediately crank them with the lug wrench or you risk cross-threading—damage to the thread that results from misaligned nuts and studs.

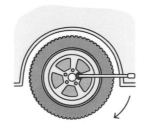

9 Turn the jack handle the opposite direction to lower the jack, returning the

tire to the ground. Once the jack is completely flattened, remove it and re-stow the jack (and the wheel chock, if you used one) in your car.

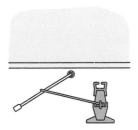

10 Use the lug wrench to tighten the lug nuts. Start by gently tightening one nut and then do the same with a nut diagonally across the circle. Continue gently tightening the nuts, each in turn, each time with a little more gusto. After driving no more than a mile, double-check the tightness of the lug nuts—spinning the tire under pressure can loosen it on the posts.

11 If you have a compact spare, the maximum speed should be listed on the sidewall. If you have a full-sized spare, you should be able to drive at full speed. Note that with the spare on your car and a flat in your trunk, you have no backup in case of another flat. Get the flat fixed quickly and reinstall it on your vehicle, or else get new tires. Make sure your spare is in good condition before re-stowing it.

The Essentials of Tire Maintenance

Tires are where the rubber meets the road. And when rubber meets road, it leaves a little piece of itself behind every time. But proper maintenance will help your tires last as long as possible.

Pressure. Contrary to popular belief, the pressure listed on a tire's sidewall is not necessarily the best pressure for your car. In general, manufacturers list the maximum pressure allowed, not the optimal level for grip or efficiency. The less air pressure a tire holds, the more it will deform to grip the roadway. The more it grips, the less gas mileage your car will get. The optimal PSI (pounds of air pressure per square inch) should balance performance against mileage. Check the owner's manual or the sticker inside the door frame to discern yours.

Storage. If you swap in snow tires seasonally, make sure you properly store your normal tires.

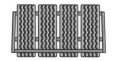

Place them in a cool, dark, dry spot, deflate them to half their normal PSI, and, rather than stacking them, set them on their treads.

Tread. While the inner workings of a modern car may require computer diagnostics, your tires do not. In fact, testing your tread will cost you exactly one cent. Yes, it's the penny test. Place the top of Abe Lincoln's head between your tire's tread and gently rest the penny against the rubber. If the tire tread comes up past the tip of the presidential hairline, the tire's good to go. Repeat the test on different areas of the tire, checking that the tread is wearing evenly along the inside and outside walls. Uneven wear on treads that pass the test signals that it's time for a tire rotation, alignment, and balancing. Uneven wear that leaves any tread below Lincoln's head means it's time to replace.

Sidewalls. The tread isn't the only place a tire can wear out. Check the sidewalls, too. Minor webs of cracks in the sidewall are likely not a major concern, but any crack that threatens to pull apart the rubber signals the end of a tire's life. Likewise, look for bubbles and bulges, which are also dangerous signs that the air inside your tire is close to getting out.

Expiration date. Over time, the essential oils in tire rubber evaporate. This is called outgassing. Enough outgassing and the tire becomes brittle.

Needless to say, a brittle tire is no good. Manufacturers and oversight agencies disagree at what age a tire has expired, but you should generally be wary of any tire more than ten years old. If you're driving a car regularly, you'll wear out tires long before their expiration date, but when buying new ones, check the date stamped in the small oval on the tire's sidewall to ensure that the tire hasn't been shelved past its useful lifespan.

Ants, known for their disciplined pace, never get into traffic jams. Because they don't make unexpected moves, their pattern of movement is much more efficient than cars on the road.

#72 How to Rotate Tires

No matter your best efforts at balancing and alignment, your car tires will wear differently. That's especially true of front tires. As you drive, twisting and turning your steering wheel, uneven pavement grates away the rubber on your front tires. On front-wheel-drive cars, where the same tires that are steering are also providing the power, wear is particularly rapid. By rotating your tires, you can ensure that wear patterns are applied evenly, extending the life of your tires. And assuming you don't drive only in a left-hand circle, you shouldn't need to switch the sides of the tires, just swap the fronts for backs.

TOOLS:

Jack • 2 jack stands • Lug wrench

1 Determine if your tires are interchangeable. For most models, a front tire can be a back and a left can be a right, but a few models use different sizes on the front and back, and some tires change tread from the inside to the outside, making them usable on only one side of the car. If you have non-interchangeable tires, they will not be able to be rotated and will instead need to be replaced.

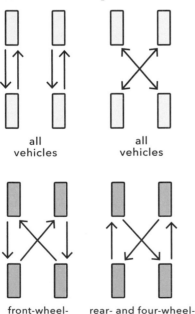

all vehicles   all vehicles

front-wheel-drive vehicles   rear- and four-wheel-drive vehicles

Most manufacturers recommend rotating your car's tires every 5,000 to 10,000 miles.

2 Park the car on a flat, level surface and engage the parking brake. Place the jack underneath the appropriate jack point (see Step 5, How to Change a Flat Tire, page 172), lift the back tire and then rest the car onto a jack stand. Repeat the procedure in the front so that both of the wheels on one side are off the ground.

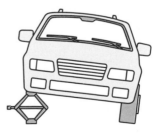

3 Swap the tires. Following the instructions in How to Change a Flat Tire, page 172, remove, switch, and reattach the front and back tires. Jack a wheel up off its stand, remove the stand and then lower the jack. Repeat with the second jack stand.

4 Repeat Step 3 to rotate the tires on the other side.

#73 How to Check and Top Off Fluids
(or, Getting Under the Hood)

There are a number of different fluids in your car, each with a way to check and fill as needed. As part of general maintenance, and especially when planning a road trip, check the oil (see opposite page) and the transmission, coolant, brake, and window washing fluids. This is a great way to get familiar with what's under the hood and is among the simplest and most satisfying ways to take your car's upkeep into your own hands.

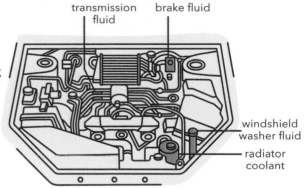

transmission fluid

brake fluid

windshield washer fluid

radiator coolant

MATERIALS:

- **Coolant**
- **Windshield washer fluid**

1 Pop the hood and prop it open. With the engine running, start by checking the transmission fluid—the cap is probably located behind the oil cap and a bit lower down. The transmission fluid should have a dipstick—pull out the dipstick, clean it, reinsert, remove, and check the fluid level. If the fluid level is low, that's a big problem—the transmission shouldn't leak. Head to your mechanic to find out what's going on.

2 Check the coolant. Make sure the engine is off and cool (not cold) before you touch the radiator. Check both the radiator cap (if your car uses a radiator) and the plastic coolant reservoir. If your car has a radiator, it's right behind the grill; the coolant reservoir should be to its side. Check that the coolant reaches the fill line on the coolant reservoir. If fluid is low, add coolant until it reaches the fill line.

MAX

3 Check the brake fluid. Consult your owner's manual to find the brake fluid

reservoir, likely in the engine compartment. Make sure brake fluid fills the reservoir up to the fill line. It shouldn't be low—if it is, take the car to the shop.

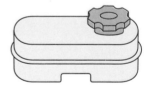

4 Check the washer fluid. This is likely in a plastic reservoir near the dashboard. Again, ensure that fluid fills the reservoir to the fill line. If needed, top it off. Car fluids can look quite similar (think radioactive blue), so be careful not to pour washer fluid into the coolant reservoir and vice versa.

#74 How to Change the Oil

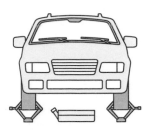

Changing a car's oil is a dirty job, but it's not hard. In fact, even the first time you change the oil, it should take you only an hour or so—half an hour once you've done it a couple of times. Consider that an oil change at the auto shop typically costs around $40. And that's only the direct savings. Consider also the role of oil: to make less friction inside your engine, which translates to less wear and tear and increased gas mileage with lower emissions. Here's how it's done.

TOOLS:

Jacks • Safety stands or ramp • Socket wrench • Oil pan • Work gloves • Filter wrench or ratchet

MATERIALS:

- Motor oil
- Oil filter

1 Buy new oil. Consult your owner's manual to learn the type and amount of oil (typically five quarts) needed for your car. The Society of Automotive Engineers standardizes the oil labeling system (e.g., 10W-30). The first number (in the example, "10") describes the oil's viscosity at 0 degrees Fahrenheit, and the second number ("30") describes the oil's viscosity at 212 degrees Fahrenheit, or approximately an engine's operating temperature. Motor oils need to be less viscous when cold to avoid being gummy in the winter and more viscous when hot to avoid becoming thin in a hot engine. Generally, the higher the second number— meaning it's more viscous at a high temperature—the better for your engine, because the oil forms better seals and a stronger friction-reducing film. That said, engines are optimized for oil of a certain viscosity. Again, consult your owner's manual and then go to an auto-supply store or gas station to buy the right kind and amount. Note that high-performance engines may require synthetic oil.

2 If needed, lift the car. To change the oil, you'll need to access the oil drain plug underneath the car. If your car doesn't naturally have enough clearance to offer access, either jack it up (see How to Change a Flat Tire, page 172) and put the car on safety stands or drive the car onto steel ramps. In either case, follow the appropriate safety precautions any time you lift a car (also see How to Change a Flat Tire, page 172). In this case, safety is doubly important, as you'll be sliding underneath the car to change the oil, and for that reason, instead of leaving the car on the jack, you will need to use safety stands. When changing oil, it's best to work with a warm, but not hot, car. Before you jack up the car, drive about a mile to loosen the oil and then let the car cool to a reasonable temperature while you prepare the rest of your tools. Keep in mind that driving the car will make the oil HOT.

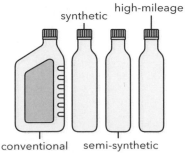

synthetic high-mileage

conventional semi-synthetic

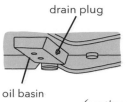

drain plug

oil basin

(continued)

3 Position the oil pan. Consider putting cardboard under the car, because spilled oil will stain the driveway or garage floor. Place a pan to catch the oil underneath the drain plug. A task-specific oil pan with a spout and screw-tight lid makes transporting and disposing of the used oil much easier. Notice that the plug points out at an angle and place your oil pan appropriately. Slide underneath the car in clothes that you don't mind staining (bring your work gloves).

4 Many newer cars include an aerodynamic under-panel that covers the drain plug and oil filter. Before you remove it, look for a small access hatch in the panel. If an under-panel exists with no easy-access hatch, you may need to call a professional to remove the panel entirely. You can remove the oil filter cap at the top of the engine to vent the drain so oil flows smoothly instead of "glugging" out. Use the correct size socket wrench to loosen the drain plug. Wearing gloves, slowly unscrew the last bit by hand. Oil will start to flow. Take this opportunity to check the oil plug washer—the O-shaped gasket that helps the plug form a strong seal. Some plugs have built-in rubber washers that may be ripped or mangled and need replacing. Once all of the oil has drained out, replace the drain plug and tighten with the socket wrench. Do not overtighten or you risk stripping the threads. And don't pour old oil down the drain! Many oil change centers will accept and properly dispose of it.

5 Locate the oil filter (if needed, check your owner's manual). Place an oil pan beneath the filter, as it will almost certainly drip. Loosen the filter with a filter wrench until you are able to work the filter loose by hand. Eventually, oil will start pouring out around the edges. Hold tight to avoid dropping the filter as you remove it. Use a rag to wipe clean any excess oil or grime and then hand-tighten a new filter in place, likely over an O-ring washer. Once the filter pulls the O-ring in contact with the sealing surface, use muscle power to turn it between three-quarters and one more full rotation. Don't overtighten.

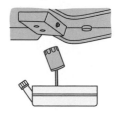

6 Add the new oil. Double-check that the drain plug and filter are secure before you start to pour. Start by adding one quart less than the recommended amount. Then start the car, let it run for a minute, turn off the engine, wait a few minutes for the oil to cool, and check the oil with the dipstick. Pull out the dipstick, clean it, reinsert the stick, pull it back out and check the bottom of the stick to see how high the oil reaches. The dipstick should have two holes to indicate low and high oil levels. Continue adding oil a bit at a time until the dipstick shows you've reached the proper amount. Continue checking your car's oil on a regular (monthly) basis using this method.

Pro tip: When replacing an oil filter, coat it with a little bit of oil before twisting it back into place.

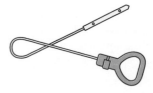

#75 How to Locate an Oil Leak

Though a car has a variety of fluids that can potentially leak out (see "What's That Puddle Under the Car?," page 180), oil—thick black or brown liquid—is the most common to do so. Depending on the source of the leak, dripping oil can be a quick fix or a major repair. Determining the source can help you gauge the seriousness of the problem. After exhausting the steps in this tutorial, take a car that's leaking oil to the mechanic and cross your fingers.

TOOLS:

Work gloves • Rags • Filter wrench or ratchet • Wheel chocks

MATERIALS:

- **Engine cleaning solvent**
- **Talcum powder**

1 Block the tires securely with wheel chocks. Put the car in park with the emergency brake on, and start the vehicle. Look underneath the car for the source of the leak, but please keep yourself safe—refrain from putting your body under a running vehicle. It's likely that an oil leak from under the car will require attention from a mechanic.

2 Check the oil plug and filter. Because these are the spots you fidget with

when changing the oil, they are also the most frequent source of a leak. If you spot a leak in one of these two places, first check that the plug or filter is attached snugly. (See How to Change the Oil, page 177, for safety precautions before diving under the car.) If that doesn't fix the leak, remove the plug and filter to check the integrity of the rubber gaskets. If needed, the gaskets are easy to replace. Note that removing either will release oil, so change into work clothes and have rags handy. (While you're at it, change the oil, if it's due!)

3 Check the valve covers. Many cars with over 30,000 miles on them will develop subtle leaks from the valve cover sealing the top of the engine. Because these leaks tend to attract and trap

dirt and grime, they should be obvious once you raise the hood and look around. If you find the leak here, breathe a sigh of relief—valve covers are inexpensive and easy for a pro to replace.

4 Check the pump. This is a common oil leak location. It's also a leak you want to catch early, as a leaking pump can be diagnostic of a bigger problem, and if the oil pump fails, it will fail to lubricate the bearings in your engine and the system can overheat and seize. Check the seals on either side of the pump to see if they are leaking oil. If you see a leak, oil pump seals are easy to replace. If the pump is leaking, but it's not the seals, you might need a whole new pump.

(continued)

5 Degrease the engine with aerosol cleaning solvent. If the location of a leak isn't immediately obvious, you'll likely need to do some cleaning to spot the problem—if everything's covered in oil, it's impossible to tell where a little extra is coming from. Wearing gloves, use a rag to clean around the valve covers, the engine block, and under the oil pan. If needed, you can get the engine professionally steam-cleaned, after which a leak location should be obvious. If oil appears to be seeping from solid metal, look for tiny cracks, which can be made visible by sprinkling the suspected leak location with talcum powder. Though you may be able to stop very small leaks temporarily with spray-on fluids that are like heavy paints (ask the folks at your local auto-supply store which brands to use), metal with hairline cracks can't spontaneously heal itself. You'll need to replace the parts.

What's That Puddle Under the Car?

As the body ages, it's increasingly prone to mysterious pains and pops and odd tweaks—if you can just ignore the discomfort for a couple of days, it generally goes away. The same is not true of your car. Unless you have a minor issue like a pebble in your tire making a clicking noise, your car's minor ailments will likely only get more severe. A leak won't spontaneously plug itself so you'll have to figure out what's leaking. Fortunately, car fluids come in a rainbow of hues, making for fairly simple diagnostics. Park your car on top of an old, white sheet for a couple of hours or overnight. Then refer to the the list below—and get thee to a mechanic, or an auto-parts shop, right away.

Red. Though some newfangled, long-life coolant is red, the rosy fluid leaking from your car is more likely power steering or automatic transmission fluid. It's time to see a mechanic.

Clear. A clear fluid might just be water from the condenser on the air conditioner unit. If you've been using the AC recently and the clear fluid seems to come from near the AC, you may be okay—a little condensation is perfectly normal. But it might also be power steering fluid, which is bad. Smell to determine which. If it's not water, get to a mechanic.

Amber. Do you smell gasoline? If so, the amber fluid is almost certainly a gas leak and it's time to visit a mechanic. If there's no gas smell, see "yellow" below for the possible fluid source.

Green. Bright green, slippery fluid is coolant, likely dripping from the radiator or engine. Unfortunately, antifreeze tastes good and is toxic to pets, so the green puddle under your car may be doing harm beyond just your vehicle. Check all the connecting hoses as well as the integrity of the reservoir. If you find either to be obviously faulty, you can consider replacing it yourself. If the source of the leak remains elusive, head to the mechanic.

Blue. Fluid that's blue is likely leaking from the windshield washing system, either from the reservoir itself or from a punctured or loose hose. Though blue is the most popular washing fluid color, it may also be pink or yellow. Again, if you can find the leaky part, you can evaluate replacing it yourself. If you can't find the leak, take it to a pro.

Yellow. Brake fluid starts out yellow and turns brown with time, so your mysterious fluid may actually be some blend of both (although keep in mind that solid brown may be an oil leak). For obvious reasons, this is not a fluid leak you should take lightly. If you can safely test your brakes in your driveway, do so, and then drive to the nearest mechanic. If you are at all nervous, have the car towed.

#76 How to Jump a Battery

The headlights and interior lights of some cars turn off automatically when the key is removed. In other cars, the lights stay on indefinitely. Combine these mechanical tendencies with the forgetfulness of the human mind, and this means that at some time in your driving life, you'll go to start the car and find that it turns over hesitantly once, and then refuses to do anything but click at you. The battery is dead. Luckily, cars are equipped with an alternator that—as long as it's functioning properly—will recharge your battery once the car is started. Of course, to get it started, you need a power source. That's where jumper cables come in. Nothing brings people together like the need for a jump. Flag down a fellow human or recruit a neighbor, and then follow these steps to ensure that you both emerge from the experience safe and un-jolted.

TOOLS:

Jumper cables • Wire brush

1 Move the cars into position. Look under the hoods to see where the battery is located in each car. Drive the car with a live battery alongside or in front of the car with the dead battery so that the batteries are close together, or at least close enough so that jumper cables will reach from one to the other.

2 Connect the two batteries together. It's not difficult to properly connect jumper cables between the live and the dead battery, but it's extremely important to do it right. First, turn both cars off. Locate the positive and negative battery terminals, which should be labeled with + and –. The positive terminal may also be covered by a red cap. Start with the live battery—if the battery terminals are corroded, use a wire brush to scrub free any rust. Then connect the red, positive strand of the jumper cables to the red, positive terminal on the good battery. Move to the dead battery and do the same thing, attaching only the positive jumper cable clip. Then attach the negative, black, clip to the negative terminal on the good battery. It used to be that batteries couldn't help but leak a small amount of flammable acid. It's not such a good idea to have sparks around flammable acid, so in the old days people clipped the negative side of jumper cables to the car's metal frame to ground the current. New batteries almost never leak acid and so this configuration is less important. To be safe,

if your battery is more than 15 years old, clip the negative end of the jumper cable to an unpainted section of your car's metal frame (likely underneath); otherwise, clip it to the negative terminal on the dead battery.

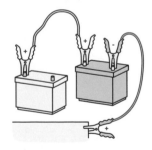

3 Start the car with the good battery and leave it running. As soon as you connect the jumper cables, the good battery will start charging the bad one. If the dead battery is really, really dead—that is, turning the

(continued)

key still does absolutely nothing—you may need to let the good battery in the running car feed some charge into the dead battery for a while before trying to start the dead car. Keep trying until it starts.

4 With the cars running, disconnect the cables. Though it doesn't matter in what order you disconnect the cables, be sure to keep

cable clips from touching each other until you've pulled the clips off at least one of each battery's terminals. If the cables remain connected to both terminals of either battery, and then you touch the other cable ends together,

you'll complete a circuit and create some rather exciting fireworks. Don't make fireworks.

5 Leave the dead car running. Assuming a depleted battery was the only problem, with the car running, the car's alternator will recharge the battery and no additional action will be required.

When You Need More than a Jump

Diagnosing your battery. After four years your car battery will start its slow fade toward the recycle bin. It might make it a few more years, but be on the lookout for signs of age and nip a fading battery in the bud before it strands you in a downpour. Unfortunately, battery testers offer imperfect diagnoses, as they are unable to tell you how long that battery is likely to *hold* a charge. So get under the hood and check the battery yourself. Remove the case and look for corrosion or leaks. Clean buildup around the terminals with a solution of baking soda and water. Keep in mind that long periods of inactivity, high gadget usage, and living in an extreme climate will all shorten battery life. And if it's been more than four years, err on the side of caution: When in doubt, replace it.

Signs of a bad starter. If you have a battery tester, use it to test the battery. Without a battery tester, it's hard to disentangle a dead starter from a dead battery. But if you've

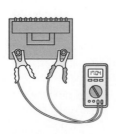

properly connected a dead battery to a live one with jumper cables and the car still refuses to start, it's a good bet the starter is to blame. In that case, call up the tow truck.

It could be the alternator. Do you notice the lights on electrical components getting dimmer while you're driving? Maybe the gauges are flickering. A warning light in your car should signal ALT or GEN when your alternator's gone south, but you can't always count on it. Instead, it might take a dead battery followed by inability to recharge to diagnose a dead alternator. That said, when you first notice your battery failing to hold a charge, check the belt running from the alternator to the starter. If it's loose, tighten it by using a socket wrench to loosen the alternator. Push the alternator back until it tightens the belt, and then retighten the alternator bolts to hold it in place. Also check the electrical connections into and out of the alternator to ensure that there are no loose or frayed wires. If everything looks good, then the alternator itself is bad.

#77 How to Sharpen a Lawn Mower Blade

Asharp mower blade will not only help you cut longer, wetter grass, but does so with less damage to the plants. That said, you don't want your blade to be sharpened to the fine edge of a samurai sword, since a lawnmower's blade's soft metal will only dull more quickly and be prone to accumulating notches and dings. Instead, after following the safety procedures below, carefully test the blade with your finger. It should be butter-knife sharp—no more and no less. If it's feeling more like a butter knife's handle than its edge, it's time to sharpen the mower blade.

TOOLS:

Socket wrench • Ratchet • Pipe (optional) • Bench vise • Metal "mill bastard" file • Rags

MATERIALS:

- Newspaper
- Scrap 2 × 4
- Penetrating oil
- Spray paint

1 Remove the spark plug wire. The chances of your lawn mower spontaneously starting while it's tipped on its side are slim—but the penalty is severe. The motion of the engine's pistons triggers subsequent spark plug firing, which in turn powers the next piston, which drives the blade another tick in its circle. If you spin the blade while underneath the mower, you can inadvertently set off this chain of events—moving

a piston, releasing a spark, and making the blade buck. Removing the spark plug wire guards against accidental starting and bucking. On most mowers, the short, rubber-coated spark plug wire is the only external wire on the mower. Pull the cap off the plug.

2 Lay the mower on its side. Tip the mower onto a layer of newspaper, resting it on the side opposite the carburetor and air filter. This will prevent oil from leaking into the parts that heat up

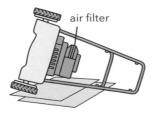
air filter

when you mow, so the mower won't belch black smoke when you start it up. Locate the carburetor by the throttle cables running into it.

3 Loosen the mounting nut. The blade should be held on to the mower by one central nut. And this nut is likely to be an absolute bear to loosen. Wedge a piece of scrap 2 × 4 between the blade and the mower's body to keep the blade from turning while you crank on the mounting nut with the appropriate-sized socket and your longest ratchet. To magnify the torque, slip a length of pipe over the handle of the ratchet. If needed, squirt a stubborn nut with penetrating oil and let it sit for 15 minutes.

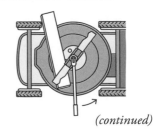

(continued)

4 Mark the blade. Before removing the nut and the blade completely, note which side of the blade was down. It's worth marking the blade with spray paint (or something similar) to avoid reinstalling it upside down.

spray paint

5 Remove the mounting nut. Grip the blade in a bench vise so its flat sides point straight up and down. Stand behind the edge you plan to sharpen and use a metal file held at a shallow angle to sharpen the edge. A long "mill bastard" file works well, which cuts only on the push stroke and so will help

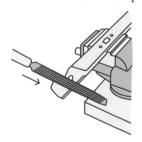

you sharpen the blade in the correct direction: with strokes running from the blade's body off the sharp edge. You don't want a razor-sharp edge on the mower blade—stop when the blade could cut butter (but not bread or tomatoes).

6 Hang the blade by its center hole on a nail. Like a wet blanket in the washing machine, if your mower blade is unbalanced it will make the machine shudder. If the blade tips to one side, use your file or grinder to remove material from that side. Work with the blade until it hangs from the nail in perfect balance.

7 Inspect and clean the mower. Tipped on its side with the blade removed,

it's a perfect time to give the underside of your mower a quick inspection and cleaning. Scrape free any caked-on grass, give it a thorough wipe-down, and consider spray-painting over any rust spots.

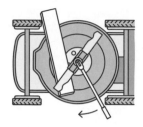

8 Reinstall the blade. Mount the blade with the proper side pointing down and hand tighten the nut. Again, wedge the 2 × 4 against the blade. If the old mounting nut is at all suspect, with gouges in the edges or other rounding, consider replacing it. Use your ratchet and socket to tighten the nut firmly onto the mounting post.

✕ ✕

Is It Time for a New Blade?

If you have a good mower, it may outlast the blade. With the blade removed, check for deep dents in the cutting edge. If you can't remove dents or other edge imperfections by filing or grinding, consider

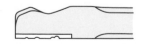

replacing the blade. Also check for bends in the blade. It's tempting to hammer a bent blade straight, but this can weaken the metal–it's best to replace it. Look also at the thickness of the metal. Over time, mower blades will simply wear thin. This will certainly happen to the cutting edge, which you'll file back into the thicker part of the blade when sharpening, but the trailing edge can also degrade. This edge has an important function–it's curved slightly upward to create suction that pulls up grass tops for cutting. If the trailing edge has gone thin, replace the blade. ✕

#78 How to Maintain a Motorcycle

I n the book *Zen and the Art of Motorcycle Maintenance,* author Robert Pirsig wrote that "the place to improve the world is first in one's own heart, head, and hands, and then work outward from there." So consider this section the first step toward a better world. Motorcycles require maintenance, just like cars, but, in the case of motorcycles, the stakes are a bit higher. Fail to maintain your car and you may end up stuck on the side of the freeway. Fail to maintain your motorcycle and you might find *yourself* on the side of the freeway.

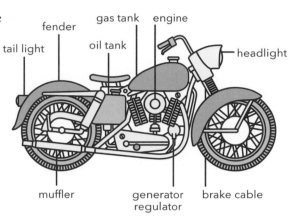

Tires

Make a habit of checking your tires before every ride. You don't have to get out the pressure gauge every morning to zip two miles to work, but a quick visual inspection can alert you of likely failures before they occur. Look for punctures like nail or screw heads and shiny shards of glass, and also for bulges or cracks that may turn into holes or slices at high speeds. Air expands as it heats, so if you do check your tire pressure, it won't be the same in your garage as it is on the road. Plan on about 5 percent increase in tire pressure once you're riding. If your tire pressure increases by more than 10 percent while you're riding (stop and check it quickly!), carry less stuff or slow down! Likewise, underinflated tires create more friction against the pavement, which in turn generates more heat, which can result in blowouts. Have a look at the treads—as with car tires (see The Essentials of Tire Maintenance, page 174), when you rest a penny with Lincoln's head down into the tread of a motorcycle tire, the top of the tread should extend past the president's hairline. Also eyeball the wheel for missing spokes and the rims for sharp cracks and dents. Even a small imperfection in a wheel can weaken the integrity of the system.

Brakes

Braided steel brake lines last longer than plastic-sleeved brake lines and include less play in the system, leading to faster and more durable braking. If you have plastic, consider replacing with steel. Frequently check the lines for kinks, abrasions, and tears, and keep an eye on your brake pads. Letting the brake pads wear down can lead to warped rotors and a much more expensive repair. Motorcycles usually have two brake fluid reservoirs, one for the front brakes and one for the back. Look for the front reservoir in the handlebars and the back reservoir under the saddle. Check them both to ensure that fluid is up to the fill line.

(continued)

Chain

It's not difficult to lubricate the chain— just spray it with commercial lubricant. It's best to do this at the end of every ride, when the chain is warm. Otherwise, get in the habit of lubricating the chain when you fill up with gas. Spray additional lubricant on the side of the chain that runs against the sprockets. It seems as if the chain should be tight, but that's not the case—it needs to sag ¾" to 1¼" to accommodate the movement of the suspension. Make sure the chain has this much play.

Oil

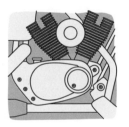

Too little oil and your bike can seize catastrophically. Too much oil and you can go smoking down the freeway. Check your oil frequently to ensure that the level is always at its maximum— in addition to keeping your bike running smoothly, the right level can prevent bigger problems. If you don't know your oil level, you can't be sure you're safe on the road. Always check your oil with the bike sitting level. Note that a motorcycle's oil needs to be monitored much more than a car's does—adhere to the manufacturer's specifications, and when in doubt change the oil at least every 2,000 miles.

Battery

Modern car batteries require little maintenance. Not so with motorcycle batteries. You still need to check the fluid level

in each cell, preferably every month. If the level is low, use distilled water to top it off. Also make sure the terminals remain clear of rust and grime, and check the cables for loose connections.

Inspections

Your motorcycle uses less gas than your car but requires more frequent maintenance. Your bike should be professionally (or very competently DIY) inspected every 3,000 miles.

Cleaning

Keeping your car clean is primarily an aesthetic choice, but keeping your bike clean is a safety requirement. Keep headlights de-bugged and de-tarred—WD-40 works for this job—and try oven cleaner to remove leather boot marks from exhaust pipes (okay, that one *is* just aesthetic). Unlike on a car, do without the tire polish, as it can compromise the tires' grip (on a motorcycle you're likely to use the rounded sides of the tire more than a car might).

Fuses and Wiring

Extra fuses should be kept clipped next to the old ones. You may notice the need for a new fuse when your horn refuses to honk . . . or your bike refuses to start. Periodically check the integrity of the fuses to nip these problems in the bud. Likewise check the integrity of your electrical wires. The wiring in your bike shouldn't give you problems—but it almost certainly will, if you roll down the road with loose connections or wires poking from their sheaths.

BICYCLE TOOL KIT

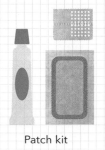

Patch kit

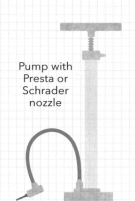

Pump with Presta or Schrader nozzle

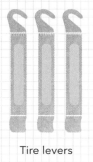

Tire levers

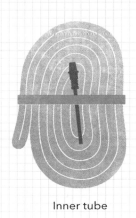

Inner tube

#79 How to Fix a Flat Tire on a Bicycle

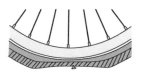

Keeping your bike tires properly inflated not only makes for a more efficient ride but also can help you avoid things like the dreaded pinch flat, which happens when an underinflated tire bumps against a curb or rock and squeezes the inner tube against the metal wheel rim, puncturing the tube. But, even with perfect inflation, if you're a bike rider, you'll almost certainly have to fix a flat, either in your garage after a period of disuse or on the side of the road during a ride. Luckily, if you have the right tools, repairing a flat is easy. Without the right tools, it's impossible. Whenever you ride, make sure you carry with you a flat kit including tire levers (also called spoons), a patch kit and new inner tube, and either a pump or a CO_2 cartridge with a nozzle matching your valve type (either Presta or Schrader) designed for refilling bike tires.

(continued)

The modern bicycle has taken many forms since its debut in 1817— from the Velocipede, or "Boneshaker" (the first model with pedals on the front wheel)—to the Penny Farthing, with its enormous front wheel and tiny back wheel.

---

1 Release the brakes. The pads of most bike brakes sit close to the rim so the tire won't slip through. A small, quick-release lever allows the brake pads to expand to the sides so the tire can be removed. Flip the quick release. Some newer bikes, especially mountain bikes, may be fitted with hydraulic disc brakes. These work just like your car's brakes, and require some model-specific finagling to release when changing the tire. If you have disc brakes, make sure you know what tool you need to release them, and keep it in your kit.

2 Remove the wheel. A bike tire is held to the fork or frame by a nut or quick-release lever that clamps onto an end of the axle. If you have a front flat, removing the wheel should be as easy as loosening the lever or nut by hand and pulling off the tire (some bikes have an additional mechanism to guard against tire loss even with the lever or nut loosened). If you have a back tire flat, you'll have to pop the

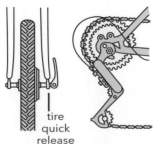
tire
quick
release

chain free first. Shift the bike so the chain runs along the smallest back-wheel cog. Then flip the bike over, release the axle lever or nut, and push in the bike's derailleur with one hand to make the chain go slack while you lift the wheel free with the other.

3 Diagnose the problem. Why did your tire go flat? If you fail to find the problem, there's a good chance that something like a thorn stuck in the tire will make a new inner tube go flat, too. Inspect the outside of the tire for punctures, tears, or excessive wear. If you find a thorn, nail, or piece of glass, remove it.

4 Remove the tire. Let all remaining air out of the inner tube and attempt to slip the tire free of the rim by hand. If that doesn't work, reach for the tire levers or spoons. Start on a section of tire opposite the valve. Use the long end of the tire lever to pry underneath the tire bead and then pop it to the outside of the wheel rim. If unseating the tire with one lever doesn't allow you to pull

the tire off by hand, work in a second lever near the first and pop a longer section of tire free of the rim. Eventually, you should be able to release all of one side of the tire bead. You needn't remove the tire completely from the wheel— just one full edge of the tire so that you can access the inner tube.

5 Remove the inner tube. Slide the valve out through the hole in the rim, being careful not to damage the valve with the rim. Then pull the entire inner tube out without damaging it further.

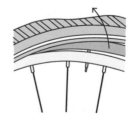

6 Inspect the inner tube. If there is an obvious gash or other catastrophic tube failure, you'll need to replace the inner tube. If there's a small puncture you can simply patch it, but these punctures can be hard to spot. If you're at home, submerge the tube in a bathtub or

bucket of water and look for bubbles. If you're on the side of the road, run the tube close to your face—look, listen, and feel for escaping air. If you still can't find the puncture, you can try running water from a water bottle along the inner tube—air from the puncture will bubble in the water, making it visible. When you find the puncture, lay the tube against the wheel and explore for matched damage in the tire itself—sometimes the source of a puncture will still be embedded.

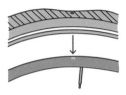

7 Patch the inner tube. Inner tubes aren't that expensive, so if you have a spare, it's worth simply replacing the tube (see Step 8). If you choose to patch it, follow the patch manufacturer's instructions. Typically, after cleaning and drying the area around a puncture, you'll rough up the surface to help the glue grab, apply the glue, and then apply the patch. If you choose

to replace the tube, double-check that your replacement is the right size for your wheel (match the tube specs listed on the box to the wheel specs listed on the rim).

8 Replace the inner tube. With the new tube slightly inflated, reinsert the valve into the hole in the rim. Gently press the inner tube along the rim inside the tire, being careful not to twist the tube or otherwise compromise the path of the tire.

9 Reseat the tire bead. This is the trickiest part, during which a mistake can result in a pinched tube and another chance to practice your tube replacement. Start near the valve and reseat the bead by hand, pressing it into the rim first in one direction and then the other. The more tire bead you seat, the harder it will get, until you're left

with a short section of tire opposite the valve that (likely) requires levers to reseat. If possible, use one lever to get the remaining tire back into the rim. If your tire is especially tight, you may need two levers—one to keep the tire bead from slipping off the rim and another to pop in a further section.

10 Once you've seated the tire bead, double-check that it doesn't pinch the tube. Then use your pump or CO2 canister to inflate the tube to the proper psi (listed on the bike tire).

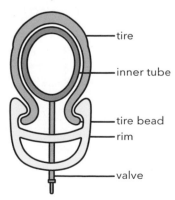

tire

inner tube

tire bead
rim

valve

#80 How to Adjust Bicycle Brakes

Biking is humankind's most efficient form of transportation—very little energy is lost to friction (as in a car), and unlike running, you can coast sometimes. In part, that's why nearly twice as many bikes as cars are manufactured annually. To keep riding at maximum efficiency, adjust your bike's brakes so you're not pushing against them as you pedal. This will also keep them from squealing and shuddering every time you come to a stop. Here's how to look at and tweak the braking apparatus on your two-wheeled machine.

brake barrel adjuster

centering adjustment screw

quick-release lever

brake shoe alignment bolt

brake shoe

brake pad

TOOLS:

Screwdriver • Needle-nose pliers

MATERIALS:

• Scrub pad and dish soap (or a degreaser such as WD-40)

1 Evaluate the brakes. With one tire off the ground, spin it and look at the position of the brakes. In most bikes with cable-pull brakes (as opposed to hydraulic disc brakes), there should be a brake pad on either side of the wheel rims. The pads should be positioned so, when closed, they grip the rim without contacting the tire rubber or touching each other. (Rubbing against the tire can cause a catastrophic flat, and

exposed pads will accumulate dirt and gunk.) Most brakes are made of two levers connected by wire—the levers should be centered so they sit at the same angle relative to the wheel and the pads are a uniform distance from the rim—you don't want one pad in contact with the rim while the other pad sits far away.

Finally, brake pads should sit so that they are slightly "pigeon-toed" in front; with the brake applied lightly, the front of the pad should contact the rim slightly before the back. When you squeeze tighter, the pad should flatten against the rim. This keeps the brakes from squeaking.

ⅩⅩⅩⅩⅩⅩⅩⅩⅩⅩⅩⅩⅩⅩⅩⅩⅩⅩⅩⅩⅩⅩⅩⅩⅩⅩⅩ

Side-Pull versus Center-Pull Brakes

There are a couple of configurations of cable-pull brakes. Most common are center-pull, in which one cable reaches straight in between two calipers, at which point the cable splits into a triangle in order to pull both calipers. You may also find side-pull brakes, in which one cable extends down the side of a horseshoe-shaped piece opposite a straight arm. Neither is necessarily better than the other and both work by essentially the same mechanism, but depending on your brake type, you may have to slightly adjust the instructions in this section. Ⅹ

side-pull brakes   center-pull brakes

2 Center the brakes. If your brakes aren't centered, one pad may rub against the rim even when the brake is released, while the other pad sits too far away to reach the rim even when the brake is applied. First, check to see if the position of the wheel might be the problem—if the wheel is slightly tilted it will push closer to one caliper than the other. If it's not the wheel, it's the brakes. First try twisting the calipers back to the center to see if the brake pads stay appropriately centered. If that doesn't work, unhook the cable and test each arm independently to see if one side pulls more strongly than the other. Rust or grime may be restricting or affecting the movement of the levers—if so, clean them using a scrub pad and a little soapy water (or a degreaser such as WD-40). Then reassemble the brake arms and, with them centered, tighten down the pivot bolt to hold them in place. If you remove and reinstall brakes and they still grab your tire, it's time for a trip to the bike shop.

As of 2016, public bicycle-sharing systems were available in over a thousand cities worldwide.

3 Adjust the cables. Lackluster braking may not be due to the pads—it could be improper cable adjustment. A cable adjustment barrel may be located at either end of the brake cable, most likely where the cable enters the handbrake. Using pliers if necessary, turn the adjustment barrel to gently adjust the length of the brake cable. If both brake calipers are contacting the wheel rim even when you're not squeezing the brake, the cable is overall too tight—after ensuring that the cable is running along its proper path without obstruction (and without the handlebars facing straight ahead), use a screwdriver to turn the brake adjustment barrel to loosen the cable. If the brake calipers sit so far away from the rim that engaging the brake fails to make the pads grab the rim, turn the adjustment barrel in the opposite direction to shorten the cable. Note that

there are also adjustment barrels for shifting cables—don't adjust the wrong ones!

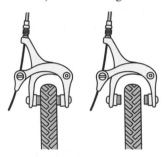

4 Adjust the brake handles. There might be a screw in the brake handle used to adjust the position of the handle itself. If you have especially large or small hands, turn this screw to adjust the openness of the brake handle to suit your grip, and then use the cable adjustment barrel to properly position the brake cable accordingly.

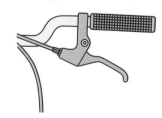

✕ ✕

If the Brakes Still Squeal . . .

While there are many things that can cause squealing brakes, the
mechanics that create the squeal are the same in all cases: The brake pad
grabs the rim, bending the caliper slightly forward, at which point the
caliper pulls against the pad and jumps backward to continue the cycle—
enough of this minor vibration at high speeds creates the sound you know
and don't love. To eliminate the noise, start by cleaning the rims with rubbing
alcohol or a citrus solvent. If that doesn't stop the noise, try using pliers (or your   front wheel
hands) to very slightly bend your brake calipers so the pads point slightly in toward
the front (pigeon-toed). This keeps the brakes from contacting the rims along the length of the
pad with a light squeeze, but allows them to flatten against the rims with a stronger pull. You may
also be able to adjust how easily your brakes pivot open to release from the rim. Try playing with
the strength of this pivot by adjusting the tightness of the nut that holds on the pivot, tightening
or loosening to see if it affects the squeal. Finally, try replacing the brake pads. New pads, or even
another model, may play better with your rims. ✕

#81 How to Maintain a Bicycle Chain

While brakes and tires get all the attention, bicycle chains are often neglected. But in
fact, chain maintenance should be at the top of your bike upkeep list. Because the
chain passes through so many of the bike's other moving parts, including the gears and
derailleurs, a little dirt on the chain can turn into a big problem. Over time, a dirty chain will
not only deteriorate, but also impact the function of the entire drivetrain.

TOOLS:

Old toothbrush • Bicycle chain
tool • Wire brush • Rags •
Pliers • Permanent marker

MATERIALS:

- Chain lubricant
- Simple Green, citrus
  solvent, or bike-specific
  solvent
- WD-40

1 Spot-check the chain.
As part of your pre-ride
checklist, eyeball the chain
for problems. Listen for
squeaks that can signal rusted
links, and look for other dirt
buildup or links that don't
seem to smoothly swivel. If
you find localized dirt, brush

it out with an old toothbrush
and apply a drop of chain
lubricant.

2 Deep-clean the chain
periodically. If you're
riding regularly, clean it
about every three months—
more if you're riding in
harsh conditions. Start by
noting the path of the chain,
taking a picture to help you
remember how to reinstall
it. Use a bicycle chain tool to
break the chain at any point.
Set the chain into the tool

and tighten the tool's screw. This should drive a small bar into the center of the pin connecting the chain links, and drive the pin out the other side. Remove the chain from the bike and aggressively clean it with a wire brush. Soak the chain in a bike-specific solvent until most of the visible grime floats free, about 30 minutes. Dry the chain and allow the solvent to fully evaporate. Reinstall the chain, using the chain tool to reinsert the pin you removed.

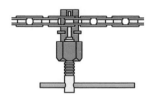

3 Lubricate the chain. Prop up the bike so that the back tire spins freely. With the chain installed on the bicycle, mark one link with a permanent marker so you know when you've cycled through all the links. Place a small drop of chain lube at each chain junction, stopping when you cycle through to the marked link. Turn the pedals for a couple of minutes to work the lube in between the links. Then hold a rag loosely around the chain and turn the pedals to drive the chain through the rag a couple of times. Any lubricant left on the surface of the chain will trap dirt and grime.

4 Fix fused or rusted links. If your bike has been under a tarp out behind the garden shed for the winter or if you've kept an imperfect eye on the condition of your chain, the next time you ride, you may notice a disturbing bump every time the chain passes over one or the other gear. Most likely this is a fused link refusing to bend or straighten. You may be able to spray a fused link with some WD-40 and use pliers to wiggle it back into pliability. Also check the pins—a protruding pin can inhibit movement, and is easily fixed with a chain tool or even by laying the chain flat and using a nail to drive a loose link back into its hole. You'll eventually need to replace a fused link—do it with a chain tool. That said, if your chain is rusted to the point of fused links, consider replacing the entire chain.

✕ ✕

Managing Chain Stretch

Chains don't actually stretch. What riders and bike mechanics call chain stretch is actually the chain metal wearing to the point that it develops play, or movement, around the pins. Enough play around enough pins can lead to a loose chain—one in which each link is a little longer than the manufacturer of the gears intended. This "stretched" chain can round the teeth of the gears, eventually necessitating that you replace the cog set. Rather than pulling a link or two to return it to its original length, replace it. A new chain costs less than new gears. ✕

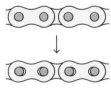

#82 How to Tighten a Single-Speed Chain

On kids' bikes or any single-speed bike without a derailleur, adjusting the chain tension requires either resizing the chain or adjusting the position of the back wheel.

TOOLS:

Wrench • Chain tool

1 Check the tension. Push down on the chain in the middle of its top length. A properly tensioned chain will bend down about an inch from its starting height.

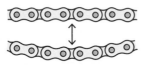

2 Move the wheel. If it bends just a bit more than an inch, use a wrench to loosen the nuts that hold the back wheel in place and slide the wheel slightly farther back along its mounting channels. Retighten the nuts and check the chain tension again.

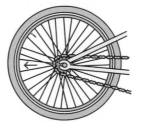

3 Remove links. If the chain pushes down 2 inches or more from its starting height, pushing back the back wheel won't be enough to pull the chain taut. In that case, remove the chain with a chain tool (see also Step 4 in How to Maintain a Bicycle Chain, see page 192).

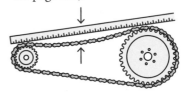

#83 How to Align Bicycle Gears
(or, Advanced Bicycle Maintenance)

On older bikes, shifting is usually done with a lever that allows you to run smoothly between the gears. This old system allowed you to fine-tune the position of derailleurs to ensure that the chain ran smoothly no matter what gear you were in. Most newer bikes include twist or click shifters, in which one notch equals one gear. It's much easier to shift gears this way—but it means your notches have to be adjusted properly to ensure that one click does, in fact, equal one change in gear. Whether your bike is new or old, if your chain is clicking or rattling while you ride, if shifting results in no change or slipping through multiple gears, or if the chain frequently pops off when you shift, it's time to align your gears. (Technically, this part of the bike is a cog, but as a unit, they're often called "gears.")

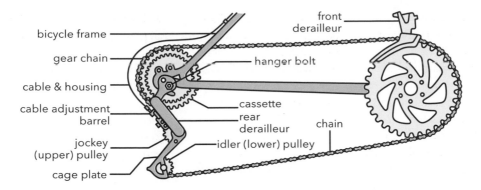

TOOLS:

Screwdriver • Ruler • Needle-nose pliers • Rags

MATERIALS:

- **Bike cable**
- **Chain lubricant**

1 Set the derailleur range. To adjust your gears, you must set the window in which your derailleur works—if the derailleur allows the chain to move too high it may pop off the largest gear, too low and it might pop off the smallest. First locate the limit screws. On most bikes, the front limit screws will be very near the gears, attached to a near vertical post on the bike's frame. There should be two Phillips head screws side by side (sometimes they are labeled "L" and "H"). The inner screw (away from the gears) is likely the "low" limit screw—adjust it so the inner plate of the chain guide is about 4 millimeters

past the inner edge of the smallest gear. Do the same with the other limit screw, which controls how high or to the outside the chain can travel, so that the inner plate of the chain guide is about 4 millimeters past the largest gear. Do the same with the limit screws in the back.

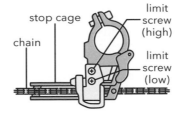

2 If needed, adjust the gear cable. A derailleur cable runs from your shifter, through a plastic sleeve, to the derailleur. If your derailleur doesn't have enough range, you may need to adjust the cable. Most cables have an anchor bolt on one end that's bigger in diameter than the cable to keep it in place. Pull the end of the cable with pliers to add tension to the

cable, or loosen the anchor bolt to give it more slack.

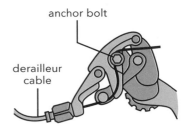

3 Check the position of the limit screws and derailleur cages. With the chain running on the largest gear, the cage should be 2 millimeters outside the chain. Likewise, with the chain running on the smallest gear, the opposite cage should be 2 millimeters inside the chain. If you have gears in the front and back, check the limit screws in both locations.

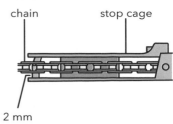

(continued)

4 Check the cable tension. The indexing (the way a shifter scrolls through gears) of modern twist or click shifters may need to be fine-tuned. You can do this by adjusting the tension of the cable. Look under the shifter where the cable enters the plastic housing. There should be a twist nut, called a barrel adjuster. Turning this adjuster by hand will slightly change the length of the plastic housing and so the tension of the wire within. Set the chain on the smallest gear. Then, with the bike's back tire off the ground, run the pedals and shift exactly one click. If the chain doesn't shift accurately to the next larger gear, turn the barrel adjuster to fine-tune the tension. The cable should be straight, no slack, and you should be able to tension it

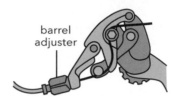

barrel
adjuster

with your fingers. Do this for all gears, both front and back if needed. Once your gears are properly adjusted, the moving chain shouldn't scrape against the gears. It may take minute turns of the barrel adjusters to get the chain running perfectly.

5 Lubricate the chain. Once the gears are running smoothly, spray them with chain lubricant and wipe off any excess with a rag.

✕ ✕
Preventing Chain Rub

Chain rub happens when your bicycle chain gets stuck between the inner ring and the chainstay. To prevent it, try these tips:

• Make sure the chain is lubricated.

• Ease up when shifting.

• Replace worn teeth as needed. ✕

INDEX

CONVERSION TABLES

INCHES TO CENTIMETERS

½ = 1.3	5 = 12.7	9½ = 24.1	18 = 45.7
1 = 2.5	5½ = 14.0	10 = 25.4	19 = 48.3
1½ = 3.8	6 = 15.2	11 = 27.9	20 = 50.8
2 = 5.1	6½ = 16.5	12 = 30.5	21 = 53.3
2 ½ = 6.4	7 = 17.8	13 = 33.0	22 = 55.9
3 = 7.6	7½ = 19.1	14 = 35.6	23 = 58.4
3½ = 8.9	8 = 20.3	15 = 38.1	24 = 61.0
4 = 10.2	8½ = 21.6	16 = 40.6	
4½ = 11.4	9 = 22.9	17 = 43.2	

FEET TO METERS

1 = .304
1½ = .456
2 = .608
2½ = .760
3 = .912
3½ = 1.064
4 = 1.216
4½ = 1.368
5 = 1.520

Use these formulas for precise conversions:

inches x 2.54 = centimeters   feet x .304 = meters

LIQUID CONVERSIONS

US	IMPERIAL	METRIC	US	IMPERIAL	METRIC
2 tbs	1 fl oz	30 ml	1 cup + 2 tbs	9 fl oz	275 ml
3 tbs	1½ fl oz	45 ml	1¼ cups	10 fl oz	300 ml
¼ cup	2 fl oz	60 ml	1⅓ cups	11 fl oz	325 ml
⅓ cup	2½ fl oz	75 ml	1½ cups	12 fl oz	350 ml
⅓ cup + 1 tbs	3 fl oz	90 ml	1⅔ cups	13 fl oz	375 ml
⅓ cup + 2 tbs	3 ½ fl oz	100 ml	1¾ cups	14 fl oz	400 ml
½ cup	4 fl oz	125 ml	1¾ cups + 2 tbs	15 fl oz	450 ml
⅔ cup	5 fl oz	150 ml	2 cups (1 pint)	16 fl oz	500 ml
¾ cup	6 fl oz	175 ml	2½ cups	20 fl oz (1 pint)	600 ml
¾ cup + 2 tbs	7 fl oz	200 ml	3¾ cups	1½ pints	900 ml
1 cup	8 fl oz	250 ml	4 cups	1¾ pints	1 liter

WEIGHT CONVERSIONS

US/UK	METRIC	US/UK	METRIC	US/UK	METRIC
½ oz	15 g	4 oz	125 g	11 oz	325 g
1 oz	30 g	5 oz	150 g	12 oz	350 g
1½ oz	45 g	6 oz	175 g	13 oz	375 g
2 oz	60 g	7 oz	200 g	14 oz	400 g
2½ oz	75 g	8 oz	250 g	15 oz	450 g
3 oz	90 g	9 oz	275 g	1 lb	500 g
3½ oz	100 g	10 oz	300 g		

OTHER USEFUL MEASUREMENTS

APPROXIMATE EQUIVALENTS

1 stick butter = 8 tbs = 4 oz = ½ cup = 115 g
1 cup all-purpose, pre-sifted flour = 4.7 oz
1 cup granulated sugar = 8 oz = 220 g
1 cup (firmly packed) brown sugar =
  6 oz = 220 g to 230 g
1 cup confectioners' sugar = 4½ oz = 115 g
1 cup honey or syrup = 12 oz
1 cup grated cheese = 4 oz

1 cup dried beans = 6 oz
1 large egg = about 2 oz or about 3 tbs
1 egg yolk = about 1 tbs
1 egg white = about 2 tbs

Please note that all conversions are approximate but close enough to be useful when converting from one system to another.

OVEN TEMPERATURES

°F	GAS MARK	°C	°F	GAS MARK	°C	°F	GAS MARK	°C
250	½	120	350	4	180	450	8	230
275	1	140	375	5	190	475	9	240
300	2	150	400	6	200	500	10	260
325	3	160	425	7	220			

Note: Reduce the temperature by 20°C (36°F) for fan-assisted ovens.